Dangerous Neighborhood

Michael S. Radu
editor

Contemporary Issues in Turkey's Foreign Relations

Dangerous Neighborhood

Transaction Publishers

New Brunswick (U.S.A.) and London (U.K.)

Library of Congress Catalog Number: 2002028929
ISBN: 0-7658-0166-3
Printed in Canada

Library of Congress Cataloging-in-Publication Data

Dangerous neighborhood : contemporary issues in Turkey's foreign relations / Michael S. Radu, editor.
   p. cm.
Includes bibliographical references and index.
ISBN 0-7658-0166-3 (alk. paper)
   1. Turkey—Foreign relations—1980- I. Radu, Michael.

DR477 .D36 2002
327.561—dc21   2002028929

Contents

Acknowledgments

Many people at the Foreign Policy Research Institute have contributed to the preparation of this volume. *Orbis* Managing Editors Steven Winterstein and Trudy Kuehner were unfailingly helpful in shepherding the manuscripts through the publication process, and my assistant, Miguel Chamorro, provided prompt and thorough research assistance and stoic shouldering of so many technical details.

The support of FPRI's staff was outstanding, as was the support and Turkish language assistance from the Assembly of Turkish American Associations (ATAA) of Washington. A grant from ATAA helped transform the original *Orbis* issue dedicated to Turkey (Winter 2001) into the present volume.

Many other friends of mine—some neutral, others well versed in the arguments on one side or another—shared their often strong views on Turkey and Turkish matters with me. These represented the whole range of opinion, and all were taken into consideration and greatly appreciated. I am especially glad that even where ultimately I decided to simply take some arguments under advisement, they remain my friends.

– Michael Radu

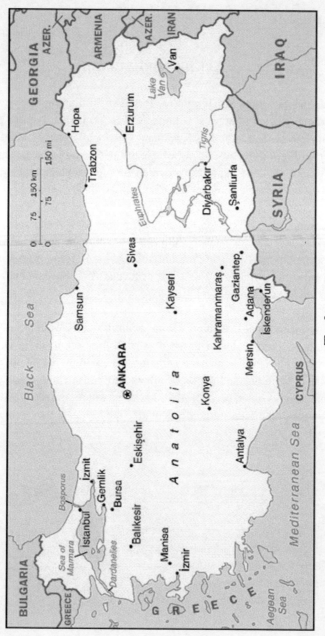

Turkey

Introduction

Turkey's Dangerous Neighborhood

by Michael Radu

In November 2001 the Ankara government announced that it would dispatch a contingent of 90 officers and noncommissioned officers to Afghanistan to train (Uzbek) elements of the United Front, as part of the U.S.-led, anti–Taliban coalition against terrorism. Foreign Minister İsmail Cem also subsequently announced that Turkey would send a much larger contingent as part of the international force being assembled for post–Taliban Afghanistan, making Turkey the only Muslim state to do so openly. The announcement came at a time when polls showed the Turkish public to be 80 percent opposed to military participation and the government coalition in general to have no more than 10 percent popular support.[1] One could wonder where here is loyalty to the legacy of reform from above left by Mustafa Kemal Atatürk, the legendary founder of the Turkish Republic These decisions speak volumes about the contemporary Turkish state and the nature of Turkish foreign policy making. The decisions underscore both Ankara's Kemalist legacy and the issues Turkey faces in shaping its relationships with the European Union and the United States.

The Search for Identity – and Policy Problems

Foreign Minister Cem's November announcements have to be seen in the context of the intense—and largely false—debate continuing in Turkey today that has led to this apparently shaky democracy and contradictory foreign policy. That debate is about Atatürk's legacy. This volume examines the parts of that legacy relevant to Turkey's foreign policy today, and the three distinct branches that have grown from it.

1

First are the Islamists, supported by some 15 to 25 percent of Turkish voters, who believe that Atatürk's nationalism, secularism, and self-reliance are contrary to Islam's notion of a religious community (*umma*) transcending national boundaries. These Islamists and their supporters also believe that the Turkish economic nationalism of the 1960s and 1970s was correct, and that economic development, which they define as consumerism, is contrary to Islam. But local elected politicians have the local interests of their electorate in mind—hence such anomalies as a Turkish town trying to cash in on "Santa Klaus."[2]

Second are those among the politically important and popularly supported military leadership, for the most part, as well as the civil servants of the Ministry of Foreign Affairs, who realize that Atatürk's economic (as distinct from cultural and political) nationalism, as expressed by Ankara's import substitution policies during the 1960s and 1970s, has failed and is not a reliable underpinning for policies for today. Significant in this respect is a press conference held on January 8, 2002 by Gen. Hüseyin Kıvrıkoğlu, the Chief of the General Staff of Turkey's military forces. Kıvrıkoğlu dealt with some decidedly non-military issues, such as corruption among civilian politicians, but also with security issues, including relations with Greece.[3] Kıvrıkoğlu "had no opinion" on the issue of the banking sector's looming bankruptcy and complained about the European Union's failure to list Turkish terrorist groups on its list of terrorist organizations, but, reflecting a more general military skepticism about the EU, he stated that he had "predicted" that decision. Most interestingly, since the press conference statements reflect the consensus of Turkey's most important and popular institution, the general stated "I think EU countries have some fears, since if they expel the terrorist organizations or make opposition to them, they become afraid of being a target of these organizations. They come to this situation as a result of their support of these organizations."[4] He was not only expressing a popular Turkish opinion, he was also correct.

This leads to the third, and least influential or popular, element of Turkey's policy makers—the "politicians," all civilian, most popularly discredited as corrupt and ineffective, none remaining in power long as the public tires of their inevitable cases of corruption.

Finally, from the 1960s on, and particularly since the 1991 collapse of the Soviet Union, there is the pull of the 4-million-strong "Turkish diaspora" in Western Europe, largely ethnic Turks and Kurds in Germany, who are far more nationalistic and Islamic-oriented than most Turkey natives are, and the tens of millions of Turkic speakers in the former Soviet republics of Azerbaijan, Turkmenistan, Uzbekistan, Khirghizstan, and Kazakstan, whose elites, if not necessarily their peoples, are interested in Turkey's unique mix of Islam and Western secular values.

As Ernest Gellner put it, unlike nineteenth-century Italy and Germany, where uniform cultures were seeking unified states (which Piedmont and Prussia eventually created), the remnants of the Ottoman Empire that Atatürk had to deal with in the 1920s were in the form of a state seeking some ethnic basis for partial survival.[5] Atatürk decided that this ethnic base should be "Turkishness": not "Turkish" but Turkishness—that is, cultural and political assimilation (voluntary if possible, forced if not) into the idea of a cultural, not ethnic, Turkish universe. Hence, decades since Atatürk died in 1938, few Turkish citizens still admit that they are originally of Laz, Albanian or Bosniak origin.

In many ways, then, Atatürk's Turkey changed everything and yet did not change much—the stubborn pursuit of nationalist goals, eliminating obstacles on the way to becoming part of the "West," all remained unchanged. On the other hand, Atatürk's own famous flexibility in pursuit of such goals remained unchanged, as well. So did his secularism and a certain Turkish superiority complex with respect to Arabs, and the Turks' vague, but episodically expressed (and mostly rhetorical) feelings of solidarity with the Central Asian Turkic speaking peoples—including Afghan Uzbeks.

One has then to consider the "Kurdish issue"—an issue that makes most Turks, particularly the military officer corps, mad, often irrationally so. The facts are simple. A majority, or close to one, of Kurds from southeastern Turkey have migrated to the more developed urban areas of Istanbul, Ankara, Izmir, and Antalya. As they did so, they also had to learn Turkish, which they did, and thus became at least in part assimilated into Atatürk's notion of Turkish nationalism. It is the same non-racial, non-ethnic "Turkishness" that made Albanians, Laz, Bosniaks, Uzbeks, Uighur, Turkoman, Abkhaz, and Chechens feel largely Turkish in their citizenship and nationalist sentiments—with some obvious exceptions among the most recent additions (the recent Chechen immigrants being an example).

One of the results is that the United States—but still not Europe—has realized the obvious: that Turkey has indeed defeated Kurdish Marxist secessionism. This is a good thing, and one has to learn the appropriate lessons from that, particularly after September 11.

Nor is that the only element of Atatürk's ideology to be discarded. As Mustafa Kemal himself would probably acknowledge, economic statism and nationalism could not and would not be applicable to his grand notion of modernizing Turkey—certainly not in a global economy and increasingly global capitalist values. Nor would Turkey's major economic crisis of 2001 help—statism, and its innevitable partner, corruption, is clearly a dead end, one Ankara reached by the end of 2001.

There are elements in Atatürk's ideology that are in clear contradiction to Ankara's latest stated national goal of joining the EU, Turkishness and nationalism being only the most obvious of them. However, other of Atatürk's personal beliefs are clear, too: join Western Europe or die (politically and nationally), and today Western Europe is not the same as Atatürk saw as a model. Nationalism is clearly on the way out, in favor of supernational organisms of the European Union; the values of socialism, hated by Atatürk (his economic statism aside) dominate it, including both such moral issues as the death penalty, and the more important issue of tolerance of ethnic divisions, seen by most Turks, and certainly by most Turkish military officers, as a recipe for national destruction. Indeed, if seen from the General Staff of the Turkish military, the EU record in dealing with the ETA and IRA is clearly not something to be emulated—a very rational approach.

Turkey's Neighbors

At the time of Mustafa Kemal, who gave himself the name Atatürk, Turkey already had dangerous neighbors—French-controlled Syria, British-invented Iraq, Persia, and Bolshevik Russia—all of whom became much more dangerous when Soviet-aligned Ba'athi Syria and Iraq came into being in the 1960s, and when the modernizing Pahlevi dynasty of Iran—a state and culture Turks have profoundly disliked but respected for centuries—was replaced in 1979 by a Shi'ite fundamentalist regime. And then, in 1989–91, the Soviet Union, a state Turkey had complex relations with from the start, collapsed, only to be replaced by the weak, unstable, and vulnerable states of Georgia, Armenia, and Azerbaijan—the relations with which are complementarily covered by Paul Henze (Chapter 3) and Ali Köknar (Chapter 4) in this volume. An always-dangerous northern border thus became a combination of three chaotic ones—not something that would improve Turkey's security situation.

Imagine a U.S. ally in Western Europe or NATO—say, Italy—sharing hundreds or thousands of miles of land borders with countries that are three of the State Department's main "countries of concern"—formerly "pariah states." Further suppose that those countries are Iran, Iraq, and Syria, and everyone at the Pentagon and Foggy Bottom would be agitated at the very least. There would be widespread U.S. sympathy and immense amounts of aid to such a country, the centuries-old Mafia, Camorra, and N'Dragheta would congressionally be seen as immediate problems to be bilaterally solved, and any criticism of Italian emergency measures against those criminal gangs would be condemned as politically incorrect discrimination. That country, and its 65 million people, happens to be Turkey rather than Italy—and there are very few Turks in this country, as opposed to Italians or, more relevant, visceral enemies of the Turks—Greek and Armenian Americans. On the other hand, few Americans even know that Turkey, a NATO ally, has an army of over 400,000—well armed, trained, and experienced and second only to the United States' in size and second to none in combat experience.

Fewer Americans still realize the difference between Turkey and all other NATO members—the only member of the Western Alliance bordering on hostile states such as Iran, Iraq, and Syria. Comfortable European members of NATO, none of whom has had a hostile border in generations, are easily overgenerous on treating enemies as friends—and as generous in condemning Turkey for being anxious about its security. Hüseyin Bağcı provides useful insights on all of this in Chapter 2.

The Balkans

And then there were the old stories of Turkey's Balkan neighbors, Bulgaria and Greece. Relations with Bulgaria were generally stable, if never really "good," until the communist regime of Todor Zhivkov decided in its waning days during the late 1980s to forcibly assimilate—or expel—hundreds of thousands of Turks. Many were forced to "emigrate" to Turkey, burdening an already stressed country and further complicating relations between Ankara and Sofia. The 1989 fall of the communist regime in Sofia and the disappointment of many Bulgarian Turks with the remote "fatherland's" actual economic situation led many of them to return—and since the neocommunists in Bulgaria lost power again in 1997, that country's ethnic Turkish party is now playing the king-maker among the various Bulgarian political forces.

Relations with Greece are an interesting element of Ankara's foreign policy. Most foreigners, including those in Washington, tend to believe that Greece and Turkey are two paranoiac regimes, each hating the other for no reason and to no purpose. This is a mistaken impression, at least as far as Ankara and most Turks are concerned. Turkey is perfectly aware of its military and demographic superiority over Greece. The only problem is that Greece, as a member of both NATO and the European Union, is widely perceived as a real or de jure ally of the West and, at least in Western Europe, is treated as such, while Turkey is not.

The history of Greek–Turkish relations is so long and complicated as to defy most rational analysis by outsiders. On the one hand, for over a century Athens has used that history, along with the alleged Turkish threat, to manipulate public opinion at home and abroad in favor of territorial and historic claims on Turkey. On the other hand, Ankara, at least since the end of World War I and the subsequent victorious war of independence (1921–23), has seen Athens as a nuisance that only posed a threat because of Western support.

Finally, there is the persistent and apparently irresoluble problem of Cyprus, which cannot be separated from relations with Greece. For all practical purposes the "Turkish Republic of Northern Cyprus" is a province of Turkey—and by far the most costly one. Whether that should be so in a rational and ideal world ought to be a matter of rational discourse, but it is not. Here, Turkish nationalism collides with national interest—with ample help from both Greece and the Greek Cypriots.

However, the Cyprus issue is only the latest, and most difficult to solve, of numerous problems between the two countries. The problem is made so difficult more by the burden of history between Greece and Turkey than by relations between Greek and Turkish Cypriots. It remains unsolved because of the asymmetry between the two sides— Greece and the Greek Cypriots have the advantage of international political support, while Turkey has the overwhelming military force.

Turkey and the West

Turkey's complicated relations with the "West" used to mean, at least in Atatürk's time, with Western Europe —England, France, and Germany—and also with "civilization": not "Western" civilization, as far as Atatürk was concerned, but the only civilization. Since Atatürk died, what could only be called the "Western temptation" of Turkey continued to dominate Turkey's intellectual and political life. The latest incarnation of that temptation is the country's main foreign policy goal of joining the European Union.

Turkey and the EU

Politicians of all stripes—some Islamists excepted—seem prepared to pay almost any price for Turkey to join the EU. This sentiment has much less support among the politically influential military, and with good reason. While it is certainly true that the EU has long tried to find excuses for avoiding the issue of admitting Muslim Turkey and her 70 million people—human rights (see Aslan Gündüz's discussion in Chapter 1), the role of the military, and the Kurdish issue being used most often for that purpose—it is also true that some of the issues are real and raise the question whether Turkey's interests are indeed best served by joining the EU.

By repeatedly raising the bar when considering Turkey's application for membership and making impossible demands such as a relaxation of Ankara's rejection of religious (Islamic) intrusion into politics—the very basis of Western secularism as well as of Kemalism—the EU contradicts its own claims to represent "Western values" and causes Turkish suspicions that Turkey's being Muslim, populous (second only to Germany in population size in a putative EU) and relatively poor (but less so than more favored applicants such as Romania or Bulgaria) are what Brussels is really concerned about when considering Turkey's accession. So far, Turkey's possible accession to the EU has not even been seriously debated in Brussels, at least in cultural and strategic terms. Indeed, questions such as "Would Turkey's identity as a secular Muslim state be threatened by membership? Would joining the economically protectionist EU—an increasingly defenseless but vocal club of small armies and creeping pacifism in a small-threat environment, where no member faces a real, serious secessionist threat—really be in Turkey's long-term interests?" are seldom addressed. The answer, paradoxically, lies in the partial way Atatürk's legacy is currently interpreted. Turkey has inherited his drive to be culturally "Western" without his nationalism and keen awareness of Turkey's security dilemmas. To understand this, one comes back again to the European view of Turkey's political system—Brussels' profound dislike of the important role the Turkish military plays and indeed has to play in Ankara.

Seen from Ankara, it appears that nothing Turkey does is satisfactory to the European human rights establishment. On learning of European complaints about overcrowded Turkish prisons, Turkey built new prisons with no more than three inmates per cell, a standard higher than that of many EU countries or the United States. The remaining terrorist group, the Revolutionary Peoples Liberation Party/Front (Devrimci Halk Kurtuluş Cephesi–DHKP/C), decided to fight that through the media—that is, through hundreds of hunger strikes. One could question whether imprisoned members of terrorist groups have the right to further indoctrinate or recruit. But judging by the reaction of the *New York Times*[6] and European human rights groups, it appears they do—an opinion Ankara does not share, and so far has remained steadfast in rejecting.

Unlike any EU state, Turkey lives in a very dangerous neighborhood indeed—one that does not allow for the kind of libertarian *cum* socialist politics of most EU states. It is one thing indeed to treat the role of the military as an afterthought when your neighbors are the Benelux, Germany, and Switzerland, but quite another when your neighbors include Syria, Iraq, Iran, and Armenia. It is easy to talk about minority rights when those minorities are small and isolated (Basques, Bretons, Welsh), or only mildly secessionist (Scotts, Welsh, Flemings) and another when they occupy a third of the national territory, are large and generously supported, in some cases, by unfriendly neighbors—as the Turkish Kurds were at various times by Iran, Iraq, the Soviet Union, and Syria. Which is not to even mention the disastrous state of the Turkish economy.

Turkey, the EU, and the PKK

Why did the EU decide to consider Turkey—a huge country of some 65 million Muslims who until quite recently had faced a Marxist–Leninist–led insurgency seeking a separate "people's republic" in the southeast—for membership? Opposition could be expected from the former terrorists of the Kurdistan Worker's Party (Partiya Karkeren Kurdistan–PKK) and their lawyers, such as European Parliament MP Daniel Cohn Bendit—an elected member of the European Parliament— and various Dutch, Greek, and Italian officials and others sympathetic to the Marxist terrorists and their leader, Abdullah Öcalan, directly responsible for 30,000 deaths in Turkey since he began the PKK insurgency in 1984, and the ideological communist parties sharing power in Italy and France and dependent upon their support in Portugal. On the other hand, we have the vacillating, although basically politically incorrect, Ankara government, which staunchly defends its right to retain the death penalty, although it has not applied it since 1983, and yet allows Öcalan himself to apply to the European Court of Justice, clear evidence of its strong interest in *not* executing Öcalan, the person most directly responsible for the largest known number of casualties in the insurgency.

Why do the Dutch, Italian, and to some extent the Spanish, French, and German—not to mention Greek—governments support totalitarian apologists like the PKK? That is a question most Turks ask themselves and cannot answer. It may be true, as Gen. Kıvrıkoğlu has suggested, that the Germans and to a degree the Dutch are simply scared: resident Kurds they accepted earlier as "political asylum" seekers have imported their own politics, exercising their right to freedom of expression by burning down Turkish embassies. For most left-wing Europeans (a majority of national activists in power in Rome and Brussels, among others), the Kurdish "cause" is the PKK—a definition Ankara can never accept. Since its beginnings as a Marxist *cum* secessionist insurgency, the PKK has caused some 30,000 deaths, Kurds and Turks alike—90 percent more than the total number of victims of all Western European terrorist groups: the Basque ETA, French Action Directe and Corsican separatists, Italian Red Brigades, the German Baader-Meinhof gang, the Irish Republican Army and its offshoots, etc. The Western European attitude toward the latest Turkish decision on terrorism— permitting the hunger strike of hundreds of imprisoned DHKP/C, with some 40 "victims" so far and 200 still waiting to be "martyred," is typical. After years of being accused by the EU of inhumane prison conditions, particularly overcrowding, Turkey is now criticized even as it builds two- or three-member prison cells for terrorists, because it refuses to deal with some of the DHKP/C terrorists' more exceptional demands. This has made Turkey the focus of protests by human rights organizations such as Amnesty International that are openly supported by European governments. Seen from Ankara, this Western European support for the PKK goes further than any mere sentimental, far-left, or misguided support for Kurdish terrorism—it amounts to actively helping the murderers of Turkish citizens (ironically, mostly Kurdish-Turkish citizens).

As I discuss in Chapter 6 of this volume, on the PKK, first the British government and then the Belgian government allowed MED-TV, a PKK creation and recruiting tool, to operate from their territory, using their technological capabilities and public relations talent, claiming that MED-TV is a "cultural" Kurdish TV satellite channel—"freedom of speech," Brussels stated. However, MED-TV was so clearly a propaganda outlet for the PKK (at a cost of some $200 million a year) that it was ultimately expelled from Britain and closed down in Belgium as well after losing its operating license. Significantly, MED-TV technical personnel were mostly Kurdish women. Nor is the pool of Western European Kurdish militants small. In 1997 the German Federal Ministry of the Interior estimated the number of PKK sympathizers in the country at 11,000, an increase of more than 1,000 from the previous year, who were capable of mobilizing "tens of thousands" of the 500,000 resident Kurds.[7] Between 1993 and 1996, when Öcalan declared that his organization would cease acts of violence in Germany, the PKK, through the Democratic People's Union (formerly the National Liberation Front of Kurdistan, or ERNK), has engaged in murder, extortion, and other violence toward rival groups and was banned. It has continued to use violence against Turkish interests in both Germany and the Netherlands through its Youth Union of Kurdistan (YCK).[8]

Not surprisingly given the numerous pro-PKK or human rights groups supporting the "Kurdish cause" as defined by PKK propaganda, the party has an abundant Western European network of highly skilled activists, once again largely (but not solely) Dutch, German, Belgian, and Scandinavian.[9] Nor is Western European support for the PKK limited to left-wing politicians and nongovernment organizations. Eva Juhnke, a German citizen and confessed ARGK militant, was captured by Turkish forces in combat in Northern Iraq in 1997,[10] while Andrea Wolf, a.k.a. "Ronahi," a German woman "internationalist" and member of PKK's "women's" front, the Free Women's Movement of Kurdistan (Yetkityia Azadiya Jinen Kurdistan—YAJK), was killed in combat in the province of Van in 1998.[11] Not surprisingly, former members of the Baader-Meinhof Gang (Rotte Armee Faktion) now associated with the German Anti-Imperialist Resistance and Internationalist groups in Germany and the Netherlands are among the most dedicated PKK supporters.[12] Members of these groups are generally university graduates or dropouts with technical training.

According to the Turkish government, based on both internal PKK documents and statements by captured militants, the PKK decided at its Fifth Congress in January 1995 to engage in suicide bombings, a decision further reinforced at the March 1996 Fourth National Conference.[13] Although there is no indication that women were particularly selected for suicide missions, the majority of such actions were committed by YAJK members.[14] Thus, the very first PKK-affiliated suicide bomber, in Tunceli Province in June 1996, was a woman; so were that year's suicides in Adana and Van, and one of the two cases in Hakkari Province's Yüksekova area (the other was an Iranian man); while in Bingöl Province in 1998, the perpetrator was a Kurdish man. Generally speaking, it appears that suicide bombers of or claiming to be associated with the PKK are generally poorly educated young women of peasant background.

Simply put, while no EU or NATO member faces these kinds of serious regional and national threats, if they did they could all rely on the United States as their ally. Turkey, on the other hand, is not an EU member, and its NATO membership is and always has been its only ace in dealing with Brussels or Washington.

Turkey and NATO

In December 2000 Turkey defeated the French-invented notion of an independent West European military force—independent of American dominated NATO, but dependent upon its infrastructure. The reason: Turkey is a NATO member but not an EU member, and, unlike her traditional enemy, Greece, has no veto in the latter's councils. On the other hand, Turkey has an unusual position among NATO—or EU— members that gives it a distinct view of security. Indeed, no NATO (or EU) member has a border with a potential, historic or openly vocal enemy—except for Turkey.

Obviously, when your neighbors are Denmark, Germany, Belgium, and Luxemburg, as is the case with the Netherlands; or NATO members Poland, the Czech Republic, France and the Benelux states and neutral Austria and Switzerland, as is the case of Germany, which also has U.S. troops, one has a different view of national security than when one has Iran, Iraq, Syria and Armenia as neighbors—not to mention Greece. Would a Germany with such neighbors be so critical of the Turkish military's role in Ankara's politics? Hardly. The problem is related to a long-standing Western European loss of any strategic viewpoint in general, and the general loss among EU members of the sense that they are under any threat. That is also a reason for the developing—at least until September 11—strategic gap between Washington and Brussels.

United States

As Birol Yeşilada points out in Chapter 8, the United States is Turkey's insurance policy against total isolation from the increasingly difficult relationship with Europe. Turkey's NATO membership and loyal support for Washington, whether in Korea in 1952, Bosnia and Kosovo during the 1990s, or in Afghanistan now, combined with the reality of its 600,000-strong, U.S.-armed and highly competent military—almost as strong as and probably better than the armies of most, if not all, of the European members of the Alliance put together—give Ankara a say in Washington.

Although American domestic politics, especially the disproportionate influence of the large and reflexively anti-Turkish Greek and Armenian lobbies, may often lead to a misunderstanding of Turkey's strategic importance for the United States, in times of crisis—like the current one in Afghanistan—the strategic reality of Turkey's position and role has a way of rearing its head, even in the U.S. Congress.

Turkish democracy is imperfect, as is readily acknowledged in Turkey as well as in the United States and Europe. But as demonstrably corrupt or incompetent as its political elites often are, Turkey remains, as it has been since the 1920s, the only Muslim country whose secularism is not in doubt. It is the only and thus the supreme demonstration of the fact that Islam and democracy, Islam and secularism, and Islam and Westernization are not incompatible. Agnostic and Turkish nationalist as Atatürk, Ismet İnönü, and their group of reformers sometimes were, they made their secularism accepted by most Turks—by means fair and sometimes foul—and this is the reality today in most of Turkey. That is obviously not the case in Egypt, Saudi Arabia, or Pakistan, and recently even less so.

Israel

The best proof of Turkey's secularism is the relationship it has established with Israel, the only other democracy in the region. It is, as Efraim Inbar discusses in Chapter 7, a symbiotic relationship based on pragmatism. But as far as Ankara is concerned, it is a relationship that involves as many risks as benefits. On the one hand, it further alienates the Turks from the rest of the Muslim, and especially the Arab, world. Osama bin Laden clearly referred to Turkey when he "wrote off" Islamic governments that support the West. It also reinforces existing disputes with neighbors like Syria, Iraq, and Iran, all staunchly anti-Israeli (and anti-Jewish).

On the other hand, the relationship with Jerusalem only continues the much older ties between Turks and Jews—and there is no need to mention, as is often done, the Ottoman willingness to give expelled

Spanish Jews asylum in Thessalonika in 1492. A more relevant case is Atatürk's staffing of Istanbul University with fleeing German Jewish academics in 1933.[15]

But the relationship is not based solely upon history—though that is widely used as a cultural explanation for a set of cold calculations. For strategic reasons Israel needs a secular, pro-American and militarily strong non-Arab Turkey to keep Syria busy to the north; for immediate military reasons Israel's Air Force needs a spacious air space for the training of its pilots, and indeed they now train over Anatolia. The Turkish military need Israeli technology (or American technology transferred via Israel) and funds, and the Turkish government needs Israeli help—funds and particularly expertise—in developing southeastern Anatolia. Turkey also needs the help of the strong Jewish-American lobby to counter the active Greek and Armenian lobbies in Washington, where Turks have little to rely on from their own local ethnic base.

For both Ankara and Jerusalem, however, this is a strictly pragmatic relationship, viewed by both as part of a general regional policy. Thus, when in October 1998 Turkey nearly went to war with Syria (or at least threatened to) over Damascus' support for the PKK, Israel publicly separated itself from the conflict, to Ankara's dismay.[16] And during the past year or so Turkey's Foreign Minister Cem has consistently stated Ankara's support for the (undefined, to be sure) concept of a Palestinian state—not something Jerusalem appreciates.

Unpleasant Neighbors—Syria, Iran and Iraq

In simple terms, Turkey's relations with her two Arab neighbors (Syria and Iraq) and Iran are centered around three issues—water, oil, and Kurdish Marxist separatism/terrorism.

As the controller of the sources of the two rivers that make Syria and particularly Iraq viable, the Tigris and Euphrates, Turkey is by far the superpower of the Middle East—it has the largest army and the largest population and owns the most important resource, which in that region is not oil but water. The Turkish use of water in its diplomacy in the region has been examined abundantly, hence one need only mention it here.[17] Syrians and Iraqis may and do feign to see this as Turkish arrogance, but the cold hard fact remains that Turkey's dams on the

Euphrates—intended, to some extent, at least, as part of the anti–PKK operations—serve a goal all of Ankara's neighbors ultimately share: hostility to the very notion of a Kurdish state.

Outsiders may be confused by this, since at various times and in various circumstances Turkey, Iran, Iraq, and Syria helped, armed, or supported Kurdish enemies of each and every other of their regional adversaries. But they only did so within limits acceptable to those enemies themselves and at no time with the goal of producing a Kurdish state anywhere. Kurds everywhere—mostly the nationalists outside "Kurdistan"—may not like this, but it remains the sentiment shared by capitals as far away as Washington, Paris, and London.

Oil is important for Turkey, a country having none of its own but neighboring closely states that do in abundance: Iraq and Iran. The infamous Ceyhan project (a proposed pipeline through Turkey between Azerbaijan and/or Turkmenistan and Kazakstan oil and gas deposits and the West) remains important in Ankara—too much so, considering the economics and politics or the matter.

Iran is a distinct problem in Turkish foreign policy—it is a potential, and sometimes active supporter of the PKK, notwithstanding that group's long-standing commitment to Marxism-Leninism. But it ultimately leads to a nuisance – just as potential Turkish support for Turkic speaking Azeris in Iran, where they make up a quarter of the population, never materialized. Furthermore, trade (both legal and illegal) between Iran and Turkey is too important to both to be endangered by religious, political, or any other considerations. Hence the apparently strange image of Turkish and Iranian foreign ministers in Ankara amiably agreeing to disagree about Israel and reaffirming the notion of closer trade and political ties, even as Iran had to extradite some PKK militants.

Syria, on the other hand, has a difficult relationship with Turkey— although, as in the Greek case, the reverse is not necessarily true. Militarily weaker, water-dependent on Turkey, with a population less than a quarter of Turkey's, and politically as well as strategically and psychologically caught between Ankara's links with Jerusalem, Syria still officially has territorial claims on Turkey, mostly in the Alexandretta (Iskenderun) area. Damascus also supported the PKK as long as its doing so was politically defensible—and protected by the Soviet Union, and while Turkey was occupied elsewhere. When that changed after the collapse of the Soviet Union, and when Turkey was able to concentrate her military efforts on the Syrian border in October 1998, the Assad regime folded, to the chagrin of the PKK and Abdullah Öcalan.

Iraq is the currently the most delicate Turkish foreign policy issue. On the one hand, most of Turkey's oil comes from Iraq,[18] and that is a fact that is not likely to change soon—Ceyhan or no Ceyhan. In addition, ideologically distant as Ankara and Baghdad are, the Kurdish separatist issue brings them together—both, not to mention Damascus or Tehran, are dead set against it—and so should Washington. For Turkey any threat to the territorial integrity of Iraq as a unitary Arab state ruled from Baghdad, is also a threat to Turkey's own territorial integrity, since it would imply some kind of independent Kurdish state in the region. There is a reason why, for some years now, Turkey has quietly established a security area in northern Iraq—under Turkish military control and presence—and did so without any protest from Iraq. Indeed, although Baghdad is prevented by the United States' no fly regime to deploy massive forces in the north, and Turkey provides the air bases for that, Ankara and Baghdad agree to accept it as long as no Kurdish state is established—*de facto* or *de jure*. Kurdish divisions and duplicity, as well as the implicit support for the present ambiguity from Tehran and Damascus also help maintain that highly ambiguous situation.

Ultimately, for Turkey a central regime in Baghdad—with or preferably without Saddam Hussein—is preferable to any scenario threatening a collapse of the Iraqi state itself. Iraqi oil supplies and trade in general are important to Turkey, and, even more so, is the avoidance of a Kurdish state—nonviable in all circumstances, and threatening as well.

The Kurdish Problem

Svante Cornell discusses the Kurdish question in Turkish politics in Chapter 5. It is significant that nobody—not supporters of Kurdish independence or autonomy nor those who would repress these movements—can accurately estimate the number of Turkish citizens of Kurdish origin. At least half of people of Kurdish background in Turkey live outside of the traditionally Kurdish areas of the southeast—

PKK's mythical "Northern Kurdistan"—and an increasing number of those have already lost, or are rapidly losing, their language and/or traditions in favor of an increasingly homogeneous Turkish identity. Nor is there anything resembling a "Kurdish" linguistic, ethnic, social, political or economic identity, uniting people speaking some Iranian-related language in Armenia, Syria, Iraq, Iran and Turkey. Kurmandji, the language (not dialect) spoken by most Turkish Kurds, is largely incomprehensible to Zaza or Soranyia speakers elsewhere. Almost a third of Turkey's Kurds are Alawites, an Islamic heresy; tribal identity in rural areas is still far more important than ethnicity; and Iraqi Kurds are once again split along tribal lines, and different from Turkish ones, even as they purport to define those differences as ideological or political. Hence, the favorite theory of human rights militants, that Kurds are the world's largest stateless nation, is meaningless.

Furthermore, *pace* human rights and other leftists in Europe as well as some scholars in the United States,[19] there is simply no such thing as a "Kurdish nation." Not only are Kurds in Syria, Iraq, Iran, and Turkey divided by clan, tribe, history, and indeed language—the two major Kurdish languages spoken in the area mutually incomprehensible, and they are only the most common, not the only ones—but there is no such thing as a "Kurdish national consciousness" —certainly not outside the West European diaspora. Not only are "Kurds" the "largest people without a state," or at least one who could never establish a viable state of their own, but there certainly will not be such a state if the other countries in the region—Islamic Iran, Ba'athist Syria and Iraq, and democratic Turkey—have a say on the matter. All of them have occasionally supported, manipulated, and armed Kurdish insurgents against their regional enemies, yet none is prepared to accept a Kurdish state anywhere in the region—for the same reason—such a state, in addition to being nonviable, will also threaten their own territorial integrity. On that matter, Damascus, Tehran, Baghdad, Ankara, even Erevan, join ranks—but not human rights militants in the Netherlands, Germany, and Switzerland, for whom the cause is politically correct and useful.

As is usual in such cases, the Turkish–Kurdish diaspora in Germany or Switzerland[20] is far more nationalistic—and effective in pursuing nationalistic goals, including support for the terrorist PKK (and Turkish Islamist elements)—than either Kurds or Islamists are in Turkey proper. That is not unusual—the Baltic and East European diaspora during the Cold War and the Cuban diaspora to this day have always been more articulate, coherent, and nationalistic in their activities—and totally unpopular at home.[21] The Turkish-Kurdish diaspora is successful only because of the outside support it receives, from the Syrian regime until 1998 and Western European political, financial, and diplomatic support before and since—an additional contentious problem between Ankara and Brussels.

The Kurdish issue is one Ankara has until recently had a hard time dealing with. However, since the 1999 capture of PKK idol Abdullah Öcalan, realism and indeed sophistication has settled in. Use of the Kurdish language in (officially overseen) media has recently been accepted. In recognizing that not all Turkish citizens are, nor do they want to be, "Turks," Ankara has discarded a fundamental precept of Atatürk's ideological framework.

The Left

Turkey likes to think of itself as a largely European country—hence her claim to European Union membership. However, in many ways, and especially politically, the Turkish Left remains as backward as it could be—a Stalinist gang committed to violence that never learned or adapted to the real word of post–Cold War politics. The Turkish Communist Party, its Maoist version (Workers and Peasants' Army of Turkey–TIKKO) and the PKK itself are all parts of an ideological *Jurassic Park*, more active now in jails than in real life. Indeed, the Maoists and Communists in jail provoked more fatalities (17), mostly among themselves, during their hunger strike and armed fight over jail conditions in December 2000 that they did through "armed action." It appears that the Turkish Left is as stubborn in its outdated convictions as it is violent in its futile attempt to "conquer political power." It was the hard Left—Maoist, Trotskyite, and "orthodox" pro-Soviet groups—that led to the 1980 military intervention in Ankara, and some of those groups, most importantly the PKK and DHKP/C, remain active—even if only marginally so. So is the Turkish Hezbollah, originally used, if not encouraged, by the Turkish intelligence as a counter to the hard Left, secessionist or not. Occasionally helped by Iran and involved in organized crime, by the late 1990s it was out of control—and a target of Ankara's wrath.

The Diaspora

Based on this author's experience—including dozens of interviews with Turkish military *jandarma*, what people in Turkey—"nationalist" Kurds, Stalinist, Maoist leftists, or politically correct intellectuals— failed to obtain significant support for, they did, with a vengeance, in exile in Western Europe. It is not that Turkish immigrants to Germany, the Netherlands, France or Scandinavia—some three million of them— exported their homeland's political disputes abroad, but that they fight abroad over ideologies long considered dead at home. In short, the Turkish diaspora is artificially kept alive ideologically and radicalized by frustrated locals seeking a totalitarian utopia among foreigners when it failed at home. Hence, the PKK's support—financial and propaganda wise—is stronger in The Hague and Berlin than in Diyarbakır or Şırnak, and Öcalan's most vocal advocates—and lawyers—are to be found among German and Dutch former members and lawyers of now defunct terrorist groups—the Red Brigades/Baader-Meinhof Gang, Action Directe, etc.

Fashionable human rights groups and individuals are also drawn to the PKK through their instinctive fascination with the absurd Left— hence Danielle Mitterand, Daniel Cohn Bendit, etc. all enthusiastically support Öcalan and his "rights" as opposed to those of 30,000 Kurds, Turks, Turkomans and others left dead as a result of his organization's activities. In fact, it is only with governmental and nongovernmental support from EU countries that the PKK continues to live at all (see Chapter 6).

Nor is the PKK's business acumen—demonstrated by its control (shared with fellow Albanian "freedom fighters" from Kosovo and Macedonia) over heroin, illegal immigrant traffic, and Mafia-like protection rackets among immigrants—taken into consideration. To the contrary, Kurdish rights advocates disregard this typical combination of a Marxist-Leninist "people's war" and simple criminality (as do human rights activists in Colombia, Sri Lanka, and Peru).

Democracy and Human Rights

When one's population is no more than 3 percent Muslim—and even that raises problems of state-church separation, as is the case in France and Germany, Muslim concerns are the subject of media arguments. When a country's population is 99.5 percent Muslim, as is the case in Turkey, the issue is quite different. As Atatürk himself noted, Islam, in its traditional form, is not compatible with democracy. It is interesting that the EU, after complaining about Algeria's lack of "democracy" following the electoral victory of a fundamentalist Islamic party, denied by army action, is now supporting the secular regime in Algiers (and its army supporters), but it also blames Turkey for not tolerating a (minority) Islamic regime, contrary to its constitution, Atatürk's legacy and everything that makes Turkey a European rather than a Middle Eastern state. It is no wonder Turks are confused.

When the United States responded to the September 11 attacks on it by attacking Afghanistan's Taliban regime and the associated terrorist networks, Turkey alone of all Muslim-majority countries declared that the U.S. is "our friend" and that Ankara supported the U.S.–led attacks —no ifs, ands, or buts. To some extent, this should prove that Turkey is completely pro-Western—as Atatürk would want it to be. Far more important, the Turkish public, unlike the Malaysian, Indonesian, Pakistani and most Arab nations' publics, did not demonstrate against the U.S. "Satan"—because it did not feel that way, thus demonstrating the continuous impact of the Kemalist ideology on the Turkish population. Once again, one has to ask why the term "Turks" is relevant—an artificial, thoroughly Kemalist, non- or multi-ethnic definition to begin with, and why it is enforced by law.

Naturally enough, it is the human rights organizations that complained about the October 7 U.S./UK counterattacks in reprisal for the September 11 terrorist attacks, voicing concern about innocent lives lost. Ankara's statement of friendship with the United States and its commitment to its NATO obligations may seem "normal," but considering that Turkey is virtually 100 percent Muslim, they are remarkable.

Conclusions

Turkish foreign policy remains largely based upon what Atatürk's strategic view was many decades ago—Turkish nationalism first, and as much as possible Western oriented—the West now meaning the United States and NATO. Most Turks are not "pro-American," although English is increasingly being treated as a natural second language in schools and universities. Turkish friendly sentiments vis a vis the United States are more the result of the impression in Ankara that Western Europe rejects Turkey, Turks and their culture, and thus that Turkey's best introduction to the "West" is via Washington rather than via Paris, Berlin, or London. Turkey also recognizes that its strategic importance is a more relevant argument than its people's cultural desires and dreams.

While some in Ankara still harbor dreams of a major Turkish influence area in Caucasus and Central Asia, the present dire economic circumstances seem to have limited their number and influence, as they limited Turkish private investments and ambitions in the former Soviet republics of that region. On the other hand, culturally and politically Ankara remains the most influential factor in the region, other than Moscow, and, from an American point of view, preferable to Tehran.

As for Europe, there is a clear difference between the perceptions of Turkey's importance between Brussels and Washington—and the latter has only a limited role in influencing the former. Ultimately, the cultural, legal and political differences between Turkey and "Europe" may well turn out to be too great for Ankara to compromise on. That, however, is still to be decided among Turks themselves.

Notes

[1] *Turkish Daily News*, Nov. 3, 2001 (http://www.turkishdailynews.com).

[2] John Ward Anderson, " Ol' St. Nick's Home Is a Very Long Way From the North Pole: Turkish Town Struggles to Save Church Where 'Santa' Served," *Washington Post*, Dec. 20, 2001.

[3] "Kıvrıkoğlu calls for strong measures against corruption," *Turkish Daily News* (http://ww.turkishdailynews.com/FrTDN/latest/for.htm).

[4] Ibid.

[5] Ernest Gellner, "The Turkish Option in Comparative Perspective," in Sibel Bozdoğan and Reşat Kasaba, eds., *Rethinking Modernity and National Identity in Turkey* (Seattle: University of Washington Press, 1997), pp. 233–44.

[6] See, e.g., Somini Gupta, "Turkish Hunger Strikers Risk Body and Mind," *New York Times*, Dec. 18, 2001.

[7] Federal Ministry of the Interior Annual Report 1997 (http://www.bmi.bund.de/).

[8] Ibid.

[9] That the Netherlands' "tolerant," if not sympathetic, government was selected by all-out terrorist Karayilan for his "asylum" request is abundant evidence of The Hague's role in helping, legitimizing, and promoting anti-Turkish terrorism.

[10] *The Kurdish Observer*, "Eva Juhnke (PKK) Has Ended Her Hunger Strike," BURN! Project, Dec. 28, 1999 (http://burn.ucsd.edu, now closed), Jan. 27, 2000. Tried in Turkey and sentenced to 15 years in jail, she made headlines by going on a hunger strike in 1999.

[11] Heval Pelda, Ruken, Sipan, and Haki, Informationsstelle Kurdistan, translated by Arm The Spirit, "Statement from Internationalists on the Death of Internationalist Andrea Wolf (Ronahi)," BURN! Project Nov. 1998.

[12] For details on these and other German radical anarchist and "anti-fascist" groups' ties with the PKK, see Federal Ministry of the Interior Annual Report, 1997.

[13] Office of the Chief Public Prosecutor, State Security Court (DGM), Indictment Regarding Accused Abdullah Ocalan (Ankara, Republic of Turkey, April 24, 1999), prep. #1997/514, principle #1999/98, indictment #1999/78, pp. 56–60.

[14] YAJK held its first National Conference in Iraq in March 1996, just before the wave of suicide bombings by its members began.

[15] Andrew Mango, *Atatürk* (Woodstock and New York: Overlook Press, 2000), pp. 481–2.

[16] Michael Radu, "The PKK," paper presented at the Conference on Toxic Terror, sponsored by the Monterrey Institute of International Studies, Washington, D.C., March 20, 2000, unpublished.

[17] Murhaf Jouehati, "Water politics as High Politics: the case of Turkey and Syria," in Henri J. Barkey, ed., *Reluctant Neighbor: Turkey's role in the Middle East* (Washington, D.C.: U.S. Institute of Peace Press, 1996), pp. 131-46.

[18] Phebe Marr, "Turkey and Iraq," in Barkey, ed., *Reluctant neighbor*, pp. 45–170.

[19] Such as respected scholars Henri J. Barkey and Graham Fuller in their *Turkey's Kurdish Question* (Oxford: Rothman & Littlefield and Carnegie Corporation, 1998).

[20] See Michael Radu, *Collapse or Decay, Cuba and the East European Transitions from Communism* (Miami: Endowment for Cuban American Studies, 1996), pp. 81–106.

[21] For an analysis of the various diasporas' attitudes and their electoral record at home see Radu, *Collapse or Decay?*

1

Turkey and Europe:
The Human Rights Conundrum

by Aslan Gündüz

Democracy and human rights in Turkey have been prominent topics in many international forums over the past ten years due to that country's unique domestic difficulties and geopolitical importance. Hardly any other country in the world has been so criticized for its human rights record, nor is the future of any other country so dependent on the promotion of human rights. And therein lies an irony: because the criticism stems not from what is appalling about Turkey, but what is laudable about it; not from what it has been in the past, but what it aspires to be.

Turkey's constitution, like those of other European countries, guarantees a long list of human rights and fundamental freedoms. The major codes and enforcement mechanisms of Turkey's legal system were taken verbatim from various European states in the early 1920s, and almost all actions of the state are subject to judicial review. Turkey has also accepted multidimensional international accountability with respect to the protection of human rights, most notably by becoming a party to the European Convention on Human Rights (the "Convention") and incorporating into its judicial system the so-called Strasbourg institutions—that is, the European Court of Human Rights (ECHR), which decides on applications concerning human rights violations, and the Committee of Ministers of the Council of Europe, which (among other responsibilities) supervises the implementation decisions of the ECHR.[1] Turkey is also a party to the European Convention for the Prevention of Torture, with its European Committee for the Prevention of Torture and Inhuman or Degrading Treatment or Punishment

(CPT),[2] as well as the European Social Charter and the U.N. Convention for the Prevention of Torture. Further links to European institutions include Turkey's membership in the Council of Europe and the Organization for Security and Cooperation in Europe (OSCE), its customs union with the European Union, and its candidacy for full membership in the EU.

In sum, the spotlight is on human rights in Turkey precisely because its government and people aspire to the highest standards of humanity and full membership in the Western club of nations. And yet, because it has grappled with virtually every kind of terrorism over the last three decades, the Turkish state has confronted considerable difficulties in meeting its international obligations in the field of human rights. The terrorism campaign of the Kurdistan Workers' Party (Partiya Karkeren Kurdistan—PKK) alone has left more than 30,000 dead. Moreover, since 1960 Turkey has experienced three military takeovers or interventions, and has not fully recovered from the most recent coup, which occurred in 1980. It is against this violent background that a portrait of democracy and human rights in Turkey must be painted.

The Anarchic Nature of the International System and Human Rights

Contemporary human rights doctrine is designed primarily to protect men and women from their own governments. It begins with the premise that the state is the main potential source of evil and must be supervised and controlled if human rights are to be protected. It ignores, however, the potential for nonstate actors to violate human rights, as well as imperfections in the institution of extradition.[3] If universal human rights are to be served, a state in custody of a murderer must either punish or extradite him. Certainly, a murderer's status should not improve when he escapes to another jurisdiction. In the real world, however, states pay lip-service to legal norms while their actions bespeak political motivations: over the last fifteen years, other European states have failed to extradite a single terrorist to Turkey.

While human rights doctrine protects the individual, it can also undermine the effective functioning of a state. Because the doctrine requires transparency, democracy, freedom of speech, and governmental accountability, it may expose a state's weaknesses. Particularly if the state is internally unstable, a hostile party can easily use human rights as a pretext to stir up domestic dissent and discontent.[4] The dilemma faced by Turkish authorities today is that the still-anarchic international system is helpless to protect the threatened state against such intrusions.[5]

After the horrendous terrorist attacks on the United States on September 11, 2001, the world has learned by bitter experience that terrorism per se is a menace to the protection of human rights, and the international system must be refashioned to combat it effectively. Otherwise the already anarchic nature of the international system shall be further exacerbated, with extremely adverse consequences for even the most fundamental human rights.

Human Rights and Turkey's Relations with the EU

A strange consensus exists across the wide Turkish political spectrum in favor of full integration of Turkey into the EU. Separatists, political Islamists, and the establishment all support efforts for full membership, albeit for sometimes contradictory reasons. Islamists and separatists hope that membership will bring a liberal democratic political environment in which they might freely campaign for their cause, while the establishment desires membership because it would anchor Turkey permanently in the West and *pari passu* reinforce secularism.

Relations between the EU and Turkey were institutionalized by the Ankara Agreement of 1963. After many ups and downs in their relations, due mainly to tensions with Greece and disagreement over democracy and human rights,[6] Turkey and the EU established a customs union in 1995. Today, Turkish goods move freely within the EU, Turkey and the European member states have a common tariff and commercial policy, and the Ankara Agreement is part of the EU's legal system.

On the question of Turkish membership in the European Union, however, no meaningful progress has been made, nor appears likely in the near future. In 1997 the Luxembourg European Council decided that the EU should enlarge to include the former socialist states of Central and Eastern Europe, but not Turkey, whereupon Ankara suspended its political relations with the EU.[7] Then, the Helsinki European Council of December 1999 changed its policy and declared Turkey to be a candidate for EU membership, agreeing to treat it on the same basis as other candidate states.[8] In practice, however, this did not make any real difference, since the EU has not even begun negotiations with Turkey for membership. On the other hand, it has already started negotiations for membership with all the other candidates—Poland, the Czech Republic, Hungary, Slovenia, Estonia, Romania, Bulgaria, Lithuania, Latvia, Slovakia, and the Republic of Cyprus. In the Nice Summit of 2000, the EU accepted an enlargement schedule, to be realized by 2010, for all the candidates except Turkey.[9] It explains this delay on the grounds that Turkey has not yet satisfied the political part of the so-called Copenhagen criteria, which states that "membership requires that the candidate country has achieved stability of institutions guaranteeing democracy, the rule of law, human rights and respect for and protection of minorities."[10] Turkey is bound to have difficulties in meeting the Copenhagen criteria, but the difference from the previous position is that the ball is now in Turkey's court. If the country satisfies the criteria, negotiations with the EU will presumably begin.

Since the Luxembourg European Council, the EU has issued two reports on Turkey's progress toward meeting the Copenhagen criteria, the conclusions of which Turkey is now hotly discussing.[11] Turkey's Supreme Coordinating Human Rights Council, working under the Ministry of State for Human Rights, in 1999 issued its own comprehensive report wherein it identifies fifty-three key legal areas in need of reform.[12] If and when it is admitted to the EU, Turkey will have to adopt and apply all of the accumulated rules, regulations, and practices of the EU (the so-called *acquis communautaire*), which will require a high degree of stability and competence from its administrative and judicial bodies.

The EU itself has established an Accession Partnership for Turkey, as it has done for other candidates, in order to prepare Turkey for the accession.[13] The Accession Partnership is a kind of road map for reforms, the implementation of which would bring Turkey in line with the EU requirements. It envisages two-stage reforms: reforms in the short term (within one year) and in the medium term (within four years). It is a preaccession project to prepare Turkey. Rising to this challenge and opportunity, Turkey has embarked on implementing the terms of the Accession Partnership. It has adopted a National Adjustment Program, a document of more than 1,000 pages that covers a host of reform areas, the timetable, and the measures to be taken. It would require Turkey to adopt about ninety-four new laws, amend some ninety-three existing laws, and take about 4,000 additional measures.

Recently the Turkish Grand National Assembly (TGNA) amended thirty-four articles of the constitution in order to implement the terms of the National Adjustment Program. The amendments have made improvements on such sensitive issues as the Kurdish question, the status of the National Security Council, freedom of expression, and the position of political parties.

Following this wave of the constitutional reforms, the TGNA is now bracing itself for a second wave of reforms and for passing the necessary implementing measures. Thus it is hoped that Turkey will have satisfied the requirements of the Copenhagen criteria before 2004 and begin accession talks.

The Role of the Strasbourg Institutions

In 1987, when Turkey applied for full membership in the European Community (EC), it also recognized the competence of the now-defunct European Commission of Human Rights to receive individual petitions from Turkish citizens with regard to violations of their human rights as guaranteed by the Convention. In 1990 Turkey recognized the competence of the ECHR as well. While the commission was abolished in 1998, the ECHR became permanent in November 1998 and exercises a decisive, if indirect, influence on the Turkish legal and political system. Anyone subject to the jurisdiction of the Turkish government may apply to the ECHR if he believes that his rights under the Convention have been violated by the state organs after he has exhausted all the relevant effective local remedies. The number of such applications against Turkey made to the ECHR since November 1998 exceeded 2,500 by June 2000.[14] For many years, applications originating from the districts of southeastern Turkey stricken by terrorism have gone directly to the ECHR before applicants have exhausted legal channels within Turkey. In other words, the ECHR has been functioning as a court of first instance with respect to such cases, on the grounds that the local remedies in the southeast are not effective. Moreover, the commission and the ECHR have virtually reversed the principle of the burden of proof in the southeast Turkish cases, in particular where the commission itself established the facts. Applicants were not required to prove their allegations against the government; instead, the Turkish government was in effect required to prove its innocence. A glance at numerous cases immediately reveals the weaknesses in that legal process.[15] In one typical case, a judgment was entered against the government (in spite of a host of exculpatory evidence) on the basis of allegations from applicants whose spouses were fighting on the side of the PKK against Turkish security forces. Thus, the resulting condemnation of Turkey was based solely on allegations by individuals with links to the PKK. Indeed, the ECHR seems to have formed an *a priori* opinion of Turkish culpability. On one notable day, it decided fifteen cases and gave the government's counsel only thirty minutes to defend the first eleven of them.[16]

In the highly publicized case of PKK leader Abdullah Öcalan, the ECHR—perhaps swayed by the prevailing political mood in Europe—seemed to exceed its powers altogether. Within hours of Öcalan's arrest, an application was made to the ECHR on his behalf that alleged violations of several articles of the Convention and requested that the ECHR order the Turkish government to comply with the terms of the Convention. The ECHR informed the government of the application and invited it to respond. Before the government could do so, however, the CPT informed Ankara that it intended to visit Imrali Island, where Öcalan was detained. The government granted the request, as required by law. Shortly after the CPT's return to Strasbourg, the ECHR—without waiting for the government's comments—called for interim measures to ensure a fair trial and the protection of Öcalan's health.[17]

The Strasbourg institutions thus seem to have politicized what ought to be judicial functions. It is Turkey's duty under both the Convention and its own laws to ensure that all detainees or suspects under its jurisdiction receive a fair trial before its courts. If the trial is not fair, then the defendant may seek a remedy from the ECHR. In fact, more than half of all applications made to the ECHR from some forty nations involve complaints of unfair trials. But all of these applications are made after the conclusion of the trial in the national court. In the Öcalan case, the CPT and ECHR acted in advance, giving the impression that they were responding to requests from EU members' governments. Nevertheless, the ECHR continues to exercise an intrusive and deep-penetrating influence on the Turkish political and legal system, although the Turkish establishment has not yet felt the brunt of the change. In fact, the ECHR has further demonstrated, in the case of the United Communist Party of Turkey (Türkiye Birlesik Komünist Partisi–TBKP), that no part of the Turkish state organization or law, including the constitution, is exempt from European supervision.[18] Quite apart from the question of whether or not the ECHR is exceeding its jurisdiction, it is important to point out that its decisions might lead to the erosion of the Turkish constitution, to the extent that the latter is not in accord with the Convention.[19] Yet the government has so far complied with the ECHR's judgments.

Democracy and the Rule of Law

The Copenhagen document of the CSCE rightly states that democracy and the rule of law are fundamental to the protection of human rights. As the European Commission's 1998 regular report acknowledged, Turkey is a constitutional republic with a multiparty parliament, a president, a government, a public administration, and a judicial system. Its political structure is laid down by the 1982 constitution, which was drawn up by the military after the 1980 coup and approved by referendum. This constitution has been substantially amended by the TGNA in light of the requirements of the Copenhagen criteria. The constitution characterizes the republic as "a democratic, secular and social state governed by rule of law." Secularism and the unitary nature of the state are the hallmarks of the entire politico-legal system, so much so that, in the eyes of many, they constitute Turkey's Achilles' heel.

The European Commission concluded in its December 1989 opinion on the Turkish application for full membership that successive reforms had resulted in "a parliamentary democracy closer to Community models." In its Agenda 2000, the commission further observed that "Turkey has a government and a Parliament resulting from multi-party democratic elections and an administration capable of framing and applying legislation compatible with *acquis communautaire*."[20]

As in other European states, the public institutions of Turkey are accountable to the law for their actions. Acts of parliament are subject to judicial review by the Constitutional Court, and those of the administration by the Council of State. Article 125 of the constitution reads: "Recourse to judicial review shall be available against all actions and acts of the administration." However, decisions of the Supreme Military Council and the Supreme Council of Judges and Public Prosecutors, independent decisions of the president, and some acts dating from the 1980 coup are exempt from judicial review.[21] Such exceptions may lead to a violation of Article 13 of the Convention, which requires a member state to make available to everyone under its jurisdiction an effective remedy against grievances by any other party. Scholars, nongovernmental organizations (NGOs), and the Supreme Coordinating Council agree that the constitution should be amended so as to extend judicial review to those acts that have been previously exempt.

In addition, the electoral law that establishes a national threshold of 10 percent for the representation of political parties in the parliament needs to be reformed. The 1999 regular report on Turkey's application for membership to the EU states that the 10-percent threshold is responsible for nonrepresentation in the parliament of approximately 5 million voters, out of 31 million votes cast in the last general election in 1999.[22] The Republican People's Party (Cumhuriyet Halk Partisi— CHP) is now a victim of the law in question. The Supreme Coordinating Council's report suggests lowering the threshold to a more reasonable 5 percent.

Civilian Control of the Military

As stated above, the Turkish military has intervened three times since 1960 to reestablish law and order when civilian authorities proved unable to control civil strife. In fact, the military has had a strong influence over the governing of the country since the Republic was established, because it views itself as the protector of Atatürk's secular, modernizing agenda. Therein lies another irony of the Turkish human rights imbroglio: the military elite is the most pro-Western force in the country.

The EU's 1998 and 1999 regular reports point to some anomalies in relations between the military and civilian authorities.[23] They note, for example, that the chief of general staff is not responsible to the defense minister but to the prime minister, and that the National Security Council exercises a disproportionate influence in the running of the state. A report of the European Parliament on Turkey reached a similar conclusion:

> As for the role played by the army in society, it must be said that its influence over Turkish political life is excessive by any standards. Its *de facto* and *de jure* position in the legal and constitutional framework is far in excess of what is used in the EU member states.[24]

In acknowledgment of the problem, the Supreme Coordinating Council has suggested amendments to the constitution that would ensure that civilian members of the NSC outnumber military members and restrict the NSC to advising the Council of Ministers solely on security issues. NGOs observing Turkey insist that the NSC be abolished altogether.[25] The TGNA now seems to have taken the middle ground. It has amended the constitution to reshuffle the Council's membership so as to give a clear weight to the civilian members, increasing the number of civilians to seven, compared to five military members. It has also brought forward the advisory nature of the Council's resolutions, formerly called "decisions," by renaming them "recommendations." However, the constitutional amendment has not gone so far as to make the chief of staff responsible to the defense minister.

An Independent Judiciary

The prominent place of the judiciary in Turkey's constitution is well acknowledged. It includes judicial and administrative courts, the Constitutional Court, the Court of Appeals, and the Council of State. The constitution expressly states that the judiciary is and must be independent. It is a punishable offense to attempt to influence judges in their judicial duties. The Supreme Council of Judges and Public Prosecutors alone has the power to appoint and dismiss judges and prosecutors, except for members of the Constitutional Court, who are appointed by the president. The membership of the Supreme Council includes, along with a majority of senior judges, the justice minister and his undersecretary. There is now a consensus to the effect that the presence of the latter two undermines the council's independence, and the next overhaul of the constitution will likely remove the minister and undersecretary from the council. Otherwise, the EU's 1998 report faulted the State Security Courts, which deal with terrorism or crimes against the state, for not "offering defendants a fair trial." The reasons cited for this included, among others, overreliance on confession rather than traditional investigative methods; the relative status of the prosecutor (who sits next to judges) and defense lawyers (who sit below and whose points of law are not entered into the trial record in full, but summarized by the presiding judge); the slowness of trials; and long detentions pending trial without giving due reason. The judicial system's excessive workload is said to undermine the efficiency of the system. In civil justice and normal criminal courts, the slowness of the procedures raises concern. All relevant circles now agree that the judiciary needs to be reformed according to EU guidelines, and both the Supreme Coordinating Council's report and the EU's Regular Reports call for an urgent reform of the judiciary.

The current amendment of the Constitution has made certain modest improvements in this field, as well. For example, under the current constitution, individuals have the "right to a fair trial" and the guarantee that any information obtained in violation of law cannot be used in court as evidence.

Freedom of Association and Political Parties

Political parties are, according to the constitution, an inseparable part of the democratic system. However, the constitution and the Political Parties Act expressly prohibit ethnic and religious parties, and since the founding of the Republic more than twenty parties that were established (under disguised names) by Islamists and separatists have been outlawed, mostly by the Constitutional Court. In recent years seven such dissolved parties have brought cases against Turkey before the ECHR. One of them, the Welfare Party (Refah Partisi—RP, sometimes called the Prosperity Party), lost, while three of them emerged victorious—the TBKP, the Socialist Party (Sosyalist Parti—SP), and the Freedom and Democracy Party (Özgürlük ve Demokrasi Partisi—ODP). The Welfare Party had been dissolved for promoting Islamic fundamentalism and the other six on the grounds that they promoted separatism or terrorism. The Constitutional Court has also dissolved the Virtue Party (Fazilet Partisi—FP) on the same grounds, and proceedings are long pending before the court for the dissolution of the pro-Kurdish People's Democracy Party (Halkın Demokrasi Partisi—HADEP). The Commission for Democracy through Law (the Venice Commission) of the Council of Europe recently reacted, in a sense, to this excessive suppression of political organization in what is known as the Venice Report, which lays down guidelines relevant to Turkish law.[26] The report made it clear that "prohibition or dissolution of political parties may only be justified in the case of parties which advocate the use of violence or use violence as a political means to overthrow the democratic constitutional order, thereby undermining the rights and freedoms guaranteed by the constitution." Specific examples of such justifiably repressed activity cited in the report include racism, xenophobia, and intolerance or involvement in terrorism or other subversive activities. But the report also emphasized that "a party that aims at a peaceful change of the constitutional order through lawful means cannot be prohibited or dissolved on the basis of freedom of opinion." The report would thus seem to conclude that ethnic or religious parties should be allowed to function. But the ECHR has most recently indicated in the *Case of the Virtue Party* that it would not look favorably upon religious parties that campaigned for the establishment of an Iranian-type political regime. The ECHR has made it clear that the Turkish court was right in dissolving the Virtue Party for having sought to use democratic means to establish a theocracy.[27] In remains unclear for the time being whether the ECHR would give the same treatment to ethnic parties that campaigned for the partition of the country along racial lines.

The fact is that a state may tolerate such parties as long as they do not have the potential to endanger public safety and national security. On the other hand, in a country where more than 30,000 people have been killed in the last fifteen years in order to establish or prevent the establishment of an ethnic state, it would be extremely difficult to persuade the majority that a separatist party whose goal it is to split the country is not a threat to the state and constitution. Likewise, a fundamentalist party that campaigns for the establishment of a theocracy may well threaten democratic order and human rights as universally understood. Therefore, much depends on the historical background and the democratic credentials of such parties and the degree of their determination to live within the same territory. Fundamentalism means to Turkey what Nazism means to Western European states. If EU member states could suspend political relations with Austria after Jörg Haider's Freedom Party became a coalition partner in the Austrian government, even though his party posed no danger to the democratic system, then it follows that Turkey has legitimate reason to act likewise toward those in its midst who hope to fuel armed ethnic terrorism.

Bearing those reservations in mind, the constitution has now been revised in a fashion that would bring the Turkish legal system closer to those of the EU member states. The constitution now makes it more difficult for the Constitutional Court to dissolve political parties, making it subject to the meeting of stricter conditions and requiring it to decide dissolution cases by a four-fifths majority instead of the previous two thirds. Furthermore, the constitution allows for a graduated series of measures short of dissolution to be taken against recalcitrant political parties.[28] Such a system would recognize the parties' right to be different so long as they remain loyal to democracy within a unitary state. Insofar as they adhere to that requirement, fear about them may dissipate over time.

A Healthy Civil Society

The EU's 1998 regular report observed that "Turkey has made an effort to gradually bring about a real improvement in the enjoyment of such rights as freedom of association, proof of this being the mushrooming number of NGOs in Turkey."[29] Indeed, Turkey is a fertile land for associations—74,617 of them are currently registered— although they remain subject to many restrictions.[30] In the fields of democracy and human rights alone, a number of well-organized associations exist, ranging from the Human Rights Association and Mazlum-Der to the Turkish Democracy Foundation, Turkey's Human Rights Foundation, and Helsinki Citizens' Assembly. Initially, the state looked on some NGOs with suspicion, and some of their activists were prosecuted for violations of law.[31] Now, however, the state and the NGOs have begun to cooperate in the interest of protecting human rights. In 1999, the former minister of state for human rights arranged a workshop in Ankara with representatives of NGOs in order to search for ways and means to strengthen democracy and human rights. The findings of that workshop have now been published by the ministry. The current constitutional amendment has further improved the right to freedom of association and assembly, which cannot fail to contribute to the development of a healthy civil society.

The Kurdish Conundrum

The question of ethnic minorities is extremely sensitive in Turkey given the country's diversity and painful history. During its decline, the Ottoman Empire suffered very much from having given an international status (through capitulations and otherwise) to minorities, who had been manipulated and in some cases created by European interventionists pursuing their own interests. Given the near-protectorate status of the empire in the nineteenth century, the Sublime Porte was almost paralyzed in its domestic and external affairs by various groups that abused their official "minority status"—often with outside assistance.[32] To this day, Turks harbor a bitter memory of some minority groups' collaboration with the occupying powers after the First World War and their attempts to thwart Atatürk's bid to forge a modern nation-state out of the ruins of the Ottoman Empire.

The Lausanne Conference of 1923 not only established the present boundaries of the Republic of Turkey, but also settled the ethnic problem once and for all by permitting special status for *non-Muslim* minorities only. The Turks fiercely and successfully refused to extend minority status to any part of its Muslim population, which included the Kurds. Because the European states agreed to those terms, Western attempts to establish, directly or indirectly, Kurdish autonomy in Turkey today arouse considerable suspicion and resentment among Turks.

In any event, in Turkey the concept of "minority" depends on one's point of view. If, for example, Kurds are a minority in racial terms, as Sunni Muslims they are certainly part of the majority in religious terms, since the Sunnis are the largest religious group. By the same definition, many non-Sunni ethnic Turks would be considered part of a religious minority. Accordingly, Ankara's common-sense policy is to recognize no minorities except those (non-Muslims) whose status was established by the Treaty of Lausanne. By the same reasoning, Turkey has accepted the Conference on Security and Cooperation in Europe's Copenhagen Document of 1990, which addresses minority rights, and the Geneva Report on National Minorities, subject to a reservation that reiterates the Lausanne formula. The government has so far refused to sign the (European) Framework Convention on Minorities or the European Charter for Regional or Minority Languages. Recently it signed the International Covenant on Civil and Political Rights, which contains an article on national minorities, but it is not clear whether or not the government will make a reservation to the document. The European Commission seems to have taken a conciliatory stance in light of Turkey's situation. Its 1998 regular report says: "The constitution does not recognize Kurds as a national or ethnic minority. There are no legal barriers to ethnic Kurds' participation in political and economic affairs, but Kurds who publicly or politically assert their ethnic identity risk harassment or prosecution." The report goes on to suggest that a political solution should be found to the problem in the southeast, which "could include recognition of certain forms of Kurdish cultural identity and greater tolerance of the ways of expressing that identity, provided it does not advocate separatism or terrorism."[33]

As the 1998 report suggested, the status of the Kurdish language remains somewhat ambiguous. The regime that was established in 1980 following the coup did indeed pass the restrictive Law on Publications in Languages other than Turkish, but that law was repealed in 1991. It is now commonly accepted that Kurdish is no longer banned in the context of cultural activities. In practice, Kurdish music, folklore, and customs are all permitted, as are publications in Kurdish in any form. All that remains prohibited is Kurdish-language education and television, but in practice the government tolerates radio broadcasts in Kurdish as well. With the current constitutional amendments this *de facto* situation has become *de jure*. Ankara will not agree to classify, categorize, and regulate minority languages, but instead will simply remove any restrictions on the use of such languages. It has taken the "residual rights" approach: anything that is not specifically prohibited by law is allowed, hence it is left to individuals to choose what language or languages to use.[34] In formal communications with government authorities, those who cannot use Turkish have always had access to free translation from and into their own native tongue.

As things stand today, Turkey will probably seek to accommodate the legitimate needs and aspirations of its citizens of Kurdish origin by promoting democracy and individual human rights.[35] Although Turkey's history and fears of separatism will not allow for a fully fledged institutionalization of minorities along racial lines, individuals will be able to realize their aspirations within the democratic system. In Turkey, all people have the right to be different, but diversity cannot come at the expense of unity.[36]

Freedom of Expression

The perceived or actual dangers that separatist terrorism and fundamentalism have posed to the integrity of the state have conditioned Turkey's policy of freedom of expression. As the European Commission stated in its 1998 regular report, "Despite improvement in recent years freedom of expression is not fully assured in Turkey."[37] In fact, the unamended constitution and a number of other laws have tended to restrict freedom of speech, but only because of the threats of separatism and fundamentalism. The TGNA, in its efforts to meet the requirements of the political leg of the Copenhagen criteria, has amended several Articles of the Constitution (Article 13, 14, 26 and 28) in order to bring freedom of expression in Turkey into substantial harmony with the terms of the European Convention on Human Rights. The government is now in the process of introducing implementing legislation.

The state so far has used two legal instruments in combating separatism and fundamentalism, two perceived "menaces": Article 312 of the Criminal Code and the Act for the Prevention of Terrorism. A number of politicians, human rights activists, journalists, trade unionists, and novelists have been prosecuted for having violated one of them, including Necmettin Erbakan, the former prime minister and chairman of the now-defunct Welfare Party. In 2000 he was sentenced to one year in prison for a campaign speech he made in 1994 that was found to promote hostility between ethnic groups (the sentence was ultimately suspended).

Article 312 expressly prohibits seditious libel, and the Act for the Prevention of Terrorism outlaws separatist propaganda, in an attempt to discourage and hopefully prevent the promotion of feelings of ill will and hostility between ethnically or religiously different segments of the population. The main problem with Article 312 is not its existence in law books, but the ambiguity surrounding its application.[38] It is couched in terms so broad that virtually anyone expressing views critical of the state's policies toward separatism or fundamentalism may find himself summoned to a prosecutor's office. The problem could have been mitigated if the judiciary had adhered to those criteria specified by the ECHR. Instead, the Turkish courts' interpretation of freedom of speech, in particular as it applies to Article 312 and the Act for the Prevention of Terrorism, is not compatible with the ECHR's case law. The state and the courts have yet to come to terms with the fact that advocating the abolition of a given law falls under the category of protected speech so long as peaceful means are used. The way to peaceful change must remain open if people are to be allowed to vent their anger or dissatisfaction and seek redress of grievances while simultaneously affirming the legitimacy of constitutional democracy.

Turkish public opinion is divided on what to do with Article 312. Secularists are opposed to its abolition, as is the Nationalist Movement (or National Action) Party (Milliyetçi Hareket Partisi—MHP). They look on it as an effective legal means to protect the integrity of the secular state. Human rights activists and some political parties such as FP and HADEP, however, would prefer to see it abolished. The Supreme Coordinating Council's report, some establishment political parties, and the president himself seek only its revision.[39] It would seem that the TGNA shall revise both pieces of legislation in a fashion that would bring the Turkish legal system in close harmony with the Convention.

The Death Penalty

The TGNA has now amended the constitution to abolish the death penalty except in cases of war, immediate war threat or crimes of terrorism. Previously, approximately forty legal provisions in Turkish law called for the death penalty.[40] In practice, however, the death penalty has been seldom carried out except in extraordinary times in which the very existence of the nation was threatened, as was the case between 1975 and 1980, when terrorism claimed more than twenty lives per day. Since 1984 no executions have taken place at all, and capital punishment would have been long abolished in law as well if not for the threat posed by organized terrorism. The death sentence given to Abdullah Öcalan has only served to renew the death penalty debate, and public opinion remains divided. Victims of terrorism press for Öcalan's execution, but the ECHR has stated that he must not be executed until his application before the court has been decided.[41] Most political parties, including one wing of the government coalition (the MHP), would agree in principle to the abolition of the death penalty, but do not wish to see Öcalan benefit from the change.[42]

Abolition of the death penalty is a requirement of the Copenhagen criteria. The European Parliament has expressly stated that it would not give its consent to the accession of any EU candidate that has capital punishment in its laws.[43] On the other hand, keeping the death penalty on the books without applying it has so far brought no good to Turkey. Other European states have refused to extradite to fugitive Turkey mafia members and common murderers in their custody on the grounds that the death penalty remains a legal possibility. The current constitutional amendment seems to have dealt with all these issues, except for Öcalan's situation, although the TGNA has yet to pass the necessary implementing legislation to give flesh to the constitutional changes.

Torture

National laws strictly prohibit torture and inhuman or degrading treatment in Turkey. Violators are subject to severe punishment and a permanent ban from civil service. Nevertheless, in several cases the ECHR has found violations of Article Three of the European Convention on Human Rights, indicating that torture is a continuing evil that the government has not been able to eradicate fully.

In legal and practical terms, however, the situation is fast improving. Amendments to Articles 243 and 245 of the Criminal Code have brought the definition of torture in line with international standards, and new provisions in several laws and regulations seek to remove its root causes. Notable changes include: more effective prosecution of allegations of torture; regulations on the apprehension, length of detention, and treatment of suspects; improvement of prison conditions; prevention of falsified medical reports; establishment of a parliamentary human rights committee to deal firmly with torture allegations; watchdog activities by NGOs; effective press coverage; access for prisoners to lawyers, doctors, and relatives; and perhaps most importantly, intensive training of law-enforcement personnel. Moreover, social opprobrium arising from greater publicity of torture tends to discourage violations.[44]

The law is fully in place, but the question of full implementation remains, to some extent, unanswered. First, the Turkish judicial system suffers from the lack of a well organized and equipped "judicial police." Public prosecutors have to rely on the police in their investigation of crimes because their own offices lack the necessary staff. But since the police come under the purview of the Ministry of Internal Affairs, prosecutors have little actual power over them. Secondly, the police, not being well trained in judicial affairs, may be less than scrupulous about their investigative methods. In cases where a police officer investigates a fellow officer, doubts naturally arise about the integrity of the process. Thirdly, most human rights violations stem from actions by law-enforcement personnel, but according to terms of the Act for Trials of Civil Servants, prosecution of the latter is possible only with the consent of their superiors (i.e., the governor or the minister of internal affairs, depending on the status of the accused). The solutions to these problems, at least, are refreshingly clear: in addition to better training for officers, improvement will require the establishment of a judicial police force and the reform or abolition of the Act for Trials of Civil Servants.

Assessing Human Rights in Turkey

Despite ethnic and religious provocations, Turkish citizens today enjoy effective democratic rule and are justifiably proud of their success. But they are also eager to preserve that progress and continue to harbor deep-rooted fears about the future of their democracy and territorial unity after decades of relentless blows from terrorism and fundamentalism. Because these fears have shaped Turkey's most basic policies and behavior, continued liberalization is contingent upon alleviating those concerns.

Turkey has every right to combat terrorism, but it needs to be more patient and attentive in distinguishing wrong from right. The Turkish people and government have now come to agree, thanks to the debate on the Copenhagen criteria, that reforms are needed in order to promote human rights and democracy. The Turkish nation has demonstrated its ability to adapt itself to new and changing conditions, a fact that gives cause for optimism. However, in order to fulfill its obligations to the EU, it must still make some difficult decisions and tackle some chronic political, structural, and legal questions. Change is always painful, but is now inexorable, even if it comes at the expense of long-standing internal balances and traditions. Insofar as EU norms and Turkish aspirations foster such change, they have a vital role to play in the future.

Notes

[1] The "Strasbourg institutions" formerly included the European Commission of Human Rights, which ceased to function in 1999.

[2] Turkey is also a party to the UN Convention for the Prevention of Torture.

[3] Cf. Nigel S. Rodley, "Can Armed Opposition Groups Violate Human Rights?" in *Human Rights in the Twenty-First Century: A Global Challenge*, ed. Kathleen E. Mahoneey and Paul Mahoneey (Boston: Martinus Nijhoff, 1993), pp. 313–14; Bülent Tanör, "Human Rights Problems in Turkey," in *Human Rights Education Project, Activity Report* (Izmir: Izmir Bar Association, Jan. 1, 1997–Dec. 31, 1997), p. 35.

[4] The Western states used the then-CSCE human dimension mechanism approximately 100 times between 1989 and 1990 against the Soviet Union. After the dissolution of the latter they lost their enthusiasm. See A. Gündüz, *Security and Human Rights in Europe: The CESCE Process* (Istanbul: M. Ü. Ayrupa Topluluğu Enstitüsü, 1994), pp. 211–13.

[5] A. Gündüz, "The Dilemma of Human Rights and Security in Combating Terrorism: An International Law Perspective" (in Turkish), in *Hukuk Devletinde Terör ve Örgütlü Suçla Mücadele*, ed. Umut Vakfı (Istanbul: BETA, 1996), pp. 190–207.

[6] See Karen Smith, "The Use of Political Conditionality in the EU's Relations with Third Countries: How Effective?" *European Foreign Affairs Review*, Summer 1998, p. 253.

[7] "Conclusions of the Luxembourg European Council, 12-13 December 1997," *Bulletin of the European Union*, vol. 12 (1997), point 1.5.

[8] "Conclusions of the Helsinki European Council," *Bulletin of the European Union*, vol. 12 (1999), point 4

[9] See Presidency Conclusions, Nice European Council Meeting, Dec. 7–9 2000, *SN 400/00, EN* and Treaty of Nice, Brussels, Dec. 12, 2000, SN 533/00 EN.

[10] "Copenhagen European Council, Copenhagen, 21-22 June, Conclusions of Presidency," *Bulletin of the European Communities*, vol. 26, no. 6 (1993), point I.13, p. 13.

[11] See European Commission, "Regular Report 1998 from the Commission on Turkey's Progress Towards Accession," *Bulletin of the European Union*, supplement 16/98 (Luxembourg: European Commission, 1999); and "Regular Report 1999 from the Commission on Turkey's Progress Towards Accession," *Bulletin of the European Union*, supplement 16/19 (Luxembourg: European Commission, 2000).

[12] Supreme Coordinating Human Rights Council of the Prime Ministry, *Measures Which Turkey Has to Take in Light of the Political Copenhagen Criteria: Calendar for Democracy, Rule of Law and Human Rights* (in Turkish) (Ankara: n.p., 1999).

[13] See, Commission of the European Communities, Proposal for a Council Decision on the Principles, Priorities, Intermediate Objectives and Conditions Contained in the Accession Partnership with the Republic of Turkey, 8.11.2000, Brussels, and Council Decision 2001-235 EC, in *Official Journal*, L-85, 24.3.2001, Brussels.

[14] Statistics supplied to the author from the Registry of the European Court of Human Rights for the period Nov. 1, 1998, the date of the Court's establishment, to June 29, 2000.

[15] See, for example, *Case of Aydin v. Turkey* (application no. 57/1996/676/866), judgment: Strasbourg, Sept. 25, 1997; *Case of Mentes and Others v. Turkey* (application no. 58/1996/677/867), judgment: Strasbourg, Nov. 28, 1997; *Case of Kurt v. Turkey* (application no. 151/1997/799/1002), judgment: Strasbourg, May 25, 1998.

[16] On July 8, 1999, the ECHR decided the following cases against Turkey: *Sürek and Özdemir* (application nos. 23927/94 and 24277/94); *Polat* (application no. 23560/94); *Tanrikulu* (application no. 23763/94); *Sürek No. 4* (application no. 2472/94); *Aslan* (application no. 23462/94); *Sürek No. 2* (application no. 24122/94); *Erdogan and Ince* (application nos. 25067/94 and 25068/94); *Okçuoglu* (application no. 24246/94); *Baskaya and Okçuoglu* (application nos. 23536/94 and 24408/94); *Sürek No. 3)* (application no. 24735/94); *Sürek No. 1* (application no. 26682/95); *Karatas* (application no. 23168); *Gerger* (application no. 24919/94); *Ceylan* (application no. 23556/94); *Cakioi* (application no. 23657/94).

[17] *Öcalan-Turkey* (no. 4622/99), European Court of Human Rights, *Information Note on the Case Law of the Court*, Mar. 1999, p. 25.

[18] *Case of the United Communist Party of Turkey and Others v. Turkey* (no. 133/1996/752/1151), judgment: Strasbourg, Jan. 30, 1998.

[19] A. Gündüz, "Has the European Court of Human Rights Become Our Constitutional Court?" (in Turkish), *Yeni Türkiye*, vol. 4, no. 22 (1998), p. 1367.

[20] "Agenda 2000 for a Stronger and Wider Union," *Bulletin of the European Union*, vol. 7/8 (1999), point I.1.

[21] According to the constitution, all but a few presidential decisions must be signed by the Council of Ministers. For example, the president may independently appoint some senior judges and university rectors and file appeals to the Constitutional Court against laws he believes are unconstitutional.

[22] "Regular Report 1999," para. B, point 1.1.

[23] Ibid.; "Regular Report 1999," para. B, point 1.1.

[24] See European Parliament, *Report on the Commission Reports on Developments in Relations with Turkey since the Entry into Force of the Customs Union*, DOC-EN\RR1356\35875, PE 221.635/fin, p. 12.

[25] Başbakanlık, *Rule of Law, Democracy, and Human Rights: A Workshop with Nongovernmental Organizations* (in Turkish) (Ankara: Basbakanlık Basımevı, 1999), pp. 44, 105.

[26] Venice Commission, *Guidelines on Prohibition and Dissolution of Political Parties and Analogous Measures, Adopted by the Venice Commission at Its 41st Plenary Session* (Strasbourg: Venice Commission, Jan. 10, 2000), CDL-INF (20 00) 1.

[27] In the ECHR's opinion, "the offending remarks and policy statements made by Refah's leaders form a whole and give a clear picture of a model of state and society organised according to religious rules, which was conceived and proposed by Refah." See *Case of Refah Partisi and Others v. Turkey*, ECHR, Judgment (merits), paragraph 76,31.7.2001, REF00002693, (http://www.hudoc.echr.coe.int). The ECHR further said that "the remarks cited as grounds for Refah's dissolution . . . give the impression that Refah did not exclude the possibility of recourse to force in certain circumstances in order to oppose certain political programmes, or to gain power and retain it." (loc. cit.) The court finally concluded that "the real chance Refah had to implement its political plans undeniably made the danger of those plans for public order more tangible and more immediate." Ibid., para. 79 in fine.

[28] Cf. Fazıl Sağlam, *Current Problems of Political Parties Law* (in Turkish) (Istanbul: BETA, 1999), p. 163.

[29] "Regular Report 1998," p. 16.

[30] Statistics supplied to the author by the General Directorate, Department of Associations of the Ministry of Internal Affairs. On the restrictions, see Hüsnü Öndül, "Human Rights and Democratic Standards in Turkey" (in Turkish), in *Rule of Law, Democracy, and Human Rights*, pp. 112–13. The current constitutional amendment is sure to meet most of the claims in that regard.

[31] See Yılmaz Ensaroğlu (chairman of Mazlum-Der), "Resolution of Human Rights Question of Turkey: Fundamental Approaches and Proposals" (in Turkish), in *Rule of Law, Democracy, and Human Rights*, p. 51.

[32] N. Sousa, *The Capitulatory Regime of Turkey: Its History, Origin, and Nature* (Baltimore, Md.: Johns Hopkins University Press, 1933).

[33] "Regular Report 1998," p. 18.

[34] See Nazli Ilıcak, "Some Obstacles on the Way to the EU" (in Turkish), *Yeni Safak*, July 20, 2000.

[35] Hüsnü Öndül stated that the Human Rights Association views the Kurdish issue as a matter of human rights and democracy. See Öndül, "Human Rights and Democratic Standards in Turkey," p. 115.

[36] Cf. Graham E. Fuller, "The Fate of the Kurds," *Foreign Affairs*, Spring 1993, pp. 109, 115.

[37] "Regular Report 1998," p. 14.

[38] Seditious libel exists, for example, in the laws of the United Kingdom, but with the difference that words would constitute seditious libel only if they were likely to cause readers to act unconstitutionally. See *McNae's Essential Law for Journalists*, ed. Walter Greenwood and Tom Welsh, 10th ed. (London: Butterworths, 1988), p. 133.

[39] "Statement by the President," *Sabah*, Aug. 5, 2000.

[40] See Öndül, "Human Rights and Democratic Standards in Turkey," p. 104.

[41] See ECHR, *Information Note on the Case Law of the Court*, Nov. 1999, p. 23.

[42] "Statement by the Prime Minister," *Sabah*, June 23, 2000.

[43] *Resolution in the Oostlander Report, A4-368/97*, adopted Dec. 4, 1997 (PE 264 945), para. 4.

[44] As to views of the Committee of Ministers of the Council of Europe on the Turkish practice concerning torture, and measures taken by the Turkish government, see "Interim Resolution DH (99) 434 on the action of the security forces in Turkey, measures of general character," *Human Rights Bulletin*, no. 46, Council of Europe, Human Rights Directorate (Sept. 1999), pp. 58, 63.

2

Turkey and Europe: Security Issues

by Hüseyin Bağcı

During the Cold War, the North Atlantic Treaty Organization provided Turkey its national security guarantee. Turkey in turn contributed to the policy of credible deterrence by its pivotal status in NATO's southeastern flank.[1] Turkey's relationship with the European Union basically evolved on the basis of the Ankara Agreement of 1963, specifying that this relationship would result in an eventual membership that would anchor Turkey to the West not only in terms of economics, politics and identity aspects, but also with respect to security.

NATO's establishment in 1949 as a collective defense organization was a response to the threat emanating from the existence of the Soviet Union. Since the dissolution of the Soviet Union in 1991, European security has undergone a radical change of character. A new threat surfaced: instability due to the transformation in Central and Eastern Europe. The crises of Bosnia-Herzegovina and Kosovo presented serious challenges to the NATO Alliance and demonstrated that meeting modern-day crises requires not only collective defense but also enhanced capabilities in crisis management and crisis prevention. As its role in Central Europe and the Balkans was gradually defined, NATO, by the New Strategic Concept, set out to create the means for reinforcing Europeans' ability to take security actions without the direct intervention of the Alliance. For the same reason, the EU has developed the European Security and Defense Identity/Initiative (ESDI) within NATO, the EU and the Western European Union (WEU) to take responsibility for managing crises and achieving a strong, comprehensive security approach. Meanwhile, under the EU's Common Foreign and Security Policy (CFSP), the Europeans are in the process of putting together a range of instruments, including the Rapid Reaction Force and a conflict prevention network, that will enhance their ability to respond to international challenges. These have been brought under the overall context of the common European Security and Defense Policy (CESDP).[2]

After the Franco-British declaration in Saint-Malo in 1998 and the Kosovo crisis in 1999, the European initiative began to take firmer shape in the European Councils of Helsinki (December 1999), Santa Maria da Feira (June 2000) and Nice (December 2000), thus gradually increasing uneasiness for Turkey in view of its reliance on recourse to NATO assets and capabilities in European-led operations, given that non EU NATO allies are excluded from the CESDP's decision-making. Turkey has raised its objections in several forums, arguing that its geographic location places it in the midst of most of the volatile areas identified by European security experts. However, in the recent efforts to give finer shape to the European security framework, there has been little development which would address Turkey's security concerns.

This paper analyzes the essentials of Turkey's security perceptions within the context of the European security initiative. Turkey played a critical role in NATO's southern flank during the Cold War and assumed a pivotal status with respect to coping with security challenges to Europe in the post–Cold War security structure. Taking into account the indivisible nature of security as a concept, the argument is that Turkey and the other non-EU European allies should be assigned an appropriate EU candidate status so that they are not excluded from the ESDP's decision-making mechanisms. After briefly discussing the national security aspect of Turkey's relations with NATO and the EU, the paper will provide an overview of the post–Cold War security architecture in Europe and a brief history of the development of the ESDI and CESDP, with an emphasis on the impact of the Kosovo crisis. The paper will then discuss Turkey's position vis-à-vis the CESDP and Turkey's arguments with respect to its role in European security. As a final remark, the paper underlines the official Turkish position that if providing security crosscuts multiple organizations, overlapping memberships are essential for a genuine security framework, and that Turkey, being a candidate for full EU membership, should be assigned an appropriate status whereby its national security would not be jeopardized by any EU operations.

Turkey and the Common European Security and Defense Policy

The significance of NATO in Turkey's National Security Culture

Since its founding in 1923, its unique geopolitical status has led the Republic of Turkey to seek security through alliances, pursue a circumspect foreign policy, and devote considerable efforts to cultivating the West.[3] After World War II, Turkey aspired to join NATO primarily to counter the Soviet threat. Its NATO membership solidified Ankara's Western orientation by establishing a long-lasting institutional and functional link with the West.[4] Turkey attaches particular importance to NATO as the linchpin of Euro-Atlantic security and stability. It believes that NATO, "with its indispensable trans-Atlantic link, core functions and the integrated military structure constitutes the basis on which Euro-Atlantic security is established."[5]

Turkey has defined strategic partnership and strategic cooperation as the key concepts of its security policy for its new geopolitical axis in the post–Cold War world. These concepts cover joint action and cooperation in regional problems and incidents that occur in different areas of the world, military partnership agreements, and the formation of permanent commissions in economic, military, political, and social fields through agreements among mutually favored states.[6] NATO membership forms the basis for any Turkish security policy to reach out to new regions with old neighbors, because NATO intervenes not only in the internal problems of Europe in the case of threats to European security, but also in out-of-area conflicts and internal crises. Ankara therefore wants to see NATO, not the EU, be the dominant security organization in Europe. It is NATO that can actually anchor Turkey as a basis of stability on NATO's southern flank.[7]

Two principles guide Turkey's understanding of national security policy: protection of territorial and national integrity and defense of legitimate rights and freedoms.[8] Turkey's recent security policy therefore does not rest upon nonviolent conflict resolution and international multilateralism. For Turkish officials, European security includes military and economic-social dimensions, the former mainly provided by an enlarged NATO and the latter by the enlarged EU.[9] It has been observed that "such a national security policy does not fit well into the overall European development characterized by multinational and multidimensional security policy organizations."[10]

Turkey has been a NATO member since 1952 and, as noted above, played a critical role in NATO's southern flank during the Cold War. Far from diminishing its strategic importance, the post–Cold War security structure made Turkey pivotal in dealing with any security threat to Europe. Thirteen out of the sixteen hotspots[11] of concern to European security determined by NATO experts surround Turkey's immediate periphery. Thus, any conflict or military operation in these hotspots concerns Turkey's national security interests as well as those of the Europeans. Moreover, the divergence between Turkey's and Europe's perceptions with respect to these areas of conflict is likely to widen when addressing these areas. For instance, Turkey's position on the Nagorno-Karabakh conflict is completely different from that of Europe and even from that of the United States, given Turkey's political, economic, and cultural relationship with Azerbaijan. Similarly, Turkey and Europe view the northern Iraq issue through different lenses. While northern Iraq poses foreign policy, security, and economic issues for Turkey, it is more a human rights concern for Europe. The Cyprus dispute is particularly significant in this context, because for the EU, Turkey itself is the problem in the accession negotiations between the EU and Cyprus. Negotiations have already started with the southern Republic of Cyprus, which is backed by the mainland—i.e. Greece, which is a member of the EU.

Turkey in the European Security Framework

Since the early 1960s, Turkey's relations with the EC/EU have been determined by security policy on the European side. In the bipolar world of two superpowers, Turkey had to be firmly bound to the Western camp to help counter the Soviet threat. Consequently, Turkey and the European Economic Community concluded the Association Agreement (Ankara Agreement) in 1963, establishing economic relations and stipulating eventual membership in the EC/EU. As foreseen by the Ankara Agreement, Turkey joined the Customs Union with the European Union in 1995. The European Commission turned down Turkey's 1989 application for full membership, and again at the 1997 European Council's Luxembourg Summit. Consequently, Turkey announced that it would suspend its relations with the European Union and that it would not accept "third-class" status. The main bulwark against Turkey had been the Greek veto, but there were also "silent no-ers." The Clinton administration urged the EU not to distance Turkey from Europe by consistently declining its application for full EU membership. Summer 1999 saw a thaw of relations between Greece and Turkey through the efforts of Greek and Turkish foreign ministers Yorgos Papandreou and İsmail Cem. The earthquakes that took place in both countries in late 1999 and the reciprocal rush for help in search-and-rescue missions intensified this dialogue. Finally, at the EU Council's Helsinki Summit in December 1999, the EU declared Turkey a candidate for full membership. The significance of the Helsinki Summit conclusions lay not only in according Turkey the candidacy status, but also in crystallizing the EU's resolve to proceed with its own defense and security structure. However, the question of where and how Turkey should fit into the new European security architecture has been conspicuously absent from the mainstream of European discussions about post–Cold War European restructuring. Yet, for Ankara, the answers to the questions how the coming European security architecture will be developed and what Turkey's place can and should be are of paramount importance.[12]

Another issue in the Turkish-EU security relations is the divergence in the perceptions of security risks. Contemporary military policy in Europe differs from traditional national defense in the sense that it is much more about military-backed intervention in conflicts outside NATO's area that may somehow affect Europe's security. In addition, the concept of security has broadened to include a variety of risks that could undermine Europe's stability. To cite a few, these risks are in the form of "armed conflicts of a limited nature deriving from unsettled border disputes or ethnic strife; the proliferation of weapons of mass destruction and their means of delivery, especially in the Middle East and South Asia; international terrorism, organized crime, drug trafficking, and uncontrolled illegal immigration; and environmental risks deriving from either modern industrial plants, transportation of dangerous substances, or military-related environmental damage."[13] These security risks are of non-military or mixed military-civilian character. They are also transnational. Hence, European governments believe that these challenges can best be met by international cooperative efforts that should be undertaken and organized by common security policy institutions. On the other hand, though these new security risks also affect Turkey, Turkey's security policy agenda only partially overlaps with this main European one.[14]

Turkey faces more numerous and more precisely defined security risks than its European allies. Despite the demise of the Soviet empire, Russia still causes concern for security on many fronts, such as Turkey's relations with the former Soviet states. Moreover, Russia poses the biggest challenge to the transportation of Caspian oil and gas via the "East-West corridor," proposing a northern route instead of the southern route through Turkey. NATO's eastward enlargement, which renders Russia uneasy, is also a concern for Turkey. Turkey incurs compound security threats from its southern neighbors in the Middle East, including weapons of mass destruction, drug trafficking, illegal migration and terrorism. Moreover, Turkey's unresolved dispute with Greece over Cyprus and the Aegean poses serious security risks, since it has a special European security dimension.

The WEU also deserves attention in considering Europe's security initiatives. The WEU was established by the Modified Brussels Treaty of 1954, based on the 1948 Brussels Treaty, to provide NATO's security guarantee to West Germany without making it a member of the Alliance (which would mean German rearmament). According to the Treaty, only EU members could be full WEU members. Turkey became an Associate Member in 1992 with the Rome Treaty. Legally, though it did not have a treaty basis, the Associate Member status provided Turkey with "acquired rights"—i.e., it gave Turkey a voice over decisions concerning the security of Europe within the WEU's domain. However, the WEU was abrogated in November 2000 and its tasks were taken over by the EU. Hence, the status of the acquired rights of the Associate Members was left vague.

For Turkey, the unclear relationship with the security policy framework developing around the reformed and enlarged EU poses the most significant problems of participation in the evolving European security architecture.[15] The crises in former Yugoslavia and the ensuing disillusionment about Europe's genuine security policy and defense abilities confirmed the importance of the United States' and NATO's contributions to European affairs. The CFSP aimed to augment the EU's political and crisis-response capabilities, but insufficient political commitment by the member states and the lack of appropriate policy instruments have severely hindered its effectiveness. Particularly, the failure of the EU to prevent the escalation of wars in Yugoslavia in the early 1990s challenged its ambitious expectations."[16] The conflicts in Bosnia in mid-90s and Kosovo in the late-90s became test cases for the CFSP's effectiveness and credibility. In Bosnia, "the hour of Europe" could neither stop the fighting nor bring about any serious negotiation until the United States intervened. The war over Kosovo demonstrated that NATO would continue to be the organization that would make the important political and operational decisions on Europe's security concerns.[17]

With respect to security in the Balkans, which poses the immediate security risks to Europe, Turkey does not want to be drawn into the domestic problems of almost any Balkan state because it is cognizant that it would not be able to impose single-handedly a solution from the outside. The Kosovo crisis is a case in point in the sense that "Turkey largely refrained from politically exploiting Greece's reluctance in taking the position of the Western institutions, which favored military intervention in Kosovo."[18]

Turkey favors a lasting negotiated settlement of all those open Balkan issues that could become the source of future instability. To contribute to stability in the Balkans, the Turkish government seeks to establish cooperative relations with all Balkan states and to promote multinational regional plans. On the other hand, it is inappropriate for the leading powers of Europe to include Turkey too intimately into the process of establishing a Balkan peace, although they also acknowledge that such a process cannot be established without Turkey's participation.[19]

The Post-Cold War European Security Architecture and the Emerging European Security Initiative

Security in the post-Cold War era is no longer identified in terms of building a massive collective defense against an identifiable enemy. Instability, national movements, and the control of natural resources in regions of turmoil all have a bearing on European security interests. To address the new challenges, there is broad agreement that Europeans should become more self-sufficient militarily and assume the responsibility for managing crises that threaten their security directly. To that end, the Maastricht Treaty (the Treaty on EU) of 1991 established the CFSP as the EU's second pillar on all EU security issues, including the progressive framing of a common defense policy.[20] The EU introduced the CFSP to respond to the challenges facing it on the international level, and to provide new means of taking action in areas of foreign relations. Conflict prevention and conflict management occupy the prime seat on the CFSP's agenda, along with its central objective of projection of stability to Central and Eastern Europe. These conflict prevention and management tasks cover humanitarian aid, election monitoring, police deployment and training, border controls, institution-building, mine clearance, arms control and destruction, combating illicit trafficking, embargo enforcement and counterterrorism initiatives. However, in crisis situations, decision-making is cumbersome and budgetary procedures inflexible.[21] In order to address the vicissitudes of security and defense matters, the TEU established several links between the EU and the WEU to provide the Union with recourse to WEU for drawing up and implementing any Union decisions and actions with defense implications. The Amsterdam Treaty of 1997 went a step further with respect to the EU's security profile, providing for "the possibility of the integration of the NEU into the Union, should the European Council so decide . . ."[22] signaling the European view that the ESDP is about being able to do those things that by force of circumstance Europe needs to do alone.[23] Consequently, the EU started to construct ESDP to substitute the WEU.

Meanwhile, in 1994, NATO endorsed the concept of Combined Joint Task Forces and of "separable but not separate forces" that could be made available for European-led crisis response operations other than collective defense. In Berlin in 1996, NATO foreign ministers decided to build up the European Security and Defense Identity/Initiative (ESDI) within the Alliance. The ESDI aimed at enabling the European allies to share more of the burden of providing European security, reinforcing the transatlantic partnership and allowing the allies to conduct EU-led operations. The Berlin decisions also established arrangements between NATO and the WEU to allow the latter to make use of NATO assets and capabilities in any operations under NATO's political control and strategic direction.

However, at Saint-Malo in December 1998 Britain and France declared their intention to improve European defense capabilities within the framework of the EU itself, shifting the focus away from the WEU.[24] The Balkan crisis had led to a new debate in European defense and security when the European Heads of State and Government recognized that Europe was not living up to its defense responsibility and potential and that CFSP's credibility was suffering for it. At the historic Saint-Malo meeting France and Britain adopted a joint declaration stating that "The European Union needs to be in a position to play its full role on the international stage. . . . To this end, the Union must have the capacity for autonomous action, backed up by credible military forces, the means to decide to use them, and a readiness to do so, in order to respond to international crises."[25] The UK and France agreed that any actual decision to embark on an EU military action would be taken by the EU Council alone:

> In order for the European Union to take decisions and approve military action where the Alliance as a whole is not engaged, the Union must be given appropriate structures and a capacity for analysis of situations, sources of intelligence, and a capability for relevant strategic planning, without unnecessary duplication, taking into account the existing assets of the WEU and the evolution of its relations with the EU. In this regard, the EU will also need to have recourse to suitable military means.[26]

The Saint-Malo declaration is significant because it left open the possibility of European military action taken outside the NATO framework and without NATO assets.

The beginning of a genuine European Security and Defense Policy came as a result of the Europeans' resolve to improve the quality of their spending for common defense through NATO. When NATO leaders met in Washington for the Alliance's 50th anniversary summit in April 1999, they approved the concept of the European Security and Defense Identity. At the Washington Summit, the nineteen NATO Heads of State and Government expressed their readiness to define and adopt the necessary arrangements to allow ready access by the EU to NATO collective assets and capabilities for crisis management operations where the Alliance as a whole is not engaged militarily. The NATO leaders adopted a New Strategic Concept that reaffirmed the Berlin decision that NATO would support European operations under the political authority of WEU by making NATO assets available to European Allies. Assistance to the European allies would take place on a case-by-case basis and by consensus.[27] NATO expressed its willingness to build on existing WEU-NATO mechanisms in the creation of a direct NATO-EU relationship and declared its readiness to "define and adopt the necessary arrangements for ready access by the EU to the collective assets and capabilities of the Alliance, for operations in which the Alliance as a whole is not engaged militarily as an Alliance."[28] It was emphasized that NATO's support to the EU was going to be improved in parallel to the active involvement of the non-EU European allies to the security dimension of the EU. In principle, it was agreed that the acquisitions of the six non-EU European allies in the WEU would be transferred to the EU.

The CFSP aimed to augment the political and crisis-response capabilities of the EU, but insufficient political commitment by the member states and the lack of appropriate policy instruments has severely hindered its effectiveness. In Kosovo, Europe relied on U.S. military capacity to manage the crisis.[29] The Kosovo crisis confirmed the major shortfalls already identified in European defense capabilities and acted as a catalyst creating a sense of urgency. "Europeans recognized the need for building a military capacity of their own to deal with those international crises that touch upon European interests, but not necessarily on American ones."[30]

In June 1992 the WEU Ministerial Council held in Petersberg, Germany, formulated specific tasks for crisis management. These were humanitarian and rescue tasks, peacekeeping tasks and combat-force tasks in crisis management, including peacemaking. The Union's common defense policy was given substance by the inclusion of the Petersberg tasks in the text of Amsterdam Treaty when it entered into force in May 1999. Moreover, the EU Councils in Cologne (June 1999) and in Helsinki (December 1999) led to important decisions on strengthening the EU's Common European Security and Defense Policy and the development of an EU rapid-reaction capability by 2003. As a result of the Kosovo conflict, the Cologne European Council of June 1999 placed the Petersberg tasks at the core of the process of strengthening the European common security and defense policy, and it focused on creating a new security and defense decision-making structure within the EU. The Cologne European Council endorsed the idea of creating "a capacity for autonomous action" as stated in the British-French declaration. It also agreed to develop a common EU policy on security and defense requiring "a capacity for autonomous action backed up by credible military capabilities and appropriate decision-making bodies." Hence it would be the Council of the EU that would take decisions on the whole range of political, economic and military instruments at its disposal when responding to crisis situations. It also called for a transfer of functions from the WEU to the EU, paving the way for a merger between the two organizations. In Cologne, four main bodies of decision-making were identified:

1. At the ministerial level, a *General Affairs Council*, composed of foreign-affairs ministers would be in charge.

2. The *Political and Security Committee* would be the key body to prepare ministers' decisions.

3. A *Military Committee* would formulate advice on military matters.

4. An EU *military staff* would inform and prepare the deliberations of the Military Committee and the PSC on defense-related issues.

The Helsinki Summit of December 1999 detailed the institutional decisions taken in Cologne. EU leaders at Helsinki acknowledged the Alliance's role in crisis management, making clear that their objective in developing an EU rapid-reaction capability was designed to enable the EU to mount and lead crisis management operations in response to international crises in which NATO as a whole is not engaged.[31] At the Helsinki Summit, the EU agreed on a common European Headline Goal, which gave member states the task of achieving the capability to deploy within 60 days and then sustain for at least one year forces of 50,000-60,000 troops able to carry out the full range of Petersberg tasks. This goal is a substantial part of the EU's resolve to develop a common European security and defense policy to underpin its CFSP militarily. In addition, the EU determined to develop arrangements for full consultation, cooperation and transparency with NATO and to set up appropriate structures to ensure the necessary dialogue, consultation and cooperation with European non-EU-member NATO members on issues related to European security and defense policy and crisis management.[32] In late 1999, under pressure from the United States, the UK sought to persuade the EU to abandon the concept of "autonomy" and to apply a formula referring simply to missions in which the United States would not be involved. So, the Helsinki Summit conclusions stressed that the process of ESDP would avoid unnecessary duplication and that it did not imply the creation of a "European army."

At the Feira European Council of June 2000, the European Heads of State and Government decided that in times of crisis management and humanitarian and peacekeeping operations, and in the case of recourse to NATO assets and capabilities, the decision-making capacity would be within the EU's authority. To allay the fears of non-EU European allies, the Council included provisions in presidency conclusions that were relevant to the status and contribution of non-EU European allies, but these did not satisfy the six non-EU allies. Official statements followed from American officials corroborating the arguments and demands of these countries.[33] The presidency conclusions mandated four EU working groups to cooperate with NATO in setting up permanent structures, to ensure full transparency and cooperation between two organizations and to continue consultation and dialogue with non-EU NATO allies. Consequently, the NATO allies agreed in July 2000 to the EU proposal to set up EU-NATO ad hoc working groups to advance the task in four specific areas: security arrangements; developing permanent arrangements for consultation and cooperation between the two organizations; defining modalities for EU access to NATO assets; and EU capability goals.[34]

At the WEU ministerial meeting in Marseilles in November 2000, those of the WEU's functions needed to take on the Petersberg tasks were taken over by the EU, exclusive of the collective defense commitments of the WEU's Modified Brussels Treaty of 1954, which would be safeguarded by a residual WEU secretariat. Thus the WEU, of which Turkey had been an Associate Member, was abrogated.

The Nice European Council and Nice Treaty followed, to give finer shape to the EU's defense pillar. During the Nice European Council Summit, the United States and Britain accorded utmost importance to the Alliance and to the status of non-EU NATO members. The presidency conclusions were "simplified" by the last-minute attempts of the British prime minister Tony Blair to exclude controversial statements that might prejudice the commitments of the NATO members.[35] At Nice the member states agreed that NATO should retain control of military planning while the new Rapid Reaction Force would be guaranteed access to NATO assets for peacekeeping and peacemaking missions. The final communiqué underlined that this new force would depend on NATO for its command structure and planning capabilities. The EU military staff would have no operational capabilities of its own, and NATO would retain the right of first refusal to engage in a mission.[36] The draft text of the chapter relating to the European Security and Defense Policy in the Nice presidency conclusions (December 9, 2000) specified that the EU would be autonomous in decision-making to initiate and advance crisis management, in which NATO would not be involved as an Alliance.

Apart from the non-EU European allies, the United States is also uneasy, not only because it would not want to see the transatlantic link lose its relevance to Europe's security and defense, but also because it attaches utmost importance to its strategic partnership with Turkey. U.S. secretary of state Madeleine K. Albright outlined the American position in a December 1998 NATO ministerial meeting, stating that the United States and Europe should work together to:

> develop a European Security and Defense Identity within the Alliance, which the United States has strongly endorsed. We enthusiastically support any such measures that enhance European capabilities. The US welcomes a more capable European partner, with modern, flexible military forces capable of putting out fires in Europe's own backyard and working with us through the Alliance to defend our common interests. The key to a successful initiative is to focus on practical military capabilities. Any initiative must avoid preempting Alliance decision-making by decoupling ESDI from NATO, avoid duplicating existing efforts, and avoid discriminating against non-EU members. . . .

In November 1999, NATO secretary general Lord Robertson suggested replacing Secretary Albright's "three D's" with a more positive "three I's": indivisibility of Alliance, improved European capabilities, and inclusiveness of all partners. The United States accordingly gives due concern to Turkish fears and uneasiness. On February 21, 2001, U.S. secretary of state Colin Powell, in his meeting with his German counterpart, Joschka Fischer, underlined that the European Force's planning function should be within NATO and warned that this new security framework should not be based on an institutional structure parallel to and competing with NATO.[37]

With respect to Turkey's unease about the ESDP, comments made by Richard Perle, Assistant Secretary of Defense for International Security Policy during the Reagan administration, are remarkable. He said in 2000 that Turkey's worries about the ESDP were justified in the sense that "Turkey sees the whole European Union's enterprise as a move away from NATO," and that "[it] do[es] not see any benefit [for itself] and they are right to be concerned."[38]

Pending ratification of the Nice Treaty, the United States has urged the EU to start formal institutional links with NATO to ensure transparency between the two organizations. As part of the U.S. approach, Washington wants the EU force to depend on NATO

members of NATO should ultimately be one and the same as this would facilitate the development of a genuine ESDI.[44]

Transparency, inclusiveness and indivisibility are fundamental principles of security for Turkey. Moreover, the actual crises that might require a European response are likely to erupt in the turbulent regions which surround Turkey. Hence, any Petersberg-type operation to be deliberated within the EU Council relating to these regions would have a direct bearing on Turkey's national security interests. Another concern on Turkey's part is the clash of interests with some EU members in the use of NATO assets and capabilities in worst-case scenarios, such as an EU intervention in Cyprus. Behind Turkey's overall uneasiness lie the particular problems stemming from the EU membership of Greece.[45] Turkey is worried that the EU might decide to intervene in a sensitive part of the Mediterranean, such as Cyprus, without consulting to Turkey.[46]

Turkey's unease about being out of the decision-making mechanisms of the ESDP is part of its concerns that it would be unable to block an EU action contrary to Turkey's interests. Hence, it wants to ensure that it will have some control over EU military operations in its region, especially given its differences with Greece--a member of the EU— over Aegean and Cyprus.[47] In a NATO-EU meeting in late January 2001, Onur Oymen, Turkey's ambassador to NATO, said that "politically, it is not inconceivable that a country of Turkey's strategic position and decades of loyalty to the Western Alliance could accept arrangements that could jeopardize its national security. . . ."[48] He outlined the Turkish concern, which is that the EU could get a blueprint from NATO, where Turkey has a voice, and then proceed to adapt and implement it in ways set up by the EU's military council, in which Ankara is non-existent. To demonstrate how things can go wrong, he gave the example of a NATO training exercise in November 2000, which turned into a near-crisis when the Greek warplanes flew over some Turkish islets in the Aegean, reopening unresolved disputes between Ankara and Athens. Mr. Oymen said that "[i]f we haven't had a problem in such situations, it is because both of us can work things out as full members of the NATO Alliance."[49] He underlined that Turkey's motivation was rooted in security concerns, and said "Turkey figures 13 out of 16 scenarios about possible future conflicts in and around Europe."[50] Therefore, Turkey argues that all NATO countries should fully participate in the decision-making process of the ESDP, because the decisions on operations led by the EU may have a strong impact on Turkish national security.

Turkey is of course also concerned about arrangements that would accord it a second-class status. Now that Turkey is a candidate for full membership to the EU, it urges for the replacement of the Maastricht formulations by an approach addressing relations with each prospective member on its own politico-strategic merits. Turkish officials have stated before and throughout the accession negotiations that Turkey is willing to contribute to the EU Rapid Reaction Force. This position deserves attention considering that Turkey's contribution to the Rapid Reaction Force can surpass those of the 15 members of the EU: Turkey has one of Europe's largest armed forces and a 20,000-man force available to operate alongside the European force. [51]Moreover, in its line of argument, Turkey departs from the thesis that, because it shouldered the European security and defense within NATO for 50 years, it is necessary for Turkey to participate in any initiative regarding European security and defense.[52]

Turkey states that "the European pillar of NATO is not the European Union, it is the European Allies."[53] Before April 1999 NATO's Washington NATO Anniversary Summit, "Turkey again stressed the necessity of its explicit agreement with any decision of the NATO council concerning the use of alliance assets for European purposes."[54] At the Summit, Turkey declared that if it was excluded from the decision-making mechanisms of the ESDI, it would veto the use of NATO assets and capabilities to assist the implementation of the decisions taken for the ESDI. From then on, Turkey drew the attention to the fact that "according to the NATO Washington Summit communiqué, the EU would require Turkey's consent to use NATO assets and capabilities such as strategic planning, defense planning, satellite communication, transportation, command and control arrangements and intelligence and that each request would be decided on a case-by-case basis and through consensus."[55] To lift its veto, Turkey wants to have a say in any European military action in its neighborhood, including the Balkans and the eastern Mediterranean. On the other hand, the EU leaders are adamant not to risk undermining the political legitimacy of their new defense role by allowing Turkey, which is not a member of the EU, to have what amounts to a seat in their military councils.[56]

As soon as it became apparent in the Feira European Council of June 2000 that the non-EU European allies (Iceland, Norway, Turkey, Hungary, Poland, and the Czech Republic) would not be included in the decision-making mechanism of the European Security and Defense Policy, the six, led by Turkey, voiced their opposition to express their concerns and warn the EU that they would exercise veto in NATO, regarding decisions taken by the EU under CFSP, pertaining to their security interests. Particularly, Turkey expressed its "mild veto" to this initiative, arguing that security is a sensitive issue and since most of the security challenges are likely to erupt in Turkey's neighborhood,[57] it wants to have a "secure seat at the table." Turkey wants active involvement in the EU-led crisis management operations, to which it would contribute, and/or for which NATO planning instruments would be used. Turkish officials refer to the WEU, in which such mechanisms actually existed.[58] They also reference the Washington NATO Summit, where it was agreed that in terms of defense and security, EU-NATO relations would be built upon NATO-WEU arrangements. Nonetheless, since the European Security and Defense Policy proceeds with the CFSP within the EU and the Headline Goal is a European construct, the EU opposes the inclusion of any non-member state in the CFSP mechanism.

Being excluded from the decision-making structures (Political and Military Committees) of the European Security and Defense Identity/Policy, Turkey reacted to the Summit conclusions by trying diplomatic channels such as official visits to some of the non-EU European Allies and giving notes to the 11 EU members, which are NATO Allies (see Table 2.1, Membership of EU, NATO and WEU). The significance of the six were expressed by U.S. ambassador to NATO Alexander Vershbow as:

> In the event of a crisis, in which the EU takes the lead, the six non-EU NATO Allies have important capabilities to offer that can enhance the effectiveness of EU forces. Moreover, it is quite possible that a crisis being managed by the EU could escalate to the point that it invokes NATO's Article V commitment. This commitment by the non-EU Allies to their eleven EU partners is reason enough for the non-EU six to have a special status in the new structures of the ESDP. The EU, with Feira decisions, now has provided a basic template for consultations with the six, as well as with the nine non-NATO countries that are candidates for EU membership. The EU

now needs to spell out how these arrangements will work in practice, so that the six will be assured that they will be first-class partners in ESDP, with a real voice in shaping EU decisions in the area of crisis management."[59]

During the year between the 1999 Helsinki European Council and the 2000 Nice European Council, the EU paid less attention to the opposition of the non-EU European allies—for whom Turkey took the lead—than to their efforts to set up the appropriate mechanisms of the ESDP to materialize the Headline Goal. Turkey argued that it had not been given the expected role within the context of the CFSP, and that the current arrangements did not alleviate its security concerns.

The differences over Turkey's crisis role form the crux of the problem. The Turkish position is that Turkey should play a full role in planning any EU military operation in which its forces take part. Moreover, it should have an explicit role in regulating NATO's support to the EU including the use of NATO's military planners. On the other hand, NATO offered the EU to use its officers to plan military operations, a formula virtually all members say would be useful to bind the union more closely to NATO and avoid duplication.[60]

As part of its policy, Turkey first tried with carrots and offered troops for the Rapid Reaction Force on November 21, 2000, right before the Nice Summit. Turkish defense minister Sabahattin Çakmakoğlu stated that Turkey was prepared to contribute a mechanized brigade of up to 5,000 men, 36 F-16 warplanes, two transport planes and a small flotilla of ships, in return for an effective role and responsibility accorded to Turkey in the ESDP framework, particularly negotiating agreements with the EU on peacetime planning and responding to a crisis. He added that Turkey could contribute even more should a satisfactory formula be found.[61] The United States and other NATO members insisted that there were sufficient safeguards to protect Turkey's interests and encouraged Turkey to reach accommodation.

As the Nice Summit approached, Turkey took up an assertive tone and turned to sticks: The Turkish Minister of Defense warned before the Nice European Council that "so long as these arrangements (of the ESDP) are not modified to satisfy Turkey, it is unlikely to be able to take steps in terms of 'guaranteed access' to NATO assets (in cases where the EU-led operations would require recourse to capabilities of NATO)."[62] Notwithstanding, the Nice Summit concluded that the EU would be autonomous in the decision-making mechanism with respect to those EU-led operations in which NATO would not be involved as an Alliance; however, whether NATO assets would be used or not was left ambiguous. The Summit emphasized the significance of relations between the EU and NATO, and the conclusions mentioned the Laeken Summit under the Belgian Presidency as the last address to agree on final modifications with respect to defense matters.

Although the outcome of the Nice Summit represents a sound rejection of efforts to develop a European defense identity apart from the United States and NATO, Turkey raised concerns about the summit decision. It insisted on a role in making decisions on deploying forces of the European Rapid Reaction Force, and on a guarantee that it would be involved in ESDP decisions that affect its sphere of interest, such as any decision involving Cyprus. The EU acknowledged that it is willing to consult Turkey closely about the use of the EU force, especially when Turkey's own security could be affected, however, they emphasized that it is only the EU which would decide to deploy it.[63] The EU, while agreeing to consult with Turkey in cases involving its interests, remained firm not to include any non-EU state in the decision-making over deploying the new rapid reaction force. The guaranteed access to NATO assets, when contemplating a military operation is one of the principal tenets of the ESDP, and it was approved by all 15 states at the Nice Summit. Shortly after the summit, on December 14, 2000, Turkey vetoed the proposal by NATO ministers to adopt the Nice conclusions, in order to prevent the EU from having assured access to NATO's planning capabilities. Hence, the Turkish opposition prevented the foreign ministers from making any progress in institutionalizing NATO-EU dialogue.[64]

In early April 2001, at the meeting of EU defense ministers held in Brussels, German defense minister Rudolph Scharping stated that it would be to Turkey's advantage to cooperate with the EU if it wishes to have a say in the decision-making mechanisms of the EU military force. Also, his French counterpart, Alain Richard, stressed that with respect to the ESDP, the next step should come from Turkey, and that unless Turkey took some concrete steps regarding the ESDP, Turkish-EU relations might be damaged.[65]

Prospects

The problem has substantial impact on the security and defense policies of EU and NATO members. The EU's goal is to share more of the burden in providing the security and defense of Europe without prejudice to the Transatlantic Alliance. The EU-NATO official contacts are mid-way between the Atlanticist and Europeanist positions. However, the Turkish veto boosts French ambitions to create a separate planning structure apart from NATO. Hence, the United States encourages both the EU and Turkey to reach accommodation. For the foreseeable future, the only option for Turkey to be included in the decision-making mechanisms of the ESDP is membership, which is unlikely before 2010. Moreover, the United States' uneasiness about the increased European role regarding continental security has not been settled firmly. One can expect that it is the next crisis that is going to test the improvements accomplished thus far in the European security dimension.

Marginalization of Turkey from the emerging European security architecture introduces substantial stumbling blocks. If the Europeans pursue the strategy of complementing a stable European security architecture by a politically and economically stable regional neighborhood, Turkey and its future relations with the EU need to be included in the design. For the EU, it should be clear that without the resolution of Turkey's status, European security initiatives cannot be sufficiently planned.

In the post–Cold War world, European security is marked by an uncertainty which must be tackled in its entirety for a genuine security framework. Turkey has contributed in NATO to European security for fifty years. Its geographical location renders it both vulnerable to security risks, and a pivotal state in its region. Considering that Turkey is also a candidate for EU membership, it should be assigned an appropriate status. In return, Turkey should underline that it is not trying to enter the EU from the backdoor, and that its main concern remains avoiding risks to its national security.

Table 2.1
Membership in EU, NATO and WEU

	NATO	EU	WEU
Austria		✓	
Belgium	✓	✓	✓
Canada	✓		
Czech Republic	✓		
Denmark	✓	✓	
Finland		✓	
France	✓	✓	✓
Germany	✓	✓	✓
Greece	✓	✓	✓
Hungary	✓		
Iceland	✓		
Ireland		✓	
Italy	✓	✓	✓
Luxembourg	✓	✓	✓
Netherlands	✓	✓	✓
Norway	✓		
Poland	✓		
Portugal	✓	✓	✓
Spain	✓	✓	✓
Sweden		✓	
Turkey	✓		
UK	✓	✓	✓
U.S.	✓		

TABLE 2.2
Membership in the WEU

Members	Associate Members	Observers	Associate Partners
Modified Brussels Treaty 1947	Rome 1992	Rome 1992	Kirchber g 1994
Belgium	Czech Republic	Austria	Bulgaria
France	Iceland	Denmark	Estonia
Germany	Hungary	Finland	Latvia
Greece	Norway	Ireland	Lithuania
Italy	Poland	Sweden	Romania
Luxembourg	Turkey		Slovakia
Netherlands			Slovenia
Portugal			
Spain			
UK			

TABLE 2.3
Defense Indicators (1999)
Source: IISS

	Defense spending per inhabitant	Force levels as a share of the overall population	Capital spending as a share of defense spending
Maximum	UK: $ 589	Greece: 1.56 %	Sweden: 52.8% (UK: 39.6%)
EU Average	$333 (US: $1,016)	0.48 %	26.4% (US: 32.7%)
Minimum	Spain: $153	Luxembourg: 0.18%	Ireland: 3.4 %
Divergence ratio	1: 3.9	1:8.7	1:15

TABLE 2.4
NATO Defense Spending as a Percentage of the GDP
Source: NATO

Country	1994	1995	1996	1997
Belgium	1.7	1.6	1.6	1.5
Denmark	1.8	1.7	1.7	1.7
France	3.3	3.1	3.0	3.0
Germany	1.8	1.7	1.7	1.6
Greece	4.4	4.4	4.5	4.6
Italy	2.0	1.8	1.9	2.0
Luxembourg	0.9	0.8	0.8	09
Netherlands	2.1	2.0	2.0	1.9
Norway	2.8	2.4	2.2	2.1
Portugal	2.6	2.7	2.5	2.5
Spain	1.5	1.5	1.5	1.4
Turkey	4.1	3.9	4.1	4.1
UK	3.4	3.1	3.0	2.8
NATO-Europe	2.4	2.3	2.3	2.2
Canada	1.8	1.6	1.5	1.3
U.S.	4.3	4.0	3.7	3.5

Input commitments: Current European defense-spending priorities make it simply impossible to reach the headline target mandated by the European Council in Helsinki, i.e. fulfilling the whole range of Petersberg tasks, including the most demanding. A sustainable corps-equivalent force in the field implies an overall reservoir more than three times the size of the fielded force, or 150,000-200,000 soldiers, let alone corresponding air and naval components. Creating a pool of up to 200,000 soldiers will be a long and costly task implying major budget reordering in view of the present situation:

- The EU's acquisition and materiel expenditure remains at around 40 percent of the U.S. level of $82 billion;
- Europe's operations and maintenance spending remains at 40 percent of U.S. levels. The readiness and sustainability of the headline force cannot be adequately ensured under such conditions; and
- Europe's capital investment per military person is one-third of the U.S. level.[66]

Notes

[1] Heinz Kramer, *A Changing Turkey: The Challenge to Europe and the United States* (Washington, D.C.: Brookings Institution Press, 2000), p. 202. (www.brook.edu/press/books).

[2] CESDP is the formal abbreviation for the European Security and Defense Policy. The "Common" refers to its being a part if the Common Foreign and Security Policy, which is the defense pillar of the European Union.

[3] Ali L. Karaosmanoğlu, "The Evolution of the National Security Culture and the Military in Turkey," *Journal of International Affairs*, Fall 2000, p. 199.

[4] Ibid., p. 209.

[5] European Security and Turkey-NATO and Turkey (www.mfa.gov.tr).

[6] Erol Mütercimler, "Security in Turkey in the 21st Century," *Insight Turkey*, vol. 1, no. 4, Oct.–Dec. 1999, pp. 16–17.

[7] Ludger Kuhnhardt, "On Germany, Turkey and the United States" in *Parameters of Partnership: The US-Turkey-Europe*, Huseyin Bagci, Jackson James, Ludger Kuhnhardt, eds. (Baden-Baden: Verlagsgesellschaft, 1999), p. 234.

[8] Kramer, *A Changing Turkey*, p. 212.

[9] Ömür Orhun, "Turkey and the West: Tension Within Cooperation," Paper presented for an IISS-SAM Conference: "Turkey-NATO Relations After Enlargement," Ankara, 1997, cited in Heinz Kramer, ibid., p. 204.

[10] Kramer, *A Changing Turkey*, p. 212.

[11] These sixteen regions are: Bosnia-Herzegovina, Sandzak, Kosovo, Montenegro, the Algania-Macedonia border, Nagorno-Karabakh, Chechnya, Georgia-Abkhazia, Georgia-South Osettia, northern Iraq, Iran, Syria, Cyprus, Voyvodina, Prevleka, and Belarus. Source: Guldener Sonumut, "Turkey Amidst Crisis Regions," *NTV-MSNBC*, Nov. 23, 2000 (http://www.ntv msnbc.com/news/46105.asp).

[12] Kramer, *A Changing Turkey*, pp. 204–5.

[13] Ibid., p. 206.

[14] Ibid., p. 207.

[15] Kramer, *A Changing Turkey*, p. 216.

[16] Raimo Vayrynen, "The European Union's New Crisis Management Capability," policy brief to the Joan B. Kroc Institute for International Peace Studies, University of Notre Dame, Feb. 2000 (http://www.nd.edu/~krocinst/polbriefs/pbrief3.html).

[17] Kramer, *A Changing Turkey,* p. 216.

[18] Ibid., p.154.

[19] Ibid.

[20] Title V of the TEU.

[21] Christopher Patten, "The Common Foreign and Security Policy," speech given in the European Institute, Washington, D.C., Sept. 11, 2000.

[22] Amsterdam Treaty, 1997, Article 17 (http://evsopa.eu.int).

[23] *The European Security and Defense Identity (ESDI) and Turkey*, Conference Report, The Institute of Turkish Studies, May 2000 (http://www.turkish studies.org/reportsb.html).

[24] *Strengthening European Security and Defense Capabilities*, (http://www.expandnato.org).

[25] The French-British Declaration on the Defense of Europe, item 2, Dec. 4, 1998 (http://fco.gov.uk).

[26] Ibid.

[27] Alfred van Staden, "Same Bed, Same Dream? Europe's Search for Autonomy in International Security," *Bologna Center Journal of International Affairs*, Spring 2000, vol. 3, no 1 (www.jhubc.it/bcjournal/print2000).

[28] Washington Summit communiqué, April 1999.

[29] The United States carried the largest burden in NATO of combat operations in Europe. During the 1999 air war against Yugoslavia, 731 of the 1,058 aircraft involved were American. The cost of the U.S. air war was $5.5 billion.

[30] Ibid.

[31] Alfred van Staden, "Same Bed, Same Dream?"

[32] NATO factsheet (http:www.nato.int).

[33] Secretary of Defense William Cohen demanded the Western Europeans not ruin NATO in Brussels in early December 2000.

[34] *Strengthening European Security and Defense Capabilities* (http://www.expandnato.org).

[35] "The NATO rift in the (Nice) Summit," *Milliyet*, Dec. 11, 2000.

[36] John C. Hulsman, "Good News at Nice: The EU Backs a Defense Plan in US Interests," Executive Memorandum, *The Heritage Foundation*, No. 707, Dec. 20, 2000.

[37] "Full Support to the Turkish Thesis from Powell," *NTV-MSNBC*, Feb. 21, 2001. (translation mine) http://www.ntvmsnbc.com/news/65663.asp

[38] Michael R. Gordon, "Turkey offers troops for new European Force, with a proviso," *New York Times*, Nov. 22, 2000.

[39] Joseph Fitchett, "Turkey puts roadblock in EU force negotiations," *International Herald Tribune*, Jan. 26, 2001.

[40] Since the members of the European Monetary Union, which includes most European NATO Allies, are required to keep government deficits under 3 percent of their GDP, all major European countries-France, Germany, Italy and the UK-project flat military spending for the next several years. Germany is actually cutting $1 billion from its $23 billion Fiscal Year 2000 defense budget. Members of the European Union

[41] Gilles Andreani, "Why Institutions Matter," *Survival*, Summer 2000, p. 91.

[42] ESDI and Turkey: www.mfa.gov.tr

[43] Ibid.

[44] Ibid.

[45] Joseph Fitchett, op.cit.

[46] Michel Evans, "Turks block development of EU army," *The Times*, Dec. 15, 2000.

[47] Gordon, "Turkey offers troops," op. cit.

[48] Joseph Fitchett, op. cit.

[49] Ibid.

[50] Ibid.

[51] Ibid.

[52] Ministry of Foreign Affairs website (www.mfa.gov.tr/).

[53] The ESDI and Turkey, op. cit.

[54] Kramer, *A Changing Turkey*, p. 217.

[55] The ESDI and Turkey, op. cit.

[56] Fitchett, "Turkey Puts Roadblock."

[57] Thirteen of the 16 hotspots, which were determined by NATO, are around Turkey. See footnote 7.

[58] Remarks by Hüseyin Diriöz, vice spokesman of the Ministry of Foreign Affairs, Turkey.

[59] Alexander Vershbow, "NATO-Europe Partnership," speech given to Norwegian Atlantic Committee, Oslo, Sept. 25, 2000.

[60] Michael R. Gordon, "Turkey offers Troops," op. cit.

[61] Ibid.

[62] Remarks by Sabahattin Çakmakoğlu, Turkish minister of defense, Brussels, Dec. 5, 2000.

[63] "Turkey force Euro army out of NATO structure," *EUObserver*, Dec. 18, 2000 (http://www.euobs.com/index).

[64] Michel Evans, "Turks Block Development," op. cit.

[65] "ESDP Message form Europe to Turkey," *NTV-MSNBC*, April 6, 2001 (http://www.ntvmsnbc.com/news/75552.asp).

[66] Francois Heisbourg, "Europe's Strategic Ambitions: The Limits to Ambiguity," *Survival*, Summer 2000, pp. 10–11.

3

Turkey and the Caucasus: Relations with the New Republics

by Paul Henze

Since the end of the Cold War, Turkish diplomacy has been active *à tous azimuths*, not least the northeastern. In the many, often contentious republics that arose in the Caucasus after the Soviet crack-up, Turkish leaders perceive opportunities to expand trade, strengthen security, and participate in the anticipated oil boom. So far, their success has been mixed, because long historical shadows still dance over the region.

A Checkerboard of Peoples

Long before the creation of the modern Turkish state, extensive links existed between the Caucasus and Anatolia. Some of the most ancient peoples of the region are believed to have entered Anatolia from the Caucasus, while Roman armies reached deep into what is today eastern Turkey and penetrated Georgia and Armenia. The Byzantine Empire enjoyed close ties to the Christian civilizations of the Caucasus, and its borderlands were an arena of competition among Rome, Byzantium, and Persia for centuries. Turkic mercenaries fought in Byzantine armies before the Battle of Manzikert (1071), when Seljuk sultan Alparslan defeated the Byzantines and captured Emperor Romanos IV Diogenes himself.[1] Once firmly established in Anatolia, the Turks moved steadily westward into Europe, but continued to be deeply involved with the Caucasus to the east. After the Ottomans captured Trabzon in 1461, another period of competition with Persia ensued. For long periods, the Ottoman Empire exercised control over Georgia, the Circassian coast, and the entire north shore of the Black Sea. The Crimean khans were vassals of the sultan, and Ottoman emissaries penetrated into the North Caucasus to establish contacts with Kabardans, Chechens, and Dagestanis and to trade with Azerbaijan. Most Caucasian Muslims looked to Turkey as the center of their civilization and their potential protector. After the Russian conquest of Crimea in 1783, the Ottomans began their gradual retreat eastward along the Black Sea coast, although they did manage to win occasional victories over Russia. They did not lose Anapa, near the outlet of the Sea of Azov, until 1829, and, with initial encouragement from Britain, continued covert support of the Circassians until their final conquest by the tsar's armies in 1864, five years after the defeat of the great Caucasian resistance leader Shamil.[2]

Turkey's struggle with Russia in the Caucasus throughout the nineteenth century is essential to understanding Turkish attitudes and policies toward the Caucasus at the end of the twentieth.[3] Each Russo-Turkish war brought a resurgence of Turkish efforts to support Caucasian peoples against the Russians, but in the end the tsarist armies won out and engaged in ethnic cleansing on a massive scale. The northeastern Black Sea coast was practically cleared of Circassians, Abaza, and Abkhaz, and historians believe that well over a million of these peoples were deported to the Ottoman Empire between 1860 and 1875.[4] They were parceled out among the lightly populated parts of Anatolia and more distant provinces of the empire, forming the core of the so-called Circassian communities in Syria, Israel, Jordan, and Saudi Arabia.[5] Simultaneously, Chechens, Dagestanis, and Azeris from the eastern side of the North Caucasus made their way to Turkey in smaller numbers in the wake of Shamil's defeat. Still other refugees arrived after the Ottomans had to cede the cities of Batum, Ardahan, and Kars to Russia after losing the war of 1876–78, because the Ottoman Empire, like the modern Turkish republic, maintained liberal immigration policies for persons of Turkic blood.

After World War I and the Bolshevik Revolution in Russia, a new wave of defeated Caucasians found refuge in Turkey, augmented by Muslims fleeing communist rule in the Volga-Ural region and Central Asia. The long Russian effort to break the "North Caucasus barrier" entailed exploitation of the Christian peoples of the Caucasus (Georgians, Armenians, Ossetes, and a few smaller groups) in order to counter the Muslims. During each Russo-Turkish war from the mid-nineteenth century to World War I, Russia sought to use Ottoman Armenians and other eastern Anatolian Christians as a fifth column. The practice had disastrous consequences for all these ancient communities during the upheavals of 1917–22, including the deaths of hundreds of thousands of Armenians as well as other Christians and Muslims.

The southern Caucasus experienced foreign intervention from several directions after the collapse of the Russian Empire in 1917. Imperial Germany attempted to establish a foothold in Georgia. Turkey was sympathetic to Azerbaijani strivings for independence and opposed to Armenian efforts to expand the territory of the emerging Armenian republic. For a brief period following the armistice of November 1918, Britain occupied Baku and actively attempted to reinforce independence movements in Georgia and Armenia.[6] These efforts proved ineffective, however, because the Bolsheviks were able to exploit serious divisions within each Caucasian republic. Their rhetoric about self-determination of nations notwithstanding, Lenin and Stalin were not about to permit the Russian hold on the Caucasus to be broken. The Red Army moved systematically to gain control of each of the South Caucasian republics and had for the most part accomplished its aim by the end of 1921. It took much longer to "pacify" the North Caucasus, where Muslim guerrilla movements continued operating for the rest of the decade.

As for Turkey, the ambitions of expansive nationalists such as Enver Pasha included assertion of Turkish dominance throughout the Caucasus and Central Asia. Enver allied himself briefly with Lenin, but turned against the Bolsheviks in Central Asia, assembled a Turkish-dominated guerrilla army, and fell to ignominious defeat near the Afghan frontier in remote eastern Bukhara (now in Tajikistan) in August 1922.[7] The much more realistic Mustafa Kemal (who later took the surname Atatürk) calculated that establishing a firm eastern frontier for his new Turkish republic was as far as his ambition should take him. He took advantage of Lenin's desire to subdue independent Armenia by making a bargain with him, formalized in the Treaty of Alexandropol (Gümrü) in December 1920. In return for restoration of Kars and Ardahan to Turkey, Russia would keep Batum, and the Bolsheviks would be free to do with Armenia as they wished.

The Turkish republic that arose in the wreckage of the Ottoman Empire in 1923 had a population of barely 13 million. Perhaps as many as 2 million—15 percent—were of Caucasian origin. Atatürk's emphasis on nationalism and pride in Turkishness led to assimilation of those living within the boundaries established by the Treaty of Lausanne in 1923.[8] Subsequent prohibition of irredentist movements left Turkey's citizens of Caucasian and Balkan origin with only limited opportunities to keep their cultural traditions alive. Education and political activity, moreover, were conducted exclusively in Turkish. Although some prominent political exiles from the Caucasus settled in Turkey, entered academic life, wrote valuable memoirs, and laid the foundations for Caucasian and Central Asian studies in Turkish universities, they were not allowed to conduct anti-Soviet activities. To be sure, Turkey's relations with the Soviet Union remained cool, and communism was strictly proscribed. But Atatürk's agreement with Moscow meant that Caucasian frontiers remained more tightly sealed during most of the twentieth century than they had been in previous thousands of years of history.

Thanks to İsmet İnönü's astute leadership, Turkey managed to stay out of World War II, maintaining formal neutrality until the war's final stages. Allied leaders concluded that Turkish nonbelligerence served their interests better than Turkey's participation would have, because the latter course might have prematurely opened a Balkan front. The German advance toward the Caucasian oil fields in 1941–42 inspired brief hopes of liberation from Soviet rule among some Caucasians and Caucasian exiles. The Caucasus was a major source of Soviet petroleum and a key link in the Lend-Lease lifeline over which the United States sent vast quantities of supplies and equipment to Russia through the Persian Gulf.

As the war in Europe came to an end, Stalin's lust for expansion led him into a blunder that propelled Turkey firmly into the Western alliance. He pressed Ankara for special rights in the Turkish Straits and generated demands from his Georgian and Armenian Soviet Republics for "rectification" of their borders, which would have required ceding Turkish territory to the Soviet Union. Turkey's response was an unequivocal refusal, and Turkish suspicion of Soviet intentions was reinforced by Stalin's attempt to maintain a foothold in Iranian Azerbaijan (frustrated by U.S. action in the new United Nations in

1946). From this time onward, Turkey shifted steadily into the Western alliance. The Truman Doctrine and a major U.S. aid program to Turkey launched in 1947 were followed by Turkish involvement with the Marshall Plan and membership in the Organization for Economic Cooperation and Development (OECD), the Council of Europe (1950), and NATO (1953).

During World War II, Turkey was a center of intelligence activity by all the powers.[9] When Stalin clearly demonstrated his desire to abet communist takeovers in East European countries and exercise heavy-handed influence around the world, Western intelligence activities in Turkey (as well as Turkey's own) became firmly focused on the Soviet bloc. Caucasian and Central Asian exiles became actively involved by publishing journals and books, staffing U.S.-sponsored radio stations such as the Voice of America and Radio Liberty, and working for Western intelligence services. The Turkish government, however, despite its firmly pro-Western and strongly anticommunist stance, remained sensitive about exiles' political activities and therefore maintained tight control over U.S. and other Western intelligence operations directed at the Caucasus.

Stalin's successors lost no time building up bases in the Caucasus for all branches of their military forces. By the end of the 1950s, the region was dotted with modern installations and the Turco-Caucasian frontier was every bit as militarized as the Iron Curtain in Central Europe. Until the end of the 1980s, the Soviet Union maintained a half-mile-deep complex of plowed strips, barbed-wire entanglements, and guard towers, and patrolled the Turkish border by helicopter. Of course, these "defenses" served more to keep Caucasians and other Soviet citizens from leaving than to keep Turks from entering. Turkish contacts with citizens of the Caucasian Soviet republics were restricted to sporadic, low-level political and cultural exchanges. Crossing points at Sarp on the Black Sea and at Gümrü (Leninakan) in Armenia remained quiet except for occasional transits of diplomats and minimal exchanges of goods.

In the 1980s, the rigid application of some of Atatürk's principles in Turkish life began to be eased. Turkey's leaders became less sensitive about ethnicity, and its citizens, now much more open to the world, found themselves free to take an interest in their heritage. Meanwhile, Turkish historians and other academic specialists had begun to produce an impressive body of research about the *Türk Dünyasí*—the Turkish world and the peoples close to it. Interest in the Caucasus, moreover, was no longer primarily the province of exiles of Caucasian origin or their descendants, though many of them made major contributions to research as they explored their own roots. By the time the Soviet Union began to crumble, Caucasians were no longer simply grouped under the heading *Çerkes*, and descendants of Chechens, Avars, Lezgins, Kumyks, Abkhaz, Karachay, Balkar, Nogay, and others formed associations of their own. As soon as Soviet power collapsed and borders opened, these groups quickly reestablished links with their long-separated kinsmen.

The Georgians and Turkey

Prime Minister (later President) Turgut Özal laid the basis for official relations with the soon-to-be-sovereign South Caucasian republics even before they broke with Moscow. By September 1991 a Turkish diplomatic delegation had already visited Baku, Yerevan, and Tbilisi to arrange for formal diplomatic relations. Although Armenia's war with Azerbaijan over Nagorno-Karabakh prevented formal diplomatic relations, Turkish embassies were soon set up in Baku and Tbilisi. The Georgian border was opened for traffic in both directions. During 1991 more than a million Georgians made shopping trips to Turkey, and a Turkish consulate general was opened in Trabzon. Daily hydrofoil service was inaugurated between Batum and Trabzon, and Georgian and Turkish airlines now provide efficient service between Tbilisi and Istanbul. New border crossing points were opened in the mid-1990s, and Georgia has now become a major avenue for truck and bus traffic across the Caucasus and northward into the Russian Federation. Turks of Georgian ancestry publish the journal *Cveneburi*, which is written largely in Turkish but includes some Georgian texts and vocabularies in Laz and other Georgian dialects.

Historical ties between Turkey and Georgia go back at least as far as the High Middle Ages, when present-day northeastern Turkey formed an important part of the Kingdom of Georgia. The Georgian monarchs King David the Builder and Queen Tamara lived in that region and constructed numerous churches, castles, bridges, and other architectural monuments that survive to this day. When the Ottomans conquered the area in the fifteenth century, the new rulers encouraged the native Georgian population to remain in place and gradually converted them to Islam. Some of the great churches were turned into mosques, their frescoes simply painted over. Prior to the spread of modern schools, radio, television, and newspapers, most of the rural population still spoke Georgian, and a Georgian dialect is widely used today among the Laz of the eastern Black Sea coast. Conversion to Islam turned both the Laz and inland Georgians into loyal subjects of the Ottoman Empire and later into citizens of the Turkish republic. Neither imperial Russians nor Soviets were successful in creating an irredentist movement among these people, who in recent years have had further reason to be thankful to belong to a rapidly modernizing, democratic country. Until World War I, families on both sides of the border managed to maintain ties to each other, and the resumption of these connections during the past decade has much to do with the rapidly improving transit and communications links between the two countries.

Good relations on a personal level have largely mirrored constructive political ties and were enhanced by the close relationship between Georgian president Eduard Shevardnadze and Turkish president Süleyman Demirel. Turkish trade with Georgia has expanded steadily, accompanied by a modest amount of Turkish investment and credit. Turkey has provided assistance to Georgia's new army and opened its service schools to Georgian military personnel. Turkey has supported Georgia's entry into the Black Sea Cooperation Organization and other regional bodies. Cooperative endeavors also include cultural and academic projects such as joint archaeological explorations. Turkish relations with Georgia's autonomous Republic of Ajaria have been especially close, not surprisingly inasmuch as Ajaria formed part of the Ottoman Empire for more than 400 years before 1878 and was given "autonomy" under Soviet rule because of its predominantly Muslim population.

For the most part, both Turkey and independent Georgia have had the good sense to refrain from any irredentist claims. One potential pitfall for Turkish-Georgian relations arose when Abkhaz refugees and descendants in Turkey sought Turkey's support for the Russian nationalist–backed effort to detach Abkhazia from Georgia immediately after independence. Although the Abkhaz managed to attract some sympathy among the Turkish population and in some quarters of the government, the realization that the Abkhaz separatists were being manipulated by former Communists and militarists in Russia for their own purposes in the North Caucasus—and falsely claimed to be oppressed Muslims—eventually prevented any serious Turkish involvement in that movement.[10] Turkish authorities intervened to keep Abkhaz freebooters from mounting operations from eastern Black Sea ports. Turkey has supported both the U.N. observer force in Abkhazia and international efforts to settle the problem. Abkhazia itself remains depressed, a sad fate for the region once dubbed the Soviet Riviera.

The Armenians and Turkey

Given the legacy of Armenian "treason" (in Turkish eyes) and Turkish "genocide" (in Armenian eyes), it is surprising that one finds almost as many Turkish products on sale on the streets of Yerevan as in Batum, Tbilisi, or Baku. However, the Armenian-Turkish border remains closed, and the only official trade between the two countries involves intermittent air and land travel for transport of emergency relief. For the most part, Turkish products as well as relief shipments enter Armenia via Georgia. When Armenia experienced a devastating earthquake in 1988, Turkey provided substantial aid, but Armenia's campaign to absorb Nagorno-Karabakh began the following year and developed into a full-scale war. Armenia's victory over Azerbaijani forces and its occupation of large sections of western Azerbaijan created a refugee population numbering in the hundreds of thousands. These circumstances, combined with the opposition of Turkish public opinion to any improvement in relations, made it impossible for any Turkish government to establish normal diplomatic or trade relations with Armenia. Ankara insists that normalization of relations must depend on Armenian withdrawal from Azerbaijani territory and resolution of the status of Nagorno-Karabakh.

The rancor and distrust born of past Turco-Armenian tensions are never far from the surface and contribute to the troubled bilateral relationship. Unlike the Georgian-derived community concentrated in northeastern Turkey, Armenians were scattered widely over Anatolia and had a strong presence in Istanbul. And unlike the Georgians residing in Turkey, few Armenians converted to Islam. Still, for centuries the Armenians were considered among the sultan's most loyal subjects, and many served the Ottoman Empire in Anatolia, the Balkans, and Arab areas. Others achieved high status as scholars, clerics, architects, doctors, and government officials in Istanbul. During the late nineteenth century, nationalist movements grew rapidly among Armenians in both the Russian and Ottoman Empires. During the last two decades before World War I, clashes between Armenians and Turks grew in intensity. During World War I, many Armenians in eastern Anatolia supported Russia, and Ottoman generals consequently ordered many of them deported to Syria. As a result of the severe hardship, a great many people perished on all sides. The Armenians also committed their own share of atrocities against Kurds and Turks.[11]

Both Armenians and Turks seemed to have moved beyond this history until the 1960s, when the extensive Armenian diaspora began to revive memories of the tragedy. Moscow, seeing in this renewed awareness an opportunity to destabilize Turkey and drive a wedge between Turkey and the United States, encouraged its own Armenians to agitate and provided clandestine support for the Armenian Secret Army for the Liberation of Armenia (ASALA), which espoused Marxism and the annexation of eastern Anatolia to the Soviet Union. The spectacular assassinations of Turkish diplomats by ASALA agents, coupled with intense Armenian lobbying against Turkey in the U.S. Congress, rekindled the old animosity that continues to hinder normal relations between the two neighbors. While some leaders in independent Armenia have called on all parties to move beyond past hatred and concentrate on future opportunities, they have not yet prevailed. Those politicians who nurture old wounds and favor a close alliance with nationalist elements in Russia have maintained their dominance. Although landlocked Armenia stands to gain far more from reconciliation than does Turkey, public opinion surveys show that most Turks would welcome normalization.

The Azerbaijanis and Turkey

Turkey's relations with independent Azerbaijan, by contrast, have been even warmer than those with Georgia. Turks regard Azeris as first cousins, and their languages are mutually intelligible, although the Azeris have adopted a somewhat more awkward Latin alphabet than the one used in Turkey. The fact that the majority of Azeris are Shi'ite Muslim while most Turks are Sunni has not dampened the enthusiasm of both peoples for each other. Azerbaijani intellectuals were leaders in the revival of Turkic nationalist consciousness in the late nineteenth and early twentieth centuries and were always sympathetically regarded by Turkish nationalists.[12] After the Red Army put an end to Azerbaijan's independence, many Azerbaijani leaders settled in Turkey. A further influx of Azerbaijani émigrés arrived after World War II, when former Red Army soldiers captured by the Germans made their way to Turkey and fit easily into Turkish life.

The Soviet KGB used Baku as a base for subversive operations against Turkey for many years. Turkey felt little affinity for Heidar Aliev and his successor, Ayaz Mutalibov, the Azerbaijani leaders of the Gorbachev era. Mutalibov found himself presiding somewhat reluctantly over Azerbaijani independence. Turkey favored Ebulfez Elchibey, who won the comparatively free election of 1992 but governed for less than a year. Of his many mistakes, perhaps the most serious was advocating the union of far more populous Iranian (southern) Azerbaijan with the smaller independent republic, an aspiration that Turkey could not support. Elchibey was overthrown in a coup in June 1993 that brought Aliev back to power. Immediate reaction in Turkey, as in much of the world, was negative, since Aliev was thought to have been restored at Russian initiative.

If such was the case, then Aliev must have proved a disappointment to Moscow, for during the next year he established himself as an Azerbaijani patriot and was soon warmly embraced by Turkish leaders. Turkish-Azerbaijani relations have been close ever since, as witnessed by flourishing trade and cultural exchanges. In Azerbaijan one now finds Turkish schools, Turkish-language television broadcasts, and even editions of Turkish newspapers. Turkish investment in Azerbaijan has grown steadily, and Turkish construction firms have been active in Baku. A bridge has been built at the narrow border between Turkey and the autonomous Republic of Nakhichevan, which is separated from the rest of Azerbaijan by a strip of Armenia that extends to the Iranian border.

Turkey is well aware of the considerable potential benefit of a good relationship with Azerbaijan. Notably, Turkey hopes (as does the United States) that most Azerbaijani oil can be transported westward via a new pipeline across Georgia that would link up with the pipeline originally built to transport Iraqi oil to Ceyhan on the Gulf of Iskenderun. Aside from the profit to be gained from putting to use a pipeline that has sat unused for a decade, a major Turkish motivation is to reduce pressure from abroad to permit increased tanker traffic through the Bosphorus and Dardanelles.

Turkey and the North Caucasus

Turkey, like the rest of the world, officially recognizes the sovereignty of the Russian Federation over the varied republics of the North Caucasus. Nonofficial contacts have increased significantly in recent years, however, particularly as Turkish citizens of North Caucasian derivation travel in and trade with the region. But the principal issue affecting Turkish relations with the North Caucasus is the Chechens' struggle for independence. The large numbers of Chechens who have fled to Turkey have attracted the attention of the Turkish media and the sympathy of the Turkish people. Mindful of the sentiments of its own citizens, the Turkish government has offered only minimal interference to Chechen exiles publicizing their cause. As a result, Russia has periodically objected to the tepid governmental response and sought to intimidate Ankara into repressing the Chechens, although so far to no avail.

After Chechnya, Turkey shows the most interest in Dagestan, a populous republic with a bewildering mosaic of peoples who reside in the mountains along the western shore of the Caspian Sea north of Azerbaijan. Many Turks are of Dagestani origin, and regular weekly flights between Makhach-Kala and Istanbul help to maintain ties on many levels, including commerce in Caucasian carpets and handicrafts, for which Turkey is a major outlet. Turkey also supports three prestigious high schools in Dagestan staffed by Turkish instructors. An impressive new Turkish-style mosque designed by a Turkish architect was dedicated in Makhach-Kala in October 1997 during celebrations of the two-hundredth anniversary of the birth of the resistance leader Shamil.[13] Shamil was an Avar, not a Turk, but like all the non-Turkic Muslim peoples of the North Caucasus, he has long enjoyed the status of "honorary Turk" and will no doubt continue to do so.[14]

Prospects for the Caucasian Frontier

The collapse of the Soviet Union rapidly restored the close but complicated relationship between Turkey and the Caucasus that had existed for centuries. Caucasians never forgot that they were neighbors of Turkey, and despite decades of anti-Turkish Soviet propaganda (perhaps even because of it) they have continued to be deeply interested in Turkey. The affinity takes many forms. For a minority the Islamic link is important, for others Turkic culture and historical ties take precedence, and to most Caucasians Turkey represents a model of the sort of successful modernization and development they soon hope to enjoy. Eventually, they also hope to follow Turkey on the path toward a much deeper relationship with Europe. No one can predict the extent to which, in years to come, the Caucasus will develop into a major highway to Asia, a "new Silk Road" that leads all the way to China. But the region will nevertheless continue to be an important avenue for Turkish traffic and trade to the east and north, and if the Baku-Ceyhan pipeline becomes reality, it will lead to expansion of Turkish ties to Georgia and Azerbaijan. Only Armenia will remain, as ever, the exception to these happy trends—unless and until it has the good fortune to find leaders focused more on future opportunities with Turkey than past injustices.

Notes

[1] Gyula Moravcsik, *Byzantinoturcica* (Leiden: Brill, 1983).

[2] Paul B. Henze, "Circassian Resistance to Russia," in *The North Caucasus Barrier*, ed. Marie B. Broxup (London: Hurst, 1992), pp. 66-111.

[3] W. E. D. Allen and Paul Muratoff, *Caucasian Battlefields: A History of the Wars on the Turco-Caucasian Border, 1828–1921* (Cambridge: Cambridge University Press, 1953).

[4] Kemal Karpat, *Ottoman Population, 1830–1914* (Madison, Wis.: University of Wisconsin Press, 1985); Justin McCarthy, *Death and Exile: The Ethnic Cleansing of Ottoman Muslims, 1821–1922* (Princeton, N.J.: Darwin Press,

1995).

5 Because the Circassians were the most numerous of the Caucasian refugees, Turks called all Caucasians Cherkess (*Çerkes*). Only recently have the descendants of the various Caucasian peoples in Turkey begun again to use their original ethnic designations.

6 Firuz Kazemzadeh, *The Struggle for Transcaucasia, 1917–1921* (New York: Philosophical Library, 1951).

7 Alexandre Bennigsen et al., *Soviet Strategy and Islam* (London: Macmillan, 1989), pp. 8–12.

8 The question of Mosul remained open. It was awarded by the League of Nations to Britain's Iraq mandate in 1926. No other adjustments of Turkey's boundaries occurred until 1939, when France transferred Hatay (the Sanjak of Alexandretta) from its Syrian mandate to Turkey. See C. J. Edmonds, *Kurds, Turks and Arabs: Politics, Travel, and Research in Northeastern Iraq, 1919–25* (London: Oxford University Press, 1957).

9 One of the best sources on this subject is Barry Rubin, *Istanbul Intrigues* (New York: McGraw-Hill, 1989).

10 Most Abkhaz Muslims migrated to Turkey in the nineteenth century, while those who remained were primarily Christian. Nothing of Islam survived in Abkhazia into the twentieth century. The notion that the Abkhaz were anticommunist Muslims gained currency in the international press in 1991–92 and was skillfully exploited by both separatists and Russians.

11 For a reasonably objective assessment of these events by an American scholar, see McCarthy, *Death and Exile*, pp. 179–253. For a comprehensive collection of documents from the Turkish viewpoint, see *Armenian Allegations: Myth and Reality* (Washington, D.C.: Assembly of American Turkish Organizations, 1986). For varied Armenian viewpoints, see Louise Nalbandian, *The Armenian Revolutionary Movement* (Berkeley, Calif.: University of California Press, 1967), pp. 161–85; Christopher Walker, *Armenia: Survival of a Nation* (London: Croom Helm, 1980), pp. 121–240; and Ronald Suny, *Looking toward Ararat: Armenia in Modern History* (Bloomington, Ind.: Indiana University Press, 1993), pp. 94–115.

[12] Audrey Altstadt, *The Azerbaijani Turks: Power and Identity under Russian Rule* (Stanford, Calif: Hoover Institution Press, 1992).

[13] Paul B. Henze, "Dagestan in October 1997—Imam Shamil Lives!" *Caspian Crossroads*, Winter/Spring 2000, pp. 16–31.

[14] This phenomenon is hardly new. Samih Nafiz Tansu's 1975 biography of Shamil, *Seyh Samil*, bore the subtitle "A Turk Who Refused to Bow to the Tsars."

4

Turkey and the Caucasus:
Security and Military Challenges

by Ali Murat Köknar

Most Western military strategists are aware of the significance Turkey's proximity to the Caucasus gave it in the Cold War, when it was assigned the role of slowing down anticipated mass Soviet armor movements southward. Fewer strategists have studied the earlier struggles of the Ottoman and Russian empires over influence in the Caucasus, both southern and northern. Czarist Russia considered the Caucasus its "near abroad," a concept that continued under the Bolsheviks and the Soviets and can indeed be seen even in President Vladimir V. Putin's foreign policy.[1] At the same time, the Republic of Turkey has, since its founding in 1923, continued the Ottoman concept of the Caucasus as Turkey's backyard.

Turkey's interest in the region flows from the close ethnic ties between the native peoples of the Caucasus and their kinfolk living in Turkey. Czarist oppression in the mid- to late-nineteenth-century drove hundreds of thousands of Azeris, Circassians, Chechens, Georgians, Ossetians, Adigei, Avars, Dagestanis and members of other ethnic groups from the Caucasus into Ottoman territory. (Except for Turks of Azeri descent, ethnic-Caucasian Turks are commonly referred to as Circassians.) After World War II, a new wave of ethnic Caucasians, this time escaping Stalin, found refuge in Turkey. Today, approximately 8 million Turkish citizens trace their roots to the Caucasus.

Since the fall of the Soviet Union, many such Turks reconnected with their kinfolk in the newly independent Azerbaijan and Georgia, as well as in semi-autonomous territories in the Russian Federation such as

Chechnya, Karachai-Circassia, and Kabartai-Balkaria. As a result of this renewed sense of identity, the Caucasian ethnic lobby in Turkey has played an important role in shaping Turkish policy toward the region, especially with respect to the Georgian-Abkhaz War of 1991–93 and the Chechen-Russian Wars of 1994–96 and 1999 onward.

Turkey's Caucasus Policy

Turkey's political/military establishment clings to the inviolability of the internationally-accepted national borders established for it after the collapse of the Ottoman Empire. The inviolability of these borders is a cornerstone of Turkey's foreign policy and therefore its approach to the Caucasus, whose economic, political, and military value is appreciable to Turkey. Opponents of Turkish influence in the region liken Turkey's security relationships to the United States' military presence in the Persian Gulf, the basis for which has primarily been protecting access to Gulf oil. Turkey's interest in the Caucasus is actually more complex. While the hydrocarbon deposits of the Caspian Basin are certainly important to it, Turkey's policy is driven by wider, often competing or even conflicting interests. Turkey wants to help secure the independence and territorial integrity of the former Soviet republics in the Caucasus, expecting that this will lead to a diminishing Russian influence in its "backyard." It also wants to establish mutually rewarding economic relations with these countries, while at the same time furthering trade and investment with the Russian Federation. These competing interests are further complicated by Turkey's inability to isolate itself from the ongoing intrastate ethnic struggles in the Caucasian states owing to its ethnic, historic and religious ties with various groups in the region.

While the current state of the Turkish economy limits the amount of economic and social assistance the Turkish government can deliver to Azerbaijan and Georgia, this deficit in Turkish influence is offset by the impressive security relationships Turkey is building with these two countries. Turkey has perhaps been best able to effectively use its security relationships as a tool to realize its foreign policy objectives in the southern Caucasus. It has achieved in Azerbaijan and Georgia the kind of tangible results it has been unable to produce in the Balkans. Turkish diplomacy in Bosnia and Kosovo has been unsuccessful even after the deployment of almost two full infantry brigades and a number of air and naval assets for the last six years. Turkey does not deploy any troops in the Caucasus, but having established a sophisticated combination of military, law enforcement, and intelligence relationships with Azerbaijan and Georgia, it has been successful in exerting its power to offset the Russian, Iranian, and other competing influences over these countries. The official Turkish foreign policy is to maintain friendly relations with both Russia and Iran. However, undeniably on issues such as Georgian territorial integrity and the re-drawing of territorial boundaries in the Caspian Sea, Turkey has positioned itself alongside Georgia and Azerbaijan, respectively, against Russia and Iran.

Turkey's conflicting interests are further complicated by the ethnic make-up of the Caucasus. Zbigniew Brzezinski calls the Caucasus the "Eurasian Balkans," given the ethnic conflicts and great-power regional rivalries of the area.[2] This complexity is best illustrated by the case of Georgia, where the secessionist Abhkaz have sided with Russia in its claims on Georgia. Despite pressure from its own ethnic Abkhaz lobby, the Turkish government is firmly behind President Eduard Shevardnadze's government in Tbilisi and stands as an official guarantor of Georgia's territorial integrity.[3]

The puzzle is perhaps easier understood if the region is viewed in blocs. From a security perspective, Turkey, with the United States' blessing, has succeeded in attracting Azerbaijan and Georgia away from the Russian sphere of influence in the southern Caucasus. There, the only remaining foothold the Russians have left is struggling Armenia, whose historic hostility towards Turkey and Azerbaijan, as well as its territorial disputes with Georgia and its dismal economy have pushed it into Russia's arms.

Turkey's Security Relationship With Azerbaijan: "Two States, One Nation"

Abulfez Elchibey, the late Azeri president, coined the slogan "two states, one nation" for the unity of the Turks in Turkey and in Azerbaijan. This slogan seems to have found acceptance even with solemn Turkish military leaders such as Chief of Staff General Hüseyin Kivrikoglu and with Azerbaijan's president Haidar Aliyev, who replaced Elchibey as president after a coup d'état in 1993. Following the Bolshevik revolution in Russia, Azeri Turks, supported by the Ottoman Caucasus Army under the command of Nuri Pasha, succeeded in driving the occupying Armenian army out of Baku, Karabag, and Dagestan. They also helped found the Republic of Azerbaijan in summer 1918. Some of the 1,130 Ottoman soldiers who died in that effort are buried in Baku, alongside the Azeris killed by the Russian army while suppressing the pro-independence Azeri demonstration in Baku in 1990 and those killed while fighting the Armenians in the early 1990s after Azerbaijan won its independence from the Soviet Union.[4] Azerbaijan and Turkey commenced their current security relationship against this historic background.

The Turkish government's long-term foreign policy goals with Azerbaijan are ambitious, including:

1)   support for Azerbaijan's independence and territorial integrity;

2)   support for Azeri sovereignty over Nagorno-Karabakh;

3)   prevention or restriction of Russian presence and influence in the southern Caucasus region;

4)   participation in Azeri oil production and export; and

5)   maintenance of a friendly Azeri administration.[5]

For all intents and purposes, Azerbaijan lost its war with Armenia, which lasted from 1991 until 1994 and resulted in over 35,000 deaths.[6] The Azeri side was ill prepared for this war.[7] Turkish covert special forces[8] and pan-Turkist paramilitary organizations[9] engaged the Armenian forces and their Russian advisors, who massacred Azeri civilians and drove them out of Nagorno-Karabakh[10] in an effort to slow down the Armenian advance, but were unable to prevent the loss of over 20% of Azerbaijani territory to Armenian rule, mostly consisting of the Nagorno-Karabakh region.

Learning from this defeat, the Azeri government under President Aliyev undertook the major task of rebuilding the Azeri armed forces. However, despite its friendly attitude towards the United States, Azerbaijan received no U.S. support for this due to the sanctions imposed by the U.S. Congress during the 1991–94 war with Armenia. Section 907 of the Freedom Support Act adopted by the U.S. Congress in 1992 under intense lobbying by the Armenian diaspora specifically prohibited any kind of aid to the government of Azerbaijan, including humanitarian aid to nearly one million Azeri refugees.[11] Belatedly, Turkey stepped in, signing a military technical cooperation agreement with Azerbaijan in 1996 and setting up a military liaison office in the ancient Salienski Barracks in Baku. Since then, Turkey has trained thousands of Azeri flag-and-staff officers in Azerbaijan and at Turkish military academies and specialist schools. This program has been successful to the extent that in 1999, an Azeri infantry platoon attached to a Turkish mechanized infantry battalion (TURKBAT) started serving as part of NATO's KFOR peacekeeping mission in Kosovo.

The Azeri armed forces, particularly the air force and the Caspian navy, are ill equipped.[12] Due to funding constraints, Azerbaijan has concentrated its military procurement on battlefield aviation, artillery, anti-tank and infantry weapons, mostly sourced from Turkey, Israel, and Ukraine,[13] spending approximately $300 million on its military annually.[14]

The U.S. Army has been preparing since 1999 to intervene in a conflict in the Caspian Basin.[15] The U.S. military leadership is no stranger to conflict in the Caucasus. In 1991, retired Major General Richard Secord and retired Brigadier General Harry C. Aderholt (both Vietnam veterans of the special operations tradition) were reportedly involved in an unofficial operation to prop up the losing Azeri army, with American advisors, as part of a multi-million-dollar contract funded by private American oil companies.[16] In 1997, then-U.S. secretary of defense William Cohen signed a joint statement on future U.S.-Azerbaijani defense and military relations with President Aliyev, making it clear that the Pentagon wanted to get involved in the training, budgeting and management of the Azeri armed forces.[17] Although the U.S. Congress has budgeted approximately $100 million in aid to Armenia every year since 1992 (making it the second largest per capita U.S. aid recipient in the world), because of Section 907, no U.S. military aid to Azerbaijan has been realized yet.

Many view the Azeri-Turkish military cooperation as a counterbalance to the Russian-Armenian military alliance. Azerbaijani policy-makers have suggested the possibility of situating NATO military bases in the country.[18] Vafa Guluzade, former foreign policy advisor to President Aliyev, made the first statement of this kind.[19]

Many other Azeri politicians support the idea, including Azerbaijan's defense minister, Colonel-General Safar Abiev. In the meantime, Russian control over the former Soviet early-warning radar station at Gabala in northern Azerbaijan continues. Since 1984, Russians have deployed approximately 2,000 troops at Gabala, from where they can conduct radar surveillance of a very large area encompassing most of the Near and Middle East, Southwest Asia and the Indian Ocean.[20] As Azerbaijan tries to use Gabala as a bargaining chip with Russia to obtain trade and defense deals, Turkey has remained silent on the issue. But Turkish generals are concerned about this facility, which can track the movement of NATO air assets all over the Caucasus.

In summer 2001, Iran started taking aggressive air and naval action in the Caspian Sea, violating Azerbaijan's sea and air borders, in an attempt to press upon Azerbaijan its version of how the littoral waters must be divided evenly among the five countries that have access to it, i.e. Russia, Azerbaijan, Iran, Turkmenistan and Kazakstan. Iran's attempt aims at barring Azeri oil exploration at some oilfields in the southern Caspian, which is unacceptable to Azerbaijan, and jeopardizes the Western oil companies' interests, as well. When Iranian gunboats began harassing Azeri exploration vessels in August 2001, Turkey came to Azerbaijan's defense, with the Turkish Foreign Ministry issuing a strictly worded note to Iran. This coincided with the arrival to Baku of the Turkish Air Force's aerial display squadron of ten F5 jet fighters. The visit of Turkish fighters and the air show carried out by them above Baku's Independence Square was witnessed by some half a million people who gathered to watch the show. On the sidelines of the crisis, Israel voiced its support for Azerbaijan.[21] The arrival of the squadron of Turkish fighters was officially timed to coincide with the visit of General Hüseyin Kıvrıkoğlu, the Chief of General Staff of the Turkish Armed Forces. Kıvrıkoğlu was there to attend graduation ceremony of more than four hundred lieutenants who had undergone a four-year education according to NATO standards under the leadership of Turkish military trainers at the Azerbaijani Military Academy.[22]

Many observers see this show of Turkish determination to stand by Azerbaijan in the face of military aggression, demonstrated as Turkish policy at the highest level, in stark contrast to the Turkish government's timid inaction back in 1993, when Ankara was unable to provide even unarmed utility helicopters to evacuate Azeri civilians from Kelbejar, captured by advancing Armenian forces.[23] Then explaining why Turkey would not intervene in the Azeri-Armenian war openly, Turkish prime minister Süleyman Demirel was reported to have commented, "It would take us two days to get in, and 20 years to get out."[24]

According to Azerbaijan expert Jayhun Mollazade, "It is very important that Georgia and Azerbaijan should build up their military institutions since they are strategically the weakest in the Caucasus. Building does not mean they are starting a war. Instead, they can be seen as building a balance. The policy of conciliation is not likely to work as there is an imbalance of power in the region. When countries in the region feel balance they will feel that peace is possible."[25] The Council of Europe has recognized the territorial integrity of Azerbaijan within its borders, as they existed at its independence on October 18, 1991. Azerbaijan is not expected to relinquish Nagorno-Karabakh from a legal point of view.[26] Since virtually no state has recognized Nagorno-Karabakh's claim to independent statehood, the armed conflict there is properly classified under humanitarian law as non-international—i.e. civil—in nature.[27] In the meantime, the self-declared Republic of Nagorno-Karabakh has organized a force of 25,000 soldiers.[28] Its leadership and equipment are said to be highly capable, thanks to a Russian infusion of almost $1 billion worth of arms, such as MIG 29 fighter jets to replace the Armenian Air Force's aging MIG-23s at the Gyumri Air Base, and S-300 air defense systems, since Armenian independence in 1991.[29] Armenian and Karabakh forces also equipped themselves with newer Russian T-62 and T-72 main battle tanks.[30] Some former Azeri officials, believing that the Karabakh problem can only be solved by force, advocate the transformation of the Azeri Armed Forces, which is made up of 87,000 conscripts organized into five army corps, into a fully professional force of 40,000.[31] Azeri veterans have formed civil/paramilitary organizations such as the National Resistance Movement (Milli Mukavemet Hareketi—MMH) and Karabakh Liberation Organization (Karabakh Azadliq Tesqilati—KAT) in anticipation of a military solution of the Karabakh problem.

Domestically, Azerbaijan's security situation is far from tranquil. Its short modern history has been marred by a string of coup d'états and attempted coups, first in June 1993 against then president Abulfez Elchibey (by Suret Huseinov), then in September 1994 against

President Haidar Aliyev (again by Huseinov, assisted by Rushen Javadov), and most recently in March 1995 (by Javadov).[32] Since then, there have also been a number of coup conspiracies that never came to fruition. The 1995 attempt was prevented by the intervention of Turkey's President Demirel, who received early warning of the conspiracy via the Turkish National Intelligence Organization (Milli İstihbarat Teşkılatı—MIT) and alerted President Aliyev.[33]

Turkish security assistance to Azerbaijan is not limited to the military and intelligence. Both Turkey's police force and its gendarmerie (the paramilitary rural law enforcement agency) have "equip-and-train" programs with their counterparts in Azerbaijan. On the civilian side, the Turkish International Cooperation Agency (Turk İsbirliği ve Kalkinma Ajansı—TIKA) trains Azeri and Georgian diplomats and civil servants in Turkey.

Turkey's Security Relationship with Georgia

President Eduard Shevardnadze of Georgia sees a key role for Turkey in the South Caucasus security system and suggests that Turkey can play an important role "in building a new algorithm of regional cooperation, a natural component of which is national reconciliation."[34] During his trip to the United States in October 2001, Shevardnadze stated his government's determination to further improve its security cooperation with Turkey and the United States. He described Georgia, "not as the southern flank of Russia's strategic zone, but rather the northern flank—extending from Israel to Central Asia—of Turkey and NATO's strategic interests."[35] Reciprocally, Turkey supports President Shevardnadze, whom its views as key to Georgia's stability.[36]

The basis of the Turkish-Georgian security relationship is the military technical cooperation treaty signed in 1996 and the military training cooperation treaty signed in 1997. Since the Russian Army handed border protection duties over to Georgia, Turkey has been playing an active role in the training of Georgian border guards. The two countries conduct joint exercises every year at the Turco-Georgian frontier near Ardahan province,[37] and Turkey is also improving the Georgian border guards' communication system with Turkish-made equipment. Georgia and Turkey have also agreed to remove antipersonnel landmines from their common 114-kilometer long land border. By removing this Soviet-era legacy, Turkey and Georgia seek to promote cross-border trade and the opening of new access roads.

The Turkish special forces command has the lead for the training of Georgian Army Units made up of 30,000 troops,[38] and they are reportedly transforming the Georgian Army's 11th Mechanized Infantry Brigade into an elite unit[39] and a light infantry battalion at Kodjori into a special operations unit[40] similar to the Albanian commando battalion the Turkish Special Forces created in 1998. The Turkish Air Force has been repairing, at its own expense, former Soviet airbases inherited by Georgia. In April 2001, President Shevardnadze signed an agreement in Ankara by which Turkey leased the Marneuli Airbase in Georgia for five years at an undisclosed sum.[41] Turkey also trains Georgian air force pilots and has extended a $5.5 million loan to Georgia for the purchase of 12 main battle tanks from the Czech Republic.[42] Turkey has continued to build up the Georgian military infrastructure, spending over $14 million in the process since 1997.[43] Like Azerbaijan, Georgia has also sent an infantry platoon to the KFOR mission in Kosovo in 1999, attached to TURKBAT near Prizren.

Another area of security cooperation between Turkey and Georgia is in law enforcement, and specifically in the prevention of illegal trafficking of narcotics and components of weapons of mass destruction. In 1994, Turkey and Georgia signed a mutual agreement on security and cooperation, and in 2000 a memorandum of understanding emphasizing their joint effort to combat terrorism, organized crime, narcotics and arms smuggling, financial crimes and money laundering and to exchange intelligence for these purposes.[44] The Turkish police has established an electronic liaison center in Tbilisi to exchange online/real-time information with Georgian law enforcement authorities about fugitives and suspected criminals.[45] It is also training Georgian and Azeri law enforcement agents at the Turkish International Academy Against Drugs and Organized Crime (TADOC) in Ankara. The Georgian defense industry exhibited their products at the last IDEF Defense Show in Ankara in September 2001 and is marketing the Russian-designed Su-25 ground attack aircraft to Turkey,[46] and Turkey has donated computers, motor vehicles, parachutes, and two coast guard patrol vessels to Georgia.[47]

Turkey has been providing five military officers to the UN Observer Mission in Georgia (UNOMIG), which has been monitoring the ceasefire between Georgian and Abkhaz forces since 1993. The Abkhaz-Georgian conflict interests Turkey a great deal. During the 1991–93 war, the ethnic Abkhaz diaspora in Turkey organized under the Caucasian-Abkhaz Solidarity Committee (Kafkas-Abhaz Dayanisma Komitesi—KADK) and worked to help Abkhazia. The KADK leaders are relatives of the key figures in Abkhaz leader Vladislav Ardzinba's government. In contrast, certain Turkish businessmen of Georgian descent are known to be funding the personal bodyguards of President Shevardnadze, the target of several assassination attempts in the last eight years. [48] These businessmen, under the leadership of former Turkish cabinet ministers Refaiddin Sahin and Hasan Ekinci,[49] have organized themselves into the Turkish-Georgian Culture and Solidarity Foundation (Türk-Gürcü Kültür ve Dayanışma Vakfı—TGKDV), a lobbying group favoring Thilisi.[50] The KADK, while cognizant that its support for Abkhaz independence plays into Russia's hand by weakening Georgia and generally making life difficult for the Chechen forces, whom they also support, is lobbying the Turkish government to cut off military aid to Georgia, or at least to place restrictions on the aid to prevent the Georgians from using it against Abkhazia.

Nevertheless, the Abkhaz diaspora has an important role to play if peace is to be achieved between Georgia and Abkhazia. The KADK was instrumental in organizing a 1999 meeting in Istanbul between the Georgian and Abkhaz governments, hosted by the Turkish Foreign Ministry. Although no solution was reached, President Shevardnadze tasked his top negotiator on Abkhazia, Malkhaz Kakabadze, to maintain regular contact with the Abkhaz diaspora in Turkey, and he personally met with KADK leaders in Ankara in January 2001. However, there is some opposition in Georgia against Turkish influence. Former Georgian defense minister Tengiz Kitovani has publicly stated that the Gudauta military base to be vacated by Russian troops should "rather be kept under the control of Christian Russians than to be given to Turkey."[51]

Turkey's Role in Chechnya

In 1995, in the middle of its own struggle with the Kurdistan Workers' Party (Partiya Karkeren Kurdistan—PKK), the separatist terrorist organization which enjoyed Moscow's political support, Ankara reportedly rendered material assistance of $20 million to Turkish Chechen volunteers fighting the Russian army in Chechnya.[52] In addition to indexing the issue to Moscow's relations with the PKK, Turkish help to the Chechens also resulted in unintended consequences, prominently the assassination of Chechen president General Dzokhar Dudayev. The Russian Air Force located Dudayev's position by tracing the signals emitted by his satellite telephone, which had been provided to him by Turkish MIT. While some Chechen nationalists believe that General Dudayev was betrayed by the Turkish and American intelligence services, the cause was more likely his choice to continue to use the satellite line even after MIT alerted him that it was no longer secure.[53] Dudayev's death, Western disinterest in Chechnya after the Chechen Republic of Ichkeria (ChRI) and Russia signed the Khasavyurt ceasefire accord in 1996, and the infiltration of Islamic extremist Wahhabi elements from the Persian Gulf countries into ChRI all contributed to the anarchy that reigned by 1999, when war broke out with Russia once again. This time, official support was lacking from Turkey, since Prime Minister Bülent Ecevit's coalition government was by then pursuing lucrative natural gas and other deals with the Russian government. In addition, neither civilian nor military authorities in Turkey wanted to be seen to be aiding radical Islamic elements, who were running a very effective public relations campaign to create the image that the Second Chechen War was waged for religious purposes. However, this did not stop the Caucasian diaspora in Turkey, led by the Caucasian-Chechen Solidarity Committee (Kafkas-Çeçen Dayanışma Komitesi—KCDK) from organizing grassroots support for the West-leaning ChRI president Aslan Maskhadov's forces resisting the Russian occupation. Despite occasional setbacks in the form of government freezes on bank accounts of charitable organizations collecting money for Chechen refugees, the Caucasian diaspora in Turkey continues to help the nationalist Chechen cause. The civil society has even stepped in to fill the void left by the Turkish government to mediate between the ChRI and Russia. Besim Tibuk, the leader of the Turkish Liberal Democrat Party (Liberal Demokrat Parti—LDP), a small party with no seats in the Turkish parliament, accompanied President Maskhadov's official representative, Ahmed Zakayev, to the first round of official peace talks held in Moscow on November 18, 2001, with Russian

President Putin's representative and former chief of the Russian forces in Chechnya, General Victor Kazantsev. Although Mr. Tibuk was not an official party to the first meeting, his presence as an observer at the talks, reportedly with the approval of the Turkish Foreign Ministry and Washington's unofficial blessing,[54] is a good indication that Turkey will continue to play a role in the resolution of the Chechnya conflict. After the September 11 attacks, Washington may have come to realize that in order to prevent Chechnya from turning into a second Afghanistan, both Turkey and the United States will have to support President Maskhadov's moderate rule, to prevent fundamentalist Wahhabi elements from infiltrating the rest of the Caucasus, as well.

Future

According to U.S. experts on the Caucasus, Russia does not welcome an increased American role in its "near abroad,"[55] especially in Chechnya. This also goes for Turkish strategic interests in the region, including its economic interests (Turkey is the top trading partner of both Georgia and Azerbaijan). It does not favor projects that will reduce Azeri and Georgian dependency on access routes controlled by Russia and Iran, such as the Baku-Tbilisi-Ceyhan pipeline, which from 2005 will carry up to a million barrels of Caspian crude oil a day from Azerbaijan to Turkey's Mediterranean coast via Georgia; the Baku-Tbilisi-Erzurum natural gas pipeline, which will bring Azeri natural gas from Shahdeniz in the Caspian to Turkey, also via Georgia; the Kars-Tbilisi railroad, which will provide easier and cheaper access to larger volumes of Turkish goods to Georgia; and the Great Silk Road Transportation Corridor highway project, which among other purposes will help keep the autonomous Adjaria region within the Georgian economic zone. These projects will facilitate interdependence in the region and contribute to stability and prosperity and will also facilitate the spread of Western influence. However, in the short term, a variety of security issues threaten their realization, which will be subject to the resolution of the existing regional conflicts.

While not yet as active and important as those ties with Azerbaijan and Georgia, Turkey has growing social and economic contacts in the autonomous Russian republics of Dagestan, Ingushetia, Karachai-Circassia and Kabartai-Balkaria. Growing Turkish presence in these regions is expected to further strengthen Russian fears that Turkey is working to weaken their hold on the northern Caucasus.

Cognizant of its limitations, Turkey realizes that it will not be able to resolve all these issues on its own. Therefore, it spearheads and participates in multilateral security arrangements in the Caucasus. A prime example of such arrangements is the creation of the Black Sea Force (BLACKSEAFOR). In 1999, the defense ministers of the six Black Sea states (Turkey, Georgia, Bulgaria, Russia, Ukraine, and Romania) signed an agreement to form a Black Sea naval cooperation task group, in order to jointly ensure environmental protection, search and rescue operations, safe navigation, and to combat smuggling in and around the Black Sea.

Since 1994 Turkey has fully supported Azeri and Georgian participation in NATO's Partnership for Peace (PfP) program, which these countries consider a prologue to building their national security relying exclusively on Western military-political guarantees and an opportunity for closer integration into NATO structures, eventually leading to accession to the Alliance.[56] Under PfP, 4,000 military officers from Caucasus countries have received military training in Turkey—a majority of them from Azerbaijan. PfP military and naval exercises, held frequently in Azerbaijan and Georgia, are expected to improve the interoperability of Azeri and Georgian forces with the NATO forces, to reanimate the military infrastructure through NATO support, and to promote military-technical cooperation.[57] Through PfP, Azerbaijan, Georgia, Uzbekistan, Kazakstan, and Turkmenistan have formal military liaisons at NATO's Supreme Headquarters.

In November 2001, a survey team led by a Turkish Air Force brigadier general completed the first phase of a project to bring former Soviet airbases in Azerbaijan, Georgia, Uzbekistan, and Tajikistan and the airspace management of these countries up to NATO standards, for possible use by the U.S. and Turkish air forces.[58] This project, to be undertaken by the Turkish Air Force, and believed to be funded by the United States and the United Kingdom, is expected to get off the ground in early 2002.[59]

Three military bases on Georgian territory—Akhalkalaki (on the southern border with Turkey), Batumi (on the Black Sea coast), and Gudauta (Abkhazia)—were recently described by Moscow as "all that Russia has left of the once formidable Transcaucasus Military

District."[60] While Russia is finally withdrawing from Vaziani, the speaker of the Georgian government has demanded that Russia should also withdraw from the Batumi and Akhalkalaki bases by 2005 at the latest. Turkey has assessed the Vaziani base near Tbilisi, where the Turkish-trained 11th Mechanized Infantry Brigade of the Georgian Army is also stationed, with a view to rehabilitating it according to NATO standards at a cost of $1 million,[61] and NATO exercise "Cooperative Best Effort - 2002" is scheduled to be held at Vaziani in June 2002.[62]

Flashpoints

Abulfez Elchibey observed over a decade ago that "We all—Azeris, Georgians, Armenians—are like prisoners, who instead of planning a joint escape, have been fighting between themselves for a better bunk bed in the prison cell."[63] The observation is unfortunately still valid today as the Caucasus states continue to be embroiled in interstate and intrastate conflicts. In the near- to mid-term the potential threats and flashpoints in the region and how these interplay with the Turkish security relationships can be summarized as follows:

Azerbaijan vs. Armenia

Nagorno-Karabakh: Despite the improvements made to Azeri Armed Forces, they would still face a formidable foe in the form of the experienced and motivated Karabakh army, should the parties decide to solve the problem through arms. Experts believe that the Karabakh army is capable of moving beyond the region between Mingechevir and Yevlakh, effectively cutting Azerbaijan in two and threatening the Baku-Supsa oil pipeline.[64] In the event of such an advance, under its mutual defense treaty with Azerbaijan, Turkey would likely intervene, triggering a similar response from Russia, since Armenia and Russia also have a mutual defense pact.

Nakhichevan: The only land border Azerbaijan has with Turkey is a mere 13-kilometer stretch of the Nakhichevan territory, which Turkish general Kazim Karabekir is believed to have secured from Iran against a payment in gold bullion in 1920.[65] This land access is of utmost importance to both countries, given the fact that Nakhichevan is cut off from the rest of Azerbaijan by a strip of Armenia that extends to the Iranian border, Armenia, Armenian-occupied Karabakh and Iran. Under the 1921 Kars Treaty it signed with Russia and under an agreement reached with Azerbaijan in 1992, Turkey has a legal right to intervene if Nakhichevan is threatened by a foreign power. The fact that the head of the Armenian presidential commission on human rights, Paruir Hairikian, has publicly demanded the incorporation of Nakhichevan and the eastern Turkish provinces of Kars and Ardahan into Armenia with Russia's help,[66] indicates that this issue is likely to become a flashpoint in future.

Azerbaijan vs. Iran

Caspian littoral waters: It appears that Iran is adamant about the division of Caspian littoral waters into five equal shares and will refuse other solutions. Azerbaijan insists that Iran does not have a right to deploy a naval flotilla in the Caspian. Under license from Azerbaijan, British Petroleum Corporation (BP) continues oil exploration and in the future will drill in the 1,400 square kilometer Alev parcel of the Araz-Alev-Sark oilfields some 120 kilometers south of Baku, 10 percent of which is actually held by the Turkish state-owned oil company, Türk Petrolleri Anonim Ortaklığı (TPAO). This is likely to attract further enmity from Iran, which claims that the parcel falls within its territorial waters.[67] If the disagreement expands the way it did last summer, when Tehran suggested that since Azerbaijan was a part of Iran 150 years ago, Iran may also consider redrawing the land borders,[68] in the future Turkey can be expected to do even more than just flying aerial acrobatics missions over Azerbaijan.

Southern Azerbaijan: Iran's population of about 70 million includes 29 million Azeri Turks, 2 million Turkic Qashqai, and 3 million Turkmen. Accordingly, approximately half of Iran's population is Turkic-speaking.[69] However, Azerbaijanis, especially the so-called National Liberation Movement of Southern Azerbaijan, claim that the Iranian authorities discriminate against Azeris, and further oppress them politically.[70] Azerbaijan's first president, Abulfez Elchibey, openly stated that he did not recognize the territorial integrity of Iran, and had expressed hopes that northern Azerbaijan (i.e. the Republic of Azerbaijan) and southern Azerbaijan (i.e. Iranian Islamic Republic's regions such as Tabriz and Kazvin) would one day be united under "Greater Azerbaijan."[71] Responding to Azerbaijan's official abandonment of the Cyrillic alphabet in favor of a Latin alphabet similar to the one used in Turkey, Iran declared a state of emergency in Tabriz. Iran has similar claims against Azerbaijan, which it accuses of discriminating against the Farsi-speaking Azerbaijanis who populate Azerbaijan's southern Talish mountainous region, bordering Iran. Furthermore, the continued sanctuary Iran provides the former *putschist* Maher Javadov, whom Azerbaijan wants extradited to stand charges in Baku stemming from his role in the 1995 coup attempt, is another source of friction between the two countries.[72] In any conflict between Iran and Azerbaijan, especially in one that involves the Turkic Iranians, Turkey can be expected to be involved, if not militarily, then diplomatically.

Azerbaijan vs. Turkmenistan

Turkmenistan also disputes the boundaries of the Caspian with Azerbaijan and has threatened to send its navy to defend its interests in the sea. Turkmenistan's major disagreement with Azerbaijan is about Azerbaijan's use of the southern Kyapaz oilfield in the Caspian sea, situated 100 kilometers from Turkmen, and 210 kilometers from the Azeri shores, to which it claims rights.[73] Turkmenistan also follows Iran's line on the redrawing of the maritime borders, as it, like Iran, also has a relatively short shoreline along the Caspian. The tension between Turkmenistan and Azerbaijan has so far kept Turkmenistan from opening an embassy in Baku. Turkey is actively working to mediate in this matter between the two Turkic countries, both of which, it is friendly with.

Azerbaijan vs. Terrorists

Wahhabi terrorism: Long before the September 11, 2001, attacks on the United States, Azeri law enforcement (Milli Tehlukesizlik Nazirliyi—MTN) was actively pursuing Wahhabi terrorists of Saudi, Yemeni, Algerian, Qatari, Jordanian, Georgian, Chechen, Dagestani, and Turkish origin affiliated with the World Assembly of Islamic Youth, Party of Liberation (Hizb-ut Tahrir), Rebirth of the Islamic Nation (Islam Irsinin Dircelis Tesqilati), and other radical Islamic organizations active in Azerbaijan.[74] By 1999, there seemed conclusive proof that Azerbaijan was being used as a base for al-Qaeda. Three members of Egyptian Islamic Jihad were extradited to Egypt; among them one who was reportedly the right-hand man of Aiman al-Zawahiri, Osama bin Laden's deputy.[75] Following September 11, Azeri authorities arrested and extradited another suspected Egyptian terrorist to Egypt.[76] Azeri authorities accuse the Iranian government of attempting to "export" its Islamic revolution to Azerbaijan.[77] The Turkish MIT, with its extensive experience in investigating fundamentalist Islamic terrorists with links to Iran, North Africa, or the Persian Gulf, is working closely with the Azeri authorities against this threat.[78]

Ethnic separatism: In 1990, a movement called Sadval was started in the then-Soviet, now Russian autonomous Republic of Dagestan, to carve out a separate territory for the 200,000 ethnic Lezgin people who inhabit southern Dagestan and northernmost Azerbaijan.[79] Today northern Azerbaijan, especially the Zagatala region, is the scene of frequent deadly attacks on Azerbaijani security forces by terrorists who cross the border from Dagestan. Azeri authorities suspect that the Sadval may have been infiltrated by Wahhabi elements, who were also working to mobilize the Avar and Tsakhur minorities in the area, to demand the transfer of parts of the Zagatala and Belokany districts to Dagestan, where Avars are in the majority[80]. Although Dagestan is part of the Russian Federation, Turkey has considerable economic and cultural clout there.[81] As some of the Wahhabi instigators of the violence in Zagatala arrested by Azeri authorities were discovered to be Turkish citizens, MIT support is expected to be forthcoming to Azerbaijan in this regard, as well.

Georgia vs. Abkhazia

Since independence, Georgia has suffered civil wars in Abkhazia and South Ossetia, and neither has been resolved up to now. This is in part due to Russia's close relations with these two separatist regions. Last year Russia imposed a visa regime on Georgia, but excluded Abkhazia and South Ossetia. In July 2001, the Russian Duma passed legislation that allows former Soviet regions to accede to the Russian Federation, encouraging the separatist regions in Georgia.[82] The October 2001 clashes between Georgian/Chechen militants and Abkhaz militia in the Kodori Gorge, which straddles the ceasefire line between Abkhazia and Georgia, illustrated that a lasting peace between the two sides is unlikely under the circumstances. Turkey and Azerbaijan have already voiced their readiness to direct peacekeepers to this zone, if such a peacekeeping operation is undertaken under the aegis of the United Nations. The Abkhaz side is willing to accept such a mission, and Georgia has extended its invitation to Turkish peacekeepers.[83] Its military ties with Georgia notwithstanding, Turkey is the only country that can persuade Abkhazia to compromise its demand for full independence from Georgia in order to reach a peaceful solution of the conflict.

Georgia vs. South Ossetia

South Ossetians, encouraged by Russia, fought Georgia between 1990 and 1991 for a separate homeland. While South Ossetia has been relatively stable over the last few years, there is always a risk of escalation. In June 2001, there was a growing demand by the Georgian opposition parties for a war to end the practical independence of South Ossetia,[84] and in November South Ossetia held parliamentary elections, which the Tbilisi government did not recognize.[85] The solution to the issues in South Ossetia, where a Russian peacekeeping battalion is deployed, depends to a large degree on how the Abkhazia situation develops.[86]

Georgia vs. Adjaria

Aslan Abashidze, the pro-Russian president of the mainly Muslim Adjaria Autonomous Republic of Georgia, is not completely satisfied with President Shevardnadze's policies. In February 2001, Abashidze refused to host NATO maneuvers scheduled to take place in late June at the Gonio training ground near Batumi, Adjaria's capitol on the Black Sea, with the participation of some 4,000 servicemen from

NATO and PfP countries.[87] In July 2001, relations between the Georgian and Adjarian governments grew increasingly hostile, as was reflected in Batumi's refusal to transfer taxes it had collected to the Georgian government, which it described as "fascist."[88] Encouraged by Russia and the Armenian power center in Javakathi, which runs a black market trade in surplus Russian arms from the Akhalkalaki military base there,[89] Abahsidze may also decide to declare Adjaria's independence from Georgia proper,[90] Turkey, with its massive economic power over neighboring Adjaria, could exert pressure over president Abashidze to prevent such a development.

Georgia vs. Mingrelia

Mingrelia (also known as Megrelia) is the native land of the first president of Georgia, the late Zviad Ghamsakhurdia, and many of his supporters (called "Zviadists," veterans of Ghamsakhurdia's presidential guard regiment) still live there. The ouster from power of Ghamsakhurdia in 1992 initiated a civil war that has continued on and off through today. Despite his death by suicide or murder in 1993, Ghamsakhurdia's followers have challenged the authority of the Georgian government through various forms of military operations and political activities. Many Zviadists, after their defeat by forces loyal to Shevardnadze in 1993, went on to fight for the Chechen side during both the first Chechen war and the ongoing second Chechen war. In July 2001, the Zviadists demanded autonomy for Mingrelia, creating a new tension point for the Tbilisi government.[91]

Georgia vs. Russia

Chechen fighters, led by field commander Ruslan "Khamzat" Gelayev, often seek refuge in the remote Pankisi Valley in northwestern Georgia bordering Chechnya, an area populated by Kists (ethnic-Chechen Georgians). This activity along with the open presence of a Chechen "embassy" in Tbilisi, is enough evidence for Russia to claim that the Georgian government supports Chechen independence from Russia. Chechen leader Maskhadov ordered his fighters to refrain from conducting military operations of any kind in Georgia, Armenia or Azerbaijan.[92] But in October 2001, Gelayev and his men, while secretly traversing Georgia to reinfiltrate Chechnya through Abkhazia, became entangled in the embarrassing and deadly debacle in the Kodori Gorge, finding themselves the target of the Abkhaz militia, who were supported by the Russian air force, flying unmarked attack helicopters and ground attack jets.[93] It is surprising that Gelayev, a powerful man in Georgia in his own right,[94] permitted himself to fall into this trap. The incident proved damaging for President Shevardnadze's government, which professed a "non-interventionist" policy with regard to the war in Chechnya. Russia also continues to blame Turkey for supporting the Chechen independence movement, with President Putin claiming "connivance" of the Georgian and Turkish authorities on the movement of Chechen fighters through their territories.[95] President Shevardnadze, denying Putin's claims, is so confident of Turkey's strategic partnership with Georgia that he denied the claims on behalf of Turkey and invited international observers to inspect Georgia's borders with Russia and Turkey.[96] In the event that the negotiations recently entered into between Russian and the Chechens prove fruitless, Russia is expected to exert more pressure on Georgia,[97] and subsequently on Turkey, to prevent the Chechen resistance from receiving sanctuary and aid in these countries.

Georgia vs. Armenia

On an issue fraught with destabilizing potential, the Turkish side showed responsibility and refrained from pressing Tbilisi to repatriate the Meskhetian Turks who had been deported by Stalin from Georgia's Javakhetia province. Feelings of Turkic solidarity notwithstanding, Ankara realizes, as does Tbilisi, that such repatriation could trigger an explosive reaction from ethnic Armenians in Javakhetia, some of whom were settled there by the Soviet authorities in place of the Meskhetian Turks. Some analysts have called Javakhetia a possible "second Nagorno-Karabakh" in southern Georgia.[98] In the event of an uprising by ethnic Armenians in Javakhetia (which would jeopardize the Baku-Tbilisi-Ceyhan pipeline and Kars-Tbilisi railroad projects),[99] Armenia proper can be expected to become involved.

Georgia vs. Organized Crime

Increasingly, traffickers are bringing illegal narcotics into Turkey, for onward transit to Western Europe, through the Hopa port and Sarp border gate with Georgia on Turkey's eastern Black Sea Coast. The street value of the heroin seized at Hopa in 1998, originating in the so-called "Golden Crescent" of Pakistan, Iran and Afghanistan, was approximately $50 million.[100] Heroin comes to Georgia from Pakistan, Afghanistan and Central Asia, and opium from Azerbaijan. Sour relations between Baku and Yerevan has cut Armenia out of the drug route, further enhancing Georgia's position as a transit point. In 1997, U.S. Drug Enforcement Agency (DEA) officials helped Georgian law enforcement seize a ton of opium and heroin originating in Azerbaijan.[101] Georgia has several elements which facilitate trafficking in illicit drugs and other organized criminal activity such as kidnapping: a relatively well-developed transport infrastructure, corruption among law enforcement, low standards of living, and high levels of unemployment. The lawless regions in and around the country's periphery exacerbate the problem. In order to better fight organized crime, both the Turkish Police Force and MIT have developed projects. In 1997, the Turkish Interior Ministry launched two projects: First was the establishment of a regional Black Sea police unit (BLACKSEAPOL), to speed up the flow of information among regional forces—namely, Turkey, Georgia, Bulgaria, Russia, Rumania, Ukraine, and Moldova, as well as Albania, Armenia, Azerbaijan and Greece.[102] The second was the establishment of a joint laboratory for the analysis and the tracing of origins of narcotic and psychotropic substances. Black Sea Economic Cooperation Council supported both projects.[103] In late 1997, MIT attempted to organize an intelligence summit of the countries, which are positioned along the route from Central Asia to Georgia to Turkey's land border post with Georgia at Sarp.[104] However, these efforts did not reach fruition due to pressure on the Central Asian republics of Turkmenistan, Kazakstan, and Kirghizistan from the Russian intelligence service, the FSB. Reportedly, the FSB feared that such close cooperation with MIT could lead to Turkey gaining intelligence resources in the Caucasus and Central Asia, which they could use for purposes other than fighting narcotics trafficking.

Hope for Peaceful Solutions with Turkey's Contribution?

In response to concerns about the upward revision of CFE flank ceilings, the former southern Soviet republics—Georgia, Ukraine, Uzbekistan, Azerbaijan and Moldova—formed the GUUAM alliance in 1997 to consult on political, economic, and security issues. [105] The establishment of GUUAM indicates the hollowness of the Commonwealth of Independent States (CIS) Collective Security Treaty in resolving regional security issues, and could have proved a useful alternative to the Russian-controlled CIS security pact. However, due to the politico-military volatilities in each member state, GUUAM has not been an effective security system, as was originally envisioned, failing to even prevent Russian violation of the CFE Treaty limits in the Caucasus. A NATO-based regional security structure along with a EU-sponsored regional stability pact may still be the preferred option of most interested parties. [106]

As a step in this direction, in January 2000, Turkish President Demirel called for the creation of a Caucasus Peace and Stability Pact modeled on the 1997 Balkan Stability Pact. Demirel proposed that under the umbrella of the Organization for Security and Cooperation in Europe (OSCE), [107] the pact be drafted jointly by all three South Caucasus states (i.e. Azerbaijan, Armenia, and Georgia) and signed by their presidents and those of the world's leading countries, underscoring that stability and peace in the Caucasus should be under Western guarantee. This proposal illustrated the idea of forming non-Russian aligned Azerbaijan and Georgia into a NATO-friendly southern Caucasus bloc that could withstand Russo-Iranian-Armenian pressures, both militarily and politically. Georgia and Azerbaijan suggested that besides the three South Caucasus states, Russia, Turkey, and Iran should also participate in such a pact. Predictably, Russia and Iran rejected President Demirel's proposal altogether. President Putin has counterproposed the establishment of a "Caucasus Four" system, which would exclude Turkey and the West, isolate Georgia and Azerbaijan, increase Armenia's dependence on Russia, and enable the latter to dominate the three small countries in the group of four. By the end of 2001, despite Turkish efforts, there were no real plans to bring the Caucasus Peace and Stability Pact into fruition. [108] Armenia also is not willing to join such a pact unless Armenian-Turkish relations are improved. Therefore, until the conflicts in Nagorno-Karabagh, Abkhazia, and Chechnya are resolved, the pact does not seem viable.

In the face of the current shortcomings of multilateral security arrangements in securing peace and stability in the Caucasus, Graham Fuller comments:

> The entire Caucasus region is becoming embroiled in a broadening geopolitical struggle with many common characteristics, even if no common strategy. In my view there is very great doubt whether Moscow will be able to retain control over the North Caucasus region at all over the longer run. Under any circumstances, political Islam is bound to play a significant role in this struggle in the years ahead. Islam serves as the ideological banner for wars of resistance against the non-Muslim Russian invaders, Russian colonialism, Bolshevism, and today's Russian neo-imperialists.[109]

The September 11 terrorist attacks on America and the ongoing American war on terrorism have highlighted the importance of the simmering ethno-religious conflicts in the Caucasus and the havoc they can play with Turkish, American, and Western interests, if left unattended. With its uniquely secular democracy, Muslim Turkey is the only bona-fide player capable of offering a workable counterbalance to Islamic fundamentalist and other totalitarian ideologies, acceptable not only to the parties in the Caucasus, but also to the West. Should Washington and Brussels worry that the only scenarios for the Caucasus are the ones that resonate with the Balkans or Afghanistan, they need to understand Turkey's goals in the Caucasus. The United States in particular, with its increasing strategic interests in the region, should support Turkish efforts to ensure that the Caucasus, free from the hegemony of its former colonial rulers, is governed by secular and democratic regimes.

During his visit to Georgia in November 2001, Turkish president Necdet Sezer proposed a security and antiterrorism agreement to which Turkey, Azerbaijan and Georgia would be parties (it is not hard to imagine Israel joining such a pact in future). This is a prime example of the kind of Turkish initiatives the West should support in order to consolidate independence in the Caucasus. The September 11 attacks created the current environment in which the United States and Turkey, taking advantage of the permissive Russian attitude to American emergency security arrangements in its "near abroad," have a window of opportunity to establish such a substantive security presence in the Caucasus.

Notes

[1] Zbigniew Brzezinski suggests that the "near abroad" concept is more a geopolitical illusion than solution to Russia. See Zbigniew Brzezinski, *The Grand Chessboard* (New York: Basic Books, 1997), p. 115.

[2] Brzezinski, *The Grand Chessboard*, p. 123.

[3] See Turkish president Necdet Sezer's statement to that effect upon his return from a state visit to Georgia on Nov. 9, 2001 (http://www.cankaya.gov.tr/ACIKLAMALAR/09.11.2001-966.html).

[4] Yaşar Kalafat, *Güney Kafkasya* (Southern Caucasus) (Ankara, Turkey: ASAM, 2000), p. 185.

[5] Süha Bölükbaşı, "Ankara's Baku Centered Transcaucasia Policy: Has It Failed?" *Middle East Journal*, Winter 1997, p. 80.

[6] For a detailed analysis of the state of the Azeri Armed Forces at independence in 1991, see Patrick Gorman, "The Emerging Army in Azerbaijan," *Central Asia Monitor*, no. 1, 1993.

[7] In the pre-Soviet period, many Azerbaijanis graduated from Russian military academies, and Azerbaijani regiments of the imperial army were noted for their fighting skill. In the Soviet military system, however, Azerbaijanis were underrepresented in the top ranks of the armed forces. Azerbaijani conscripts were regularly assigned to non-combat arms units. The Azeri side lacked a professional officer cadre when war with the Armenian separatists in Nagorno-Karabakh began. For these and other reasons, the Azerbaijanis were not prepared for long-term warfare in Nagorno-Karabakh when independence arrived ("Azerbaijan Country Profile," *Turkistan Newsletter*, Feb. 17, 2000).

[8] John E. Sray, "Turkish SOF train Azerbaijani forces," U.S. Army Foreign Military Studies Office, Fort Leavenworth, Kansas (Jan. 1994).

[9] Arslan Tekin, *Alparslan Türkeş'in Liderlik Sıirları* (Leadership secrets of Alparslan Turks) (Istanbul: Okumus Adam Publishing, 2000), pp. 354–63.

[10] *The Guardian*, "Nowhere to hide for Azeri refuges," Sept. 2, 1993. See also "Massacre by Armenians," *New York Times*, March 3, 1992.

[11] Following Azerbaijan's close cooperation with the U.S. in its war on terrorism in the aftermath of the Sept. 11 terrorist attacks, the U.S. Congress amended the law, allowing the president to waive the Section 907 sanctions on national security grounds.

[12] Formed in mid-1992, the Azeri Caspian Navy has about 3,000 personnel, five minesweepers, four landing ships, and two Soviet-era patrol boats. The air force has about 2,000 troops, 48 combat aircraft, and one helicopter squadron ("Azerbaijan Country Profile"). The 1991 Conventional Forces in Europe (CFE) Treaty limits Azerbaijan to 100 combat aircraft and 50 combat helicopters.

[13] "Nagorno-Karabakh: Diplomats talk as both sides rebuild forces," *Jane's Defense Weekly*, Oct. 16, 1996.

[14] Its expenses have increased almost 50% from their 1992 level per *U.S. Arms Control and Disarmament Agency (ACDA),* "World Military Expenditures and Military Transfers," Washington, D.C., 1996.

[15] Steven Lee Myers, "A Modern Caspian Model for US Wargames," *New York Times*, Mar. 15, 1999.

[16] Alexis Rowell, "US Mercenaries Fight in Azerbaijan," *Covert Action Quarterly*, Spring 1994, pp. 23–27.

[17] Uğur Akıncı, "US wants to train Azeri Army," *Turkish Daily News,* Aug. 6, 1997.

[18] Gulnara Ismailova, "Behind the Turkish Stars: The depth of Turkish-Azerbaijani military cooperation," *The Analyst*, Sept. 2001.

[19] Vafa Guluzade, "To delay the stationing of NATO forces in Georgia and Azerbaijan is a crime not only against those two countries but against the world community as well," Turan News Agency, Baku, June 28, 1999.

[20] Dr. Garip Kafkaslı, "Azerbaycan Bıçak Sırtında" (Azerbaijan on the Knife's Edge), *Yeni Düşünce* (Turkey), Dec. 8, 2000.

[21] "Ariel Şaron Türkiye ziyareti esnasında 'İran'a karşı Azerbaycan'ın yanındayız' mesajını verdi" (Ariel Sharon indicated 'We are with Azerbaijan against Iran' during his visit to Turkey), Kanal D Television, Aug. 13, 2001.

[22] Ismailova, "Behind the Turkish Stars."

[23] Bölükbaşı, "Ankara's Baku Centered," p. 85.

[24] Cited by Daniel Sneider, *Christian Science Monitor*, April 16, 1993.

[25] Jayhun Mollazade, "Future Prospects for the Eurasian Corridor," a series of roundtable discussions at Harvard University, JFK School of Government, Cambridge, Mass., April 23, 1998, p. 28.

[26] Interview with former Turkish president Süleyman Demirel, AZTV1, Oct. 15, 2001.

[27] Robert Kogod Goldman, "Bloodshed in the Caucasus: Escalation of the Armed Conflict in Nagorno-Karabakh," *Helsinki Watch*, Sept. 1992, p. 67.

[28] Abdülhamit Bilici, "ABD'nin yeni Avrasya stratejisi (The new Eurasian strategy of the USA)," *Aksiyon* (Istanbul), no. 347, July 28, 2001. Armenia proper fields a force of 60, 000 conscripts.

[29] Hafiz M. Pashayev, "Russian arms shipments to Armenia are a major threat to Azerbaijan," *Washington Times*, April 15, 1999; Faruk Arslan, "Second S-300 Crisis on Our Doorstep," *Zaman* (Istanbul), Dec. 31, 1998. See also "Russia reinforcing Armenian air defense base with MIG-29s," BBC Worldwide Monitoring, Jan. 21, 1999.

[30] "Nagorno-Karabakh," *Jane's Defense Weekly*, p. 27.

[31] "Azeri general says Karabakh should be liberated by means of war," ANS TV, Baku, Dec. 23, 2000.

[32] Bölükbaşı, "Ankara's Baku Centered," p. 93.

[33] However, in a speech to the Turkish Parliament in 1997, President Aliyev alleged that the failed Javadov coup attempt had been planned at the instigation of certain Turkish pan-Turkist elements affiliated with MIT.

[34] From a lecture delivered by Georgian president Eduard Shevardnazde at the Yerevan State University in Armenia on October 24, 2000, as reported by Noyan Tapan news agency.

[35] Text of lecture delivered by Georgian president Eduard Shevardnadze at Harvard University, Oct. 3, 2001.

[36] Margarita Antidze, "Turkish leader backs embattled Georgian president," *Reuters*, Nov. 9, 2001.

[37] See *Dilis Gazeti* (Tbilisi), Oct. 29, 1999, p. 2.

[38] "Türkiye yardıma hazır" (Turkey is ready to help), *Zaman*, Mar. 3, 1999. See also *Svobodnaya Gruzia,* Oct. 12, 1999, and *Kavkasioni* (Tbilisi), Oct. 13–19, 1999.

[39] Sozar Subeliani, "Georgian Army in Crisis," *CRS* No. 19, Feb. 18, 2000, Institute of War and Peace Reporting, London, UK.

[40] Georgi Divali, "Tblisi accounts to Ankara," *Kommersant* (Moscow), June 4, 2001.

[41] This $1.5 million upgrading project is similar to the Turkish Navy's modernization of the Pashaliman Naval base in southern Albania. Opponents of Turkish military presence in the Balkans and the Caucasus have quickly condemned both projects as "Turkish expansionism."

[42] "Georgia takes delivery of Czech army tanks," Radio Free Europe/Radio Liberty (RFE/RL), Oct. 5, 2000.

[43] Ekrem Dindarol, "Vaziyani'ye TSK uzmanı" (Turkish Armed Forces experts to Vaziani), *Zaman*, Aug. 17, 2001. The annual Georgian defense budget is $23 million.

[44] "Turkey, Georgia To Cooperate Against Terror, Other Crimes," Anatolian News Agency, Ankara, Feb. 23, 2000.

[45] "Suçluya online takip" (Online tracking of criminals), *Milliyet* (Istanbul), Oct. 24, 2000.

[46] While Turkey is in the process of purchasing U.S. Bell-made King Cobra attack helicopters for ground attack missions, possible technology transfers from the aircraft factory near Tbilisi interests the Turkish military industrial establishment.

[47] "Karadayı visit signals new era in Turkish-Georgian military ties," *Turkish Daily News*, April 17, 1998.

[48] Mim Mansuroğlu, "Etnik Lobiler, Insan Hakları ve Türk Dışpolitikası" (Ethnic Lobbies, Human Rights and Turkish Foreign Policy), *Turkistan*

Newsletter, Nov. 11, 1999.

[49] Tuncay Özkan, *Bir Gizli Servisin Tarihi* (History of a Secret Service) (Istanbul, Turkey: AD Publishing, 1996), p. 261.

[50] Arslan Tekin, "Kafkas barışını Ankara saglar" (Ankara secures peace in Caucasus), *Türkiye* (Istanbul), Aug. 10, 1999.

[51] *"Gurcistan'da aykırı bir ses"* (A dissenting voice in Georgia), *Zaman*, Aug. 15, 2001.

[52] Özkan, *Bir Gizli Servisin Tarihi*, p. 260.

[53] The satellite telephone line was reportedly intercepted weeks before the Russian Air Force finally dropped a guided bomb on General Dudayev's compromised position. See Mehmet Eymür, "Avrasya'dan Swissotel'e Eleştiriler (Comments on 'From Eurasia to Swisshotel')," *Anatolian Turkish Information Network* (ATIN), July 5, 2001 (http://www.atin.org).

[54] Sabahattin Onkibar, "Rus-Çeçen görüşmesinin perde arkası ve Tibuk" (Behind the scenes at the Russian-Chechen talks and Tibuk), *Star* (Istanbul), Nov. 11, 2001.

[55] Martha Brill Olcott in *New York Times*, Nov. 19, 1999.

[56] Ismailova, "Behind the Turkish Stars."

[57] Turkish Ministry of Foreign Affairs press release, "NATO/PfP Exercise Cooperative Partner–2001," June 12, 2001.

[58] Metehan Demir, "Özbek üslerini NATO standardına Türkiye yükseltecek" (Turkey will upgrade Uzbek bases to NATO Standards), *Hürriyet*, Oct. 3, 2001.

[59] *Hürriyet*, Nov. 20, 2001.

[60] *Kommersant*, Aug. 1, 2000.

[61] Dindarol, *"Vaziyani'ye."* See also "Türkiye'den Gürcistan'a 1 Milyon Dolar us parasi" ($1 million from Turkey to Georgia for the base), Ajans Kafkas, Nov. 15, 2001.

[62] "NATO training will be carried out on former Russian military base," Independent Information Center Glasnost (Moscow), Nov. 28, 2001.

[63] Wojciech Jagielski, "The Caucasus: Fighting for a bunk bed in the prison cell," *Gazeta Wyborcza* (Poland), Aug. 31, 2001.

[64] Bilici, "ABD'nin yeni."

[65] Kalafat, *Güney Kafkasya*, p. 13.

[66] Karine Kalantarian, Harry Tamrazian, "Hairikian demands return of Nakhichevan, Kars, Ardahan," *RFE/RL* The Caucasus Report, March 16, 2001.

[67] Azerbaijan suggests that the Caspian body of water is a "sea," and its littoral must be divided in proportion to the length of the shoreline of the countries, which border it (i.e. Russia, Azerbaijan, Iran, Turkmenistan, and Kazakstan). This division would grant Azerbaijan 35% of the Caspian littoral waters, leaving only 14% for Iran. Iran, on the other hand, suggest treating the Caspian as a "lake," which would guarantee it an even 20% when the littoral waters are divided evenly among the five Caspian nations. The variations in percentages of access to oilfields under the Caspian matter greatly to Azerbaijan's and Iran's oil-dependent economies.

[68] Abdülhamit Bilici, "Tam yerine rastgeldi tavır koyduk" (We showed our posture at the right time), *Aksiyon*, no. 352, Sept. 1, 2001.

[69] A. William Samii, "New Statistics on Minorities in Iran," *RFE/RL* Iran Report, Aug. 30, 1999.

[70] "Azerilere baski var" (http://www.internethaber.com/detay.php?d=6145).

[71] Macit Gürbüz, Cabbar Sıktas, "Çatlı'nin savaş planı (Catli's battle plan)," *Milliyet*, Nov. 14, 1997.

[72] Maher Javadov's brother, Rovshan, the commander of Azerbaijan's OMON troops (Interior Forces Special Detachment) was killed in a standoff with Azerbaijani army troops in March 1995. Javadov fled to Austria after that debacle, but since late 1998 he has lived in Iran. Maher Javadov has repeatedly expressed his intention of mounting a coup against the present Azerbaijani leadership (See: *RFE/RL* Caucasus Report, Mar. 23, 1999).

[73] Marat Gurt, "Turkmens warn Azeris over disputed Caspian oil," *Reuters*, Aug. 8, 2001.

[74] "Azerbaycan Xususi Xidmet Orqanlari Terrorculari Axtarir" (Azerbaijani Special Services Agents Arrest Terrorists), *Azerbaycan Weekly Analytical-Information Bulletin*, Oct. 11, 2001, Azerbaijan National Democratic Foundation, Baku.

[75] Samir Razimov, "Bin Laden's Azeri Connections," *CRS* No. 100, Oct. 5, 2001, Institute of War and Peace Reporting, London, UK.

[76] "Azerbaijan hands over Egyptian terrorist suspect," *AFP*, Oct. 12, 2001.

[77] *Turan* (Baku), Oct. 1, 2001. See also Liz Fuller, "Is There an Islamic Threat to Azerbaijan?" *RFE/RL Caucasus Report*," March 23, 1999).

[78] *"Dışışlerıi Bakanı Ismail Cem Bakü'de"* (Foreign Minister Ismail Cem is in Baku), *Habertürk* news agency, Oct. 21, 2001.

[79] *RFE/RL* Research Report, vol. 1, no. 41, Oct. 16, 1992.

[80] Mamed Suleimanov, "Baku Alarmed Over Wahhabi Menace," *CRS* No. 97, Sept. 7, 2001. Institute of War and Peace Reporting, London, UK.

[81] Paul B. Henze, "Turkey's Caucasian Initiatives," *Orbis*, Winter 2001, p. 90.

[82] Zeyno Baran, "The Caucasus and Caspian Region: Understanding United States Policy," *Testimony to House Committee on International Relations, Subcommittee on Europe*, Oct. 10, 2001.

[83] "Gürcistan'ın umudu Türkiye" (Georgia's hope is Turkey), Ajans Kafkas, Nov. 10, 2001.

[84] Hooman Peimani, "Rising tension and the danger of unrest in the Caucasus," *The Analyst*, Aug. 2001.

[85] "Güney Osetya seçimlerinde sonuc ikinci tura kaldı" (Elections in South Ossetia to be finalized in the second round), Ajans Kafkas, Nov. 20, 2001.

[86] Zeyno Baran, *The Caucasus*.

[87] "Aslan Abashidze Jeopardizes Planned NATO Maneuvers," *RFE/RL*, Feb. 9, 2001.

[88] Peimani, "Rising tension."

[89] Yaşar Kalafat, *Baku-Ceyhan Kültür Hattı* (Baku-Ceyhan Cultural Pipeline), Ankara, Turkey: ASAM, 2000, pp. 76–77.

[90] In November 2001, President Shevardnadze appointed Abashidze his envoy to Abkhazia, no doubt to honor him and to secure his assistance in keeping Georgia intact.

[91] Peimani, *"Rising tension."*

[92] Aslan Maskhadov, "Order No. 328: On the tasks of the military formations of the ChRI Armed Forces at the current moment," *ChechenPress* news agency, Sept. 1, 2001.

[93] Mumin Shakirov, "The Fatal Attraction of Abkhazia," *NAA Georgia*, Nov. 16, 2001.

[94] Gelayev was rumored to have put a quick end to the May 2001 mutiny against President Shevardnadze by a Georgian infantry battalion under the command of Colonel Giorgi Krialasvili, simply by telephoning the mutinous colonel and informing him that he would personally intervene with his Chechen fighters on behalf of President Shevardnadze to "put an end to the nonsense."

[95] "Meeting of RF President Vladimir Putin with Chief Correspondents of the Moscow Bureaus of the Leading US Mass Media the Kremlin," Nov. 10, 2001.

[96] "Iddialar asılsız" (Allegations are unfounded), Ajans Kafkas, Nov. 13, 2001.

[97] Such as bombing suspected Chechen guerilla camps in Pankisi Valley near the border with ChRI. See "US: Helicopters attack Georgian area," AP, Nov. 28, 2001.

[98] Ara Tadevosian, "Violence Flares in Armenian Enclave," *CRS* No. 48, Sept. 8, 2000, London, UK: Institute of War and Peace Reporting.

[99] Hasan Kanbolat, "Rusya Federasyonu'nun Güney Kafkasya'daki Varlığı ve Gürcistan Boyutu" (The military presence of the Russian Federation in southern Caucasus and the Georgian dimension), *Stratejik Analiz*, July 2000. Also see Uğur Akıncı, "The Bottle Neck of Baku-Ceyhan Pipeline," *Silk Road*, Dec. 1997.

[100] "Eroinin Karadeniz seferi" (Heroin's Black Sea trip), *Radikal* (Turkey), Jan. 12, 1999.

[101] Irakli Chikhladze, "Traffic Control," *CRS* No. 95, Aug. 24, 2001, London, UK: Institute of War and Peace Reporting.

[102] *Reuters*, Oct. 21, 1997.

[103] "Karadeniz Polisi Kuruluyor" (Black Sea Police Being Established), *Zaman*, Oct. 23, 1997.

[104] Enis Berberoğlu, "MIT'in Orta Asya Zirvesine Sabotaj" (NIO's Central Asian summit sabotaged), *Hürriyet*, Sept. 2, 1997.

[105] "US imperialism and Caspian oil (part II)," *The Guardian*, Feb. 9, 2000.

[106] Lt. Col. James DeTemple, "Expanding Security Eastward: NATO and US Military Engagement in Georgia," *Briefing from the Institute for the Study of Conflict, Ideology and Policy*, Oct. 26, 2000.

[107] Hasan Kanbolat, "Rusya Federasyonu'nun Kafkasya politikasi ve Çeçenistan savaşı" (The Russian Federation's Caucasus policy and the Chechen war), *Avrasya Dosyasi*, Winter 2001, p. 175.

[108] Selcuk Gültaşlı, "Georgia asks for Turkey's support vis-à-vis Russia," *Turkish Daily News*, Dec. 19, 2000.

[109] Graham E. Fuller, *The Future of Islamic Fundamentalism* (Palgrave Publishers, forthcoming 2002).

5

The Kurdish Question in Turkish Politics

by Svante E. Cornell

In November 1998, Turkey's Kurdish question returned to the top of the international agenda with the seizure in Italy of Abdullah Öcalan, leader of the rebellious Kurdistan Workers' Party (Partiya Karkeren Kurdistan—PKK). Demonstrations in support of Öcalan's release wreaked havoc throughout Europe and served as a reminder of the war between the PKK and the Turkish state that has claimed over 30,000 lives since 1984. A month before his seizure, Öcalan had been expelled from Damascus, his base for the last nineteen years, after Turkey had threatened Syria with war unless it ceased to provide a safe haven for the PKK. Having failed to find asylum in Russia, Belgium, or the Netherlands, Öcalan—apparently acting on an invitation from Italian leftists—believed he could find refuge in Italy. After heavy Turkish and American pressure, Öcalan was nevertheless forced to leave Italy and seek asylum elsewhere, but was eventually apprehended by Turkish security forces on February 16, 1999, in Nairobi, Kenya.

The Kurdish question is arguably the most serious internal problem in the Turkish republic's nearly eighty-year history and certainly the main obstacle to its aspirations to full integration with European institutions. Most Westerners define the problem simply as a matter of oppression and denial of rights by a majority group (the Turks) of an ethnic minority (the Kurds). The civil war in southeastern Turkey that raged between 1984 and 1999 is accordingly viewed as a national liberation movement and enjoys widespread sympathy both in the West and in the Third World. The Turkish political elite, for its part, promotes an entirely different view of the problem, which is often misunderstood and ridiculed in the West. In official Turkish discourse, there is no Kurdish problem, but rather a socioeconomic problem in the southeastern region and a problem of terrorism that is dependent on external support from foreign states aiming at weakening Turkey. In reality, neither the official Turkish view nor the dominant Western perception holds up to close scrutiny. A deeper study of the problem reveals its extreme complexity, with a number of facets and dimensions that tend to obscure the essentials of the conflict.

One observation that should be made at the outset is that the Kurdish issue in Turkey differs in many respects from such recent ethnic conflicts as those in Bosnia, Chechnya, Kosovo, Liberia, Nagorno-Karabakh, and Rwanda. Despite almost two decades of armed conflict and thousands of casualties, open tensions in society between Turks and Kurds remain, under the circumstances, minimal. Foreigners are startled by the discovery that a significant portion of Turkey's political and business elite is of Kurdish origin, including three of the country's ten presidents—something unthinkable for Kosovars or Chechens—and that Kurds' representation in the country's parliament is larger than their proportion of the population.[1] At the same time, it is difficult to refute the assertion that there is an ethnic dimension of the conflict, in the sense that a portion of the country's population holds on to an identity distinct from that of the majority and feels discriminated against on the basis of that identity, resulting in at least a limited ethnic mobilization. In addition to the irrefutable ethnic aspect, the Kurdish problem contains oft-neglected social, economic, political, ideological, and international dimensions that have carried different weight at different times.

Several points need to be understood with regard to the origins and future prospects of the Kurdish problem in Turkey. A thorough grasp of the problem requires, first, an understanding of the national conception underlying the Turkish state and society. Secondly, it must take into account the social (and not only ethnic) distinctiveness of the Kurds and their relationship with the republic's leadership. Thirdly, the Kurdish problem in Turkey must be understood as distinct from the problem of PKK terrorism. Finally, the Kurdish question must be understood within the analysis of the general process of democratization in Turkey.

The National Conception of the Turkish Republic

The Turkish republic is the successor state of the Ottoman Empire, which dissolved during the First World War after more than a century of decay. However, the republic is a dramatically different construct from its predecessor. The Ottoman Empire was an authoritarian monarchy with a religious foundation derived from the sultan's claim that he was also the caliph, the spiritual head of all Muslims of the world. The empire recognized minorities and accorded them extensive self-rule, but it defined minorities in religious terms. Hence, no Muslim people was ever accorded minority rights, while Jews and Christian Armenians, Serbs, Greeks, and others were. Before the twentieth century, this approach posed few problems, especially given that the Muslim peoples in the empire developed national identities considerably later than the empire's Christian subjects in the Balkans, and did so at least partly as a result of the latter's emerging national awareness. Collective identities were based primarily on religion— Islam at the broadest level and various religious orders and sects at the local level—and regional or clan-based units.

The Turkish republic, by contrast, was modeled upon the nation-states of Western Europe, particularly France. It was guided by six "arrows" or principles enunciated by its founder, Mustafa Kemal Atatürk: republicanism, nationalism, secularism, populism, étatism, and reformism. Among these, the first three principles form the foundations of the republic. Although Turkey was no democracy in Atatürk's lifetime, the principles of republicanism and populism suggest the goal of popular rule, that is, a democratic political system.[2] In the speeches and writings of Atatürk, republicanism unmistakably meant a break with the monarchy of the past.[3] The second pillar, secularism, entailed a break with the Islamic character of the state. Although religion was to be kept out of political life, however, this is not to imply that Kemalist Turkey was in any way atheistic. Indeed, as Dogu Ergil has noted, Atatürk's highest goal in the religious field was the translation of the Quran into Turkish. In fact, the aim of the new regime was twofold: to dissociate the state from religious principles, and to "teach religion in Turkish to a people who had been practicing Islam without understanding it for centuries."[4] The regime's policies, most blatantly the abolition of the caliphate, nevertheless enraged the more religious parts of the population. This included the Kurds, who have been described as being at that time "a feudal people . . . of extreme religious beliefs."[5] Indeed, the Kurdish population was ruled by local hereditary chieftains whose power often stemmed from the backing of the Naqshbandi or Qadiri religious orders.

The founding principle most relevant to the Kurdish question, however, is nationalism. The new state was based on Turkish nationalism, but the territory comprising the republic was a highly multiethnic area even before the large migrations that took place in the late nineteenth and early twentieth centuries.[6] As the Ottoman Empire was retreating from the Balkans, large numbers of Muslims, predominantly Slavic by ethnicity, fled to the heartland of the empire, the present-day Turkish republic. In addition, the Russian suppression of Muslim highlanders' resistance in the North Caucasus in the 1850s forced additional hundreds of thousands of people to migrate to Anatolia. As a result, when the Turkish republic was created in 1923, a large proportion of its population consisted of recent immigrants of Slavic, Albanian, Greek, Circassian, Abkhaz, and Chechen origin, whereas people that could claim descent from the Turkic tribes that had come from Central Asia were certainly a minority of Anatolia's population. It was in this complex setting that Atatürk and his associates aimed to create a modern nation-state, an integrated, unitary polity of the French type. For that reason, the model of the nation that Atatürk and his associates adopted was civic, as expressed by the maxim that lies at the basis of Turkish identity: *"Ne mutlu Türküm diyene,"* best translated as "Happy is whoever *says* 'I am a Turk'"—not whoever *is* a Turk. To be a Turk meant to live within the boundaries of the republic and thereby be its citizen. The very use of the word *Turk*, moreover, was a breakthrough, since it had been a derogatory term during Ottoman times, referring to the peasants of the Anatolian countryside. Thus, the word *Turk* defined a new national community into which individuals, irrespective of ethnicity, would be able to integrate. Language reform and the introduction of the Latin alphabet added to the novel character of the nation. It is against this background that every person living within the borders of the republic and accepting its basic principles was welcome to be its citizen. Immigrants to Anatolia of Caucasian or Slavic origin and indigenous populations of Kurdish, Laz, or Arabic origin all became Turks in their own right, whereas ethnically Turkish minorities outside the boundaries of the republic, in the Middle East or the Balkans, were disqualified from membership in the national community. But whereas the Turkish national conception was benign compared with the fascist ones triumphing in Europe in the 1920s and 1930s, becoming a Turk entailed the suppression of an individual's own ethnic identity. In other words, Atatürk's maxim was generous in allowing everyone who desired to do so to become a Turkish citizen, but it did not provide a solution for those who were not prepared to abandon their previous identities in favor of the new national idea. This, in a nutshell, was the problem of a significant portion of the Kurdish population, which differed from the rest of the population not only because of language, but also because of its clan-based feudal social structure.

In retrospect, Atatürk's nation-building project appears to have been largely successful. Out of the melting pot of the 1920s has emerged a society in which an overwhelming majority of individuals feel a strong and primary allegiance to a Turkish identity. The only group that has escaped this process seems to have been the Kurds, though by no means all of them. In fact, a great number of Kurds, especially those that willingly or forcibly migrated to western Turkey, integrated successfully into Turkish society and adopted the language, values, and social organization of the republic. Kurds today are active in all spheres of social and political life, and are even present in the ranks of the Nationalist Movement (or National Action) Party (Milliyetçi Hareket Partisi—MHP), which is often characterized in the West as fascist and anti-Kurdish. This remarkable level of assimilation can be attributed in part to the policies of the state, but clearly the ethno-linguistic heterogeneity of the Kurdish population was an additional factor.

It remains a fact, however, that the Kurds are the one ethnic group that to a large degree has retained a distinct identity. There are several reasons for this, of which a major one is demography. The Kurds are by far the largest non-Turkish-speaking group in the country. A second reason is geography: the Kurds were settled in a single area of the country that is distant from the administrative center and inaccessible because of its topography. Thirdly, the Kurds differed from other large groups such as Slavs or Caucasians in that they were an indigenous group and not comparatively recent migrants. Uprooted immigrant populations that have suffered severe upheavals and hardships are significantly more likely to embrace a new national identity than are indigenous groups. Fourthly, the Kurds, unlike other populations, were organized according to a tribal and feudal social structure, a factor that remains crucial to this day. Paradoxically, the Turkish nation-building project (with its one major exception) has been so successful that it is doubtful that state policies can still be described as seeking integration rather than assimilation. As the Turkish identity has strengthened and previous identities vanished or receded, Turkish identity itself has become more homogeneous; as such it carries the risk of growing less civic and more ethnic in nature.

The Distinctiveness of Kurdish Society

The Kurds are not a homogeneous ethnic group and evince differences in religion, language, and ways of life. In Turkey, the clear majority of the perhaps 12 million people that are referred to as Kurds are Sunni Muslims and speak Kurmandji. Nevertheless, some Kurdish groups speak Zaza, which is not mutually intelligible with Kurmandji, or adhere to the Alevi faith, a heterodox branch of Islam with strong non-Islamic features. Moreover, these groups overlap, especially in the Tunceli and Bingöl areas of Turkey, where most Kurds are both Zaza-speaking and Alevi. Hence there are important divisions among Kurds, a fact emphasized by most analysts as an important reason for their lack of political unity.[7] Even among Sunni Kurds, adherence to different religious orders (*tariqat*) has been a divisive factor. A more important element of the problem is Kurdish social organization, which has traditionally been, and essentially remains, tribal and feudal. The tribes, usually referred to as *ashiret* in Turkey, are "fluid, mutable, territorially oriented and at least quasi-kinship groups" that range in size between tribal confederacies of thousands of members to small units of several dozen individuals.[8] At the head of a tribe is an agha, the leader of a ruling family, who seeks to—and often does—command absolute loyalty from the members of the tribe. Tribes are often, but not always, held together by kinship ideology: an underlying myth of common ancestry, at times going back to a descendant of the Prophet Muhammad, has been a strong source of legitimacy keeping the tribe together. Numerous shaykhs, or leaders of the religious orders, have also been tribal aghas, thereby exercising dual authority over their followers. Practically speaking, some tribes have nevertheless been no more than what McDowall calls "a ruling family that has attracted a very large number of clients."[9] During Ottoman times, the state used tribal leaders as a means to exert territorial control over Kurdish areas. Those that sided with the Ottomans in their wars with Persia were rewarded with the recognition of their autonomous rule over essentially semi-independent principalities, in return for which they paid an annual levy and pledged military support for the empire in times of war. A number of tribal leaders received the title of emir through such agreements.[10] But whereas tribal leaders were co-opted by the state, shaykhs and aghas also led rebellions against the state. However, the very fact of these rebellions' tribal rather than national nature led to a lack of cohesion vis-à-vis the state. When one tribal leader revolted, for example, others saw it fit to collaborate with the state to quell the rebellion. As Gérard Chaliand notes, perpetual competition was the hallmark of relations between tribes: "Allegiances can . . . fluctuate, but division itself . . . remains a constant."[11]

Moreover, the relationship between a tribal society and the state is by no means easy. As displayed not only in Kurdish-populated areas but also in places such as Afghanistan and Chechnya, there is a fundamental incompatibility between the tribal hierarchy and the modern nation-state. Tribal leaders "act as arbitrators of disputes and allocators of resources, benefits and duties . . . [and] jealously guard [their] monopoly of all relations with the outside world."[12] A centralized state is a direct threat to tribal leaders' authority because by definition it seeks to exercise direct control over all citizens. There are two basic ways for a state to exercise control over predominantly tribal areas: either to break down the tribal structures and integrate the population into the social structures of the state, or to co-opt tribal leaders and use them as instruments of power in the tribal areas. Most states facing this dilemma have employed a mixture of these two strategies, often playing tribal leaders against one another. Needless to say, the strategy of breaking down tribal structures risks provoking armed resistance on the part of the tribal leaders, and so the Turkish republic, much like the Ottoman Empire before it, adopted a strategy of co-optation. Among the numerous members of parliament from the predominantly Kurdish southeast, many if not most belong to families of feudal lords or are endorsed by them. This is especially the case for the rightist parties with an origin in the now-defunct Democratic Party (Demokrat Partisi—DP).[13] In the southeast, where it is not uncommon to find up to 80 percent electoral support for a given political party in one province and equally strong backing for a different party in a neighboring province, such curious parliamentary election results should be interpreted with that history in mind.[14] A tribal leader's endorsement of one party is likely to ensure the votes of an overwhelming majority of tribal members. It is small wonder, then, that the political leaders in Ankara have resorted to the policy of co-optation, which not only is much safer than trying forcibly to break down tribal structures, but also carries the distinct advantage of winning large numbers of votes without significant campaigning. Turkish governments until the 1990s therefore had little incentive to integrate southeastern Anatolia socially with the rest of the country.[15]

Whereas this strategy has been beneficial both for Ankara and the tribal leaders, it has been less so for the Kurdish population as a whole. The Kurdish areas have consistently lagged behind the rest of Turkey in terms of economic development, due largely to the preservation of the tribal structures and the neglect of the central government. Tribal leaders, of course, have an interest in preventing rapid modernization, which would inevitably weaken the traditional social structures that perpetuate their power. As a result, they have in all likelihood encouraged a certain lack of attention to their region on the part of central authorities. This is not to say that the rapid development of Turkish society has wholly bypassed the Kurds. Although the government may have neglected the area, considerable development has taken place, especially through the introduction of nationally standardized educational norms and compulsory military service, and through the spread of mass media, which have all brought dramatic changes to the perceptual environment of a generation of Kurds. In addition, as noted above, numerous Kurds have migrated to urban areas in western Turkey. Some of them left the southeast in search of better economic conditions and others were relocated by the state in an effort to integrate Kurds into society, but in both cases the result was to expose thousands of young Kurds to previously alien ways of living and thinking. In this context, leftist ideologies have had a specific attraction to many of the Kurds who have studied in Turkish universities since the 1960s.

The Militant PKK

Kurdish rebellions before World War II had a strong tribal and religious character that often overshadowed the national component, but in the postwar period this pattern underwent significant change. Turkey held its first multiparty election in 1950, resulting in the electoral defeat of Atatürk's Republican People's Party and a transfer of power to the center-right DP. The new government allowed exiled shaykhs and aghas to return, co-opting them into the system as outlined above.[16] The strengthened position of tribal leaders gave further impetus to the migration of Kurds to the urban areas of western Turkey, where a number of them benefited from the increasingly market-oriented economic policies of the government. Within a short time, a movement called "Eastism" (*Doğuculuk*) emerged, advocating economic development efforts in eastern and southeastern Anatolia. After the military coup of 1960, a new and more liberal constitution was adopted that included substantial protections for democracy, freedom of expression, and human rights. Indeed, the 1961 constitution (which was superseded in 1982) was the most liberal that Turkey has ever had. These freedoms led to a mushrooming of leftist activity among Kurds and others in Turkey. Although more-radical groups with various Marxist-Leninist affiliations emerged, the most prominent was the Workers' Party, whose public statements calling attention to an oppressed Kurdish minority eventually led to its closure.[17] Meanwhile, the increasing stature of Mullah Mustafa Barzani and his Kurdish Democratic Party (KDP) in northern Iraq and the rise of Kurdish nationalism there had a profound effect on more right-wing Kurdish activities in Turkey. From the 1960s onward, therefore, one can speak of a clear ideological division among politically active Kurds. A Marxist wing cooperated with ideological brethren of Turkish origin and often formed parts of Turkish-dominated groups, while a more traditionally nationalistic wing identified closely with Barzani's KDP. A main item on the agenda of the leftist Kurds was the socioeconomic restructuring of the southeast into a more equitable society through the dismantling of tribal institutions and, in its more extreme versions, the creation of a socialist system. This agenda was naturally anathema to the right-wing groups, which were closely linked to the tribal hierarchy. The right-wing Kurdish nationalists nevertheless failed to prevail for two main reasons: internal tribal divisions among them weakened their strength and appeal, and both their main leaders were forced into exile after the 1971 military intervention and eventually assassinated in northern Iraq. During the 1970s, leftist radicalization intensified as migration to urban areas of western Turkey continued and enrollment in higher education increased. These parallel processes heightened awareness of economic and political disparities between the southeast and the rest of the country, and Kurds were socioeconomically predisposed to be absorbed into the leftist climate predominant among the student body in Turkish universities. Gradually, however, Kurdish leftists became alienated from their Turkish colleagues and formed separate political movements.

Having its origins in an informal grouping around Abdullah Öcalan dating back to 1973, the PKK was formally established as a Marxist-Leninist Kurdish political party in 1978 and advocated the creation of a Marxist Kurdish state. From the outset, the PKK defined Kurdish tribal society as a main target of the revolutionary struggle. It described Kurdistan as an area under colonial rule, where tribal leaders and a *comprador* bourgeoisie colluded to help the state exploit the lower classes. In particular, it advocated a revolution to "clear away the contradictions in society left over from the Middle Ages," including feudalism, tribalism, and religious sectarianism.[18] It should be noted that in the 1990s the PKK toned down its Marxist rhetoric and instead emphasized Kurdish nationalism in the hopes of attracting a larger following among Turkish Kurds. Marxism-Leninism found little resonance among the population in agricultural, rural southeastern Turkey.

The PKK suffered heavily from the 1980 military coup, and Öcalan and some associates fled Turkey for Syria and the Beka'a Valley of northern Lebanon. But the repression of other leftist and Kurdish movements allowed the PKK to emerge as the sole credible Kurdish challenger to the state, and with the start of military operations in 1984, the PKK left Turkish Kurds with few choices. Unless they decided to stay out of politics completely, Kurds were forced either to side with the state, thereby expanding their opportunities as Turkish citizens at the price of suppressing their ethnic identity, or else join the PKK and fight the state. Any option ranging between these two extremes became highly dangerous, since any form of *peaceful* advocacy of Kurdish rights would attract the wrath of both the state and the PKK. The Turkish state painted itself into a corner by equating virtually all expressions of Kurdish identity with PKK terrorism. The PKK, in turn, suffered from several drawbacks that would ultimately precipitate its demise. Most significantly, its violence against the very population it claimed to represent disillusioned many Kurds, who saw little difference between the repressive Turkish state organs and a repressive PKK. To this should be added the megalomania that has been attributed to Öcalan. Beyond disallowing intraparty opposition, Öcalan developed a true personality cult around himself, leading other Kurdish leaders to abandon him as a madman. Jalal Talabani, the leader of the northern Iraqi Patriotic Union of Kurdistan (PUK), stated that "Öcalan is possessed by a *folie de grandeur* . . . he is a madman, like a dog looking for a piece of meat." The other Iraqi Kurdish leader, Masoud Barzani of the KDP, compared him to the Ugandan dictator Idi Amin.[19] Thirdly, the PKK's Marxist-Leninist ideology, which never really commanded much enthusiasm in Kurdish society at the outset, became a liability after the collapse of communism worldwide. Fourthly, despite its ideological zeal, the PKK failed to stay out of the tribal politics it aimed to destroy. In light of the authority commanded by tribal leaders, the PKK was forced to negotiate with the aghas, since winning over a tribal leader meant winning the support of the whole tribe, an advantage the PKK could not afford to forgo. As a result, the PKK had a stake in preserving tribal structures.[20] A fifth source of weakness derived from the westward migrations that were partly a result of the war. By the mid-1990s only a minority of Turkey's Kurds actually lived in the southeast. The sixth and final flaw was that the prospect of a separate Kurdish state did not enjoy the support of a majority of Kurds. The failure of the Kurdish "Federated State" in northern Iraq in the early 1990s, which culminated in economic misery and factional infighting, heightened the appeal of remaining within Turkey, especially as Turkish attempts to gain membership in the European Union were likely to bring increased democratization and economic development.

The longevity and intensity of the PKK rebellion are partly explained by the party's organizational skills and the support it managed to muster as a result of dissatisfaction among Kurds in Turkey. Of equal or greater importance, however, has been the PKK's mobilization of international resources, which can be divided into three basic categories: support from Kurds in exile, primarily in Western Europe; financial resources stemming from the narcotics trade; and indirect and direct support from states with an interest in weakening Turkey. Reliable PKK support has come from the Kurdish communities in Western Europe, especially Germany and, to a lesser degree, Sweden, where it has commanded the loyalty of a majority of exiled Kurds. This is not surprising, given that Kurds in exile include large numbers of politically motivated migrants, and given that the political mobilization of Kurds in Europe, including the (sometimes forced) levy of "taxes," is considerably easier than in Turkey, where state restrictions are far more stringent.[21] As concerns the drug trade, significant circumstantial evidence suggests that the PKK derives a large part of its financing from the production, refining, and smuggling of illicit narcotics to Europe, although the importance of the drug factor in the PKK rebellion should not be overestimated.[22]

Unquestionably, the most important factor in the PKK's survival has been the support of several foreign countries. During the 1980s the PKK was funded mainly by its ideological brethren in the Soviet Union. Evidence that other states supported or tolerated its operations on their soil has also surfaced, notably Greece, Iran, and the Republic of Cyprus. The PKK's most crucial and stable ally, however, has been Syria, which hosted Öcalan for twenty years and provided training facilities in the Beka'a Valley of Syrian-controlled northern Lebanon. Syria's reasons for opposing Turkey are manifold.[23] Most fundamental is a border dispute over the Hatay province, which is claimed by Syria but was ceded to Turkey by France (Syria's League of Nations mandatory) in 1939. Furthermore, Turkey's economic development program for southeastern Anatolia, which was inaugurated in the 1980s, planned to use water from the Euphrates and Tigris Rivers to irrigate large tracts of the arid region. Syria, fearing this would jeopardize its own access to water from the Euphrates, increased its support not only for the PKK, but also for Armenian terrorist organizations targeting Turkey.[24] Syria's role as the PKK's main patron became increasingly evident as the Soviet Union dissolved. Although Russia has utilized the PKK as a lever against Turkey, especially to deter possible Turkish support for Chechen insurgents, Russian support in no way approaches that which the Soviet Union provided in the

1980s.[25] It is doubtful whether the PKK could have attained anything close to the position it did without foreign support.

Whereas the end of the Cold War entailed a series of problems for the PKK, the Persian Gulf War was highly beneficial. The coalition against Iraq and Operation Provide Comfort/Northern Watch for all practical purposes removed northern Iraq from Baghdad's jurisdiction, and a U.S.-backed Kurdish "Federated State" was created there. At the heart of this new entity was a power-sharing agreement between Barzani's KDP and Talabani's PUK, an arrangement achieved partly through the efforts of the Turkish government, which stepped in as a patron of the deal in order to keep the PKK out of the area. However, conflicts between the KDP and PUK prevented the scheme from being implemented, and northern Iraq became a power vacuum, which coincided nicely with the aims of the PKK. Öcalan's organization soon based its operations there, and by 1994 it had managed to deny the Turkish state effective control of large tracts of its southeastern territory.[26] At the same time, the Turkish army's demonstrable lack of preparation for mountain and guerrilla warfare undermined discipline in the ranks. As soldiers continually failed to differentiate between civilians and rebels, the PKK enjoyed increasing popular support.

But the situation began to change in the mid-1990s. The Turkish army, having apparently realized the importance of not alienating the civilian population, emphasized discipline within the ranks and initiated a public-relations campaign that included the introduction of health and educational facilities for the population of the southeast. Meanwhile, the Turkish military eventually adapted successfully to guerrilla warfare (in stark contrast to the disastrous performance of the Russian army in Chechnya at roughly the same time) and gathered enough strength to strike the problem at its roots in northern Iraq. Since 1995, regular and massive troop incursions (some involving up to 35,000 troops) and the establishment of a security zone reminiscent of the Israeli zone in southern Lebanon have caused the PKK's position in northern Iraq to wither away. By 1998 the PKK's only lifeline was Syria. Spurred by its alliance with Israel, the Turkish government felt strong enough to threaten Syria with war unless it expelled Öcalan and the PKK bases in the Beka'a Valley. Unable to rule out the prospect of Israel's joining a Turkish punitive expedition, Damascus complied and expelled Öcalan in October 1998. After the PKK's forces relocated to northern Iraq, a subsequent Turkish incursion dealt a severe blow to their military capabilities. Since Öcalan's capture, his unreserved submission to Turkish authorities seems to have damaged the PKK so seriously that it is doubtful that it will ever again become a credible actor.

In sum, the PKK's intrinsic weaknesses that shrank its base of popular support, the Turkish military's change of policy toward the civilian population, and especially Turkey's growing ability to crush the insurgents and stamp out its sources of foreign support combined to defeat the insurgency. In late 1999 the PKK declared its withdrawal from Turkish territory and in early 2000 publicly laid down its arms, apparently emulating the PLO by trying to gain recognition as a political movement instead.

The Kurdish Question and Turkey's Democratization

Having defeated the PKK, Turkey has still not resolved its Kurdish question, since the PKK never represented the opinions of a majority of Turkey's Kurds. Although few reliable sources are available on Kurdish attitudes, there is conclusive evidence that only a minority of Kurds see the PKK as their main representative organ and that the majority desires to remain within the Turkish state. In the PKK's heyday in 1992, a poll conducted in the southeast showed that only 29 percent of the population viewed the PKK as the best representative of the Kurdish people.[27] Moreover, a great part of the Kurdish population has taken on Turkish identity in whole or in part. Indeed, Kurds in Turkey have three options: to reject Turkish identity altogether, to accept it in its civic version while retaining their Kurdish ethnic identity (which amounts to integration), or to accept Turkish identity in both its civic and ethnic forms (which amounts to assimilation). A 1993 poll showed that over 13 percent of Istanbul's population claimed Kurdish roots, while 3.9 percent considered themselves Kurds, and 3.7 percent identified themselves as "Turks with Kurdish parents." Apparently, the remainder considered themselves simply "Turks." Even accounting for the less-than-ideal polling conditions at the height of the conflict (including state restrictions on expressions of Kurdish identity), this outcome clearly shows that a significant number of Kurdish people have integrated into Turkish society.

That said, these figures should not be taken as evidence corroborating the view that Turkey does not have a Kurdish problem. Clearly, a large portion of the Kurdish population feels a significant frustration at the state-imposed restrictions on cultural and other rights. However, these figures do show that any solutions based on autonomy or federalism, which have often been advocated by outsiders, are obsolete. Since a majority of Kurds live in western parts of Turkey or are otherwise integrated into Turkish society, autonomy and federalism are impractical alternatives. Moreover, despite the bitterness of the armed conflict, tensions on the grassroots level between Turks and Kurds remain low. Any solution that would institutionalize ethnic distinctiveness would therefore risk fueling ethnic antagonism.[28]

The solution to the Kurdish question, pragmatically speaking, depends on several factors. First, the Turkish state needs to act in accord with its own rhetoric stipulating that the Kurdish issue is distinct from PKK terrorism. With the PKK militarily vanquished and Öcalan behind bars, the time has come for Turkey to accelerate its democratization, including the removal of restrictions on cultural rights. Turkey has long opposed any easing of its strict legislation governing terrorism, freedom of expression, and cultural rights, and justifies its position with the argument that reform would imply concessions to terrorists.[29] Now that the specter of PKK terrorism has significantly diminished, a window of opportunity has emerged for the country to press forward with reforms on human rights and democratization. In so doing, Turkey could take significant steps to prevent separatist organizations from receiving popular support, and it could do so with little risk of harming its own interests. Some activists claim that Turkey should permit school instruction in Kurdish and other minority languages, but such provisions may be counterproductive. Lack of command of the state language has proven to be a major socioeconomic impediment in countries where similar policies have been in effect, such as the Soviet Union. While retaining its unitary state structure and preserving Turkish as the sole official language of the state and the medium of education in schools, the liberalization of language laws to allow private and supplementary school instruction in minority languages would enable Kurds (and others) to retain their identity while integrating with society. Television broadcasts in Kurdish would serve a similar purpose and deal a significant blow to the PKK-aligned channel MED-TV, which (via satellite from Europe) has had a virtual monopoly on Kurdish-language programming. If the Turkish government allowed private or state-controlled Kurdish media to exist, its ability to influence the local population would increase significantly, as some high Turkish officials have acknowledged. Such measures would also improve Turkey's image in the West. In its relations with the European Union and international human rights bodies, Turkey's very defeat of the PKK rebellion makes it increasingly difficult to justify restrictions on cultural rights. An even more important step, however, would be to lift the state of emergency in the southeast. Until that happens, the country is effectively split into two juridically, with a significantly stricter legal system applied in one part of the country.

In this context, the role of Kurdish political parties deserves mention. Most Kurdish-oriented parties in the 1990s have been closed by the Constitutional Court due to alleged links to the PKK. Presently the People's Democracy Party (Halkin Demokrasi Partisi—HADEP) is under the same threat. However, the results of the 1999 general elections indicate the wide popularity of HADEP in the southeast. Although the party received only 4.7 percent of the total votes in the parliamentary election, this poor showing is largely related to the 10 percent threshold for representation in the parliament. With little chance of attaining that level nationwide, many voters concluded that a vote for HADEP was wasted. Results in the simultaneous municipal elections suggested a different picture. In many towns in the southeast, including the large cities of Van and Diyarbakir, HADEP candidates won landslide victories with up to 70 percent of the vote. This is a clear sign that large parts of the population of the southeast strongly favor a democratic representative of Kurdish rights. State attempts to destroy HADEP, either by closing down the party through legal measures or through the harassment or arrest of its leaders, are thus likely to be counterproductive. Removing the possibility of a democratic outlet for Kurdish sentiment will only fuel new illegal movements or enable the PKK to regain some strength. Despite its sometimes warranted suspicions, the state needs to tolerate and, if possible, engage HADEP and other democratic Kurdish movements instead of suppressing them.

Secondly, the economic measures consistently touted by the Turkish state must be realized. After the capture of Öcalan, the government did launch yet another large-scale investment program for the southeast, and as a result there is now a distinct possibility to attract foreign investments to the region. However, the government must take measures to ensure that development benefits the entire population and not just the tribal leaders who own most of the land and industry. Development efforts that enrich only aghas and their client networks but not the Kurdish population as a whole could provide a spark for a social explosion. The educational system, which suffered greatly from the war, also needs to be reestablished so that the Kurdish region's population can compete on equal terms in the increasingly competitive Turkish society.

Finally, the crucial issue for both democratization and economic development is the proper implementation of existing legislation. Previously, Turkey's main problem stemmed not from the legislation itself, but from a state bureaucracy that was often unable or unwilling to implement reforms. There is, however, reason to hope that this problem may be somewhat alleviated in the future. Civil associations in Turkey are growing in strength and exerting increasingly effective pressure on the government. At the same time, the end of large-scale hostilities should increase the transparency of state organs. The presidency of Ahmet Necdet Sezer, a prominent democrat from the judicial establishment, could also have a positive effect in this context.

The multifaceted Kurdish question is central to Turkey's future, including its relations with the European Union. Its international ramifications, moreover, make it an issue of utmost importance in the regional politics of the Middle East. However, the issue is often understood or depicted in simplistic ways. A deeper understanding of the matter must take into account the tribal character of Kurdish society, the dynamics of the PKK rebellion's rise and fall, and the larger context of Turkey's ongoing democratization. It is noteworthy that the current Turkish government is dominated by parties generally branded as "nationalist." Besides the MHP, the Democratic Left Party (Demokratic Sol Partisi–DSP) of Bülent Ecevit is a center-left party with strong nationalist tendencies. However, the electoral victory of these two parties in the 1999 general elections should not be dismissed as "a nationalist wind" sweeping through the country after the capture of Abdullah Öcalan.[30] The anticorruption profile of these two parties and the infighting of the center-right played at least as important a role as the seizure of Öcalan. Nevertheless, the dominant political forces in Turkey today subscribe to a definition of the Kurdish problem that denies its ethnic dimension. Although the current government promotes economic development programs in the southeast, it seems unwilling, close to two years after Öcalan's capture, to release the pressure on Kurdish-oriented political parties or to consider the easing of cultural restrictions. Without broadening its understanding of the Kurdish question and the measures needed to address it, the government is unlikely to resolve this problem. The Turkish state must therefore take advantage of the opportunity created by its victory over the PKK, because conditions have never been better to address the Kurdish question constructively and bring an end to the political instability and economic backwardness of southeastern Turkey. Having won the war, Turkey now needs to win the peace.

Notes

[1] Based on estimates, given that the ethnicity of members of parliament is not published and that census data do not include ethnicity.

[2] Populism (*halkçılık*) carries the meaning of a "government for the people" rather than the present-day meaning of the term, used to define political opportunism.

[3] For Atatürk's ideas, see e.g. Mustafa Kemal Atatürk, *Nutuk* (Ankara: Kültür Bakanlığı Yayınları, 1980). *Nutuk* is the Great Six-Day Speech held by Atatürk on Oct. 15–20, 1927.

[4] Doğu Ergil, *Secularism in Turkey: Past and Present* (Ankara: Foreign Policy Institute, 1988), p. 61.

[5] Patrick Kinross, *Atatürk: The Rebirth of a Nation* (London: Weidenfeld, 1964), p. 397.

[6] Justin McCarthy, *Death and Exile: The Ethnic Cleansing of Ottoman Muslims, 1821–1922* (Princeton, N.J.: Darwin Press, 1995).

[7] For a useful introduction, see David McDowall, *A Modern History of the Kurds* (London: I. B. Tauris, 1996), pp. 1–18.

[8] See, for example, Jack David Eller, *From Culture to Ethnicity to Conflict* (Ann Arbor: University of Michigan Press, 1999), p. 149–51.

[9] McDowall, *A Modern History of the Kurds*, pp. 15–16.

[10] See Martin van Bruinessen, *Agha, Shaikh and State* (Utrecht: Rijswijk, 1978).

[11] Gérard Chaliand, *The Kurdish Tragedy*, trans. Philip Black (London: Zed Books, 1994).

[12] McDowall, *A Modern History of the Kurds*, p. 15.

[13] The center-right True Path Party (Doğru Yol Partisi—DYP), Motherland Party (Anavatan Partisi—ANAP), Welfare Party (Refah Partisi—RP), Virtue Party (Fazilet Partisi—FP), and Nationalist Movement Party all originate from the DP, which existed from 1950 to 1960.

[14] For the 1995 elections, see Harald Schüler, "Parlamentswahlen in der Türkei" (Parliamentary elections in Turkey), *Orient*, vol. 37, no. 2 (1996).

[15] See Erik Cornell, *Turkey in the Twenty-First Century: Challenges, Opportunities, Threats* (Richmond, U.K.: Curzon Press, 2000), p. 101.

[16] McDowall, *A Modern History of the Kurds*, pp. 396–400.

[17] See Nader Entessar, *Kurdish Ethnonationalism* (Boulder, Colo.: Lynne Rienner, 1992), p. 90. The Workers' Party is unrelated to the PKK.

[18] See Michael M. Gunter, *The Kurds in Turkey: A Political Dilemma* (Boulder, Colo.: Westview Press, 1990), p. 60.

[19] See Nicole and Hugh Pope, *Turkey Unveiled* (New York: Overlook Press, 1998), p. 261.

[20] Ismet G. Imset, *PKK: Ayrılıkçı Şiddetin 20 Yılı* (The PKK: Twenty years of separatist terror) (Ankara: TDN, 1992).

[21] Henri J. Barkey and Graham E. Fuller, *Turkey's Kurdish Question* (Lanham, Md.: Rowman and Littlefield, 1998), p. 30.

[22] Nimet Beriker-Atiyas, "The Kurdish Conflict in Turkey: Issues, Parties, Prospects," *Security Dialogue*, vol. 28, no. 4 (1997), p. 440; Nur Bilge Criss, "The Nature of PKK Terrorism in Turkey," *Studies in Conflict and Terrorism*, vol. 18, no. 1 (1995), pp. 17–38.

[23] See Süha Bölükbaşı, "Ankara, Damascus, Baghdad, and the Regionalization of Turkey's Kurdish Secessionism," *Journal of South Asian and Middle Eastern Studies*, Summer 1991, pp. 15–36.

[24] See Philip Robins, *Turkey and the Middle East* (London: Pinter/RIIA, 1991), p. 50.

[25] Robert Olson, "The Kurdish Question and Chechnya: Turkish and Russian Foreign Policies since the Gulf War," *Middle East Policy*, vol. 3, no. 4 (1996), pp. 106–18.

[26] See Kemal Kirişçi and Gareth Winrow, *The Kurdish Question and Turkey* (London: Frank Cass, 1997), pp. 161–67.

[27] See *Milliyet*, Sept. 6, 1992, for the results of the poll; and Hugh Poulton, *Top Hat, Grey Wolf and Crescent: Turkish Nationalism and the Turkish Republic* (London: C. Hurst, 1997), pp. 245–48.

[28] On the perils of autonomy, see Svante E. Cornell, "Autonomy: A Catalyst of Conflict in the Caucasus?" paper presented at the Fifth Annual Convention of the Association for the Study of Nationalities, New York, Apr. 2000 (http://www.geocities.com/svantec/ASNCornell.pdf). Also see Henry J. Steiner, "Ideals and Counter-Ideals in the Struggle over Autonomy Regimes for Minorities," *Notre Dame Law Review*, vol. 66 (1991), pp. 1539–60.

[29] On human rights problems and legislation in Turkey, see Dilnewaz Begum, *International Protection of Human Rights: The Case of Turkey*, report no. 43 (Uppsala, Sweden: Department of East European Studies, 1998).

[30] For a development of this argument, see Svante E. Cornell, "Turkey: Return to Stability?" *Middle Eastern Studies*, vol. 35, no. 4 (1999), pp. 209–34.

6

The Rise and Fall of the PKK

by Michael Radu

In 1992 Turkey was in the midst of a war with the Kurdistan Workers' Party (Partiya Karkeren Kurdistan—PKK), whose forces were credibly estimated to be 10,000 strong.[1] In 1996 the journalist Franz Schurmann called the PKK "the biggest guerrilla insurgency in the world" and wrote of its founder and uncontested leader, Abdullah Öcalan, that "he alone among Kurdish leaders understands that a social revolution is going on in Kurdish society everywhere. . . . Öcalan will go down in the history books as the Saladin of the late 20th century."[2] By summer 1999, however, senior officers of the Turkish military and *Jandarma* (militarized police) estimated the PKK's total strength inside the country at 1,500 and declining rapidly.[3] In May 2000 the *Turkish Daily News* reported that "PKK armed militants have largely left Turkish territory after the PKK executive council called on them to cease armed struggle and leave Turkey."[4]

What brought about such a dramatic decline in just three years? Three developments provide a short, albeit incomplete, answer: the February 1999 capture of Öcalan; the increasing disenchantment of Turkey's Kurdish citizens with the PKK's armed struggle; and dramatic changes in the regional balance of power in the Middle East, which weakened the PKK's traditional supporters. Of these, the capture of Öcalan in Nairobi, Kenya, by Turkish commandos was the most obviously devastating blow, but was in fact symptomatic of military and political troubles that were years in the making. This is amply demonstrated by the fact that, after fifteen years of safe haven in Syria, Öcalan was on the run and desperately seeking asylum in Africa.

The PKK's evident vulnerability in the late 1990s raises the question of the depth and strength of its support among the Kurdish population, which had long been considered the source of the party's military and political successes over a decade and a half. The far from simple answer is that the degree of PKK support is a matter of definition. While some Kurdish clans actively backed Öcalan's party, others rejected it and joined the government's efforts to combat it. Clearly, then, the hitherto widespread impression of the PKK as a grassroots movement with broad popular support needs revisiting. To arrive at a greater understanding of the origins, ideology, leadership, and goals of the PKK, this article will rely heavily on the PKK's own statements and documents—all freely available on the Internet.[5] Obviously, such material constitutes propaganda rather than objective analysis, but that does not limit its value. To the contrary, what the PKK wants the world to know about it says a great deal about the way it sees itself.

Ideology, Leadership, and Strategy

On occasion, the PKK has presented itself as the defender and chief advocate of Kurdish nationalism. Its weak claim to such a position, however, reveals not any true conviction, but rather astute political instincts and sheer opportunism. Since the beginning, the PKK has been Marxist-Leninist in its ideology, Stalinist in its leadership style, and Maoist in its strategy for the conquest of power.

Marxism, not Kurdish nationalism, has always defined the PKK. Given that the founders of the PKK included ethnic Turks as well as Kurds, their common interest was never based on ethnicity. The history of the PKK, as portrayed in the records of its congresses prior to Öcalan's capture in February 1999, makes abundantly clear the party's unwavering loyalty to Marxism-Leninism. Most important is the "Fifth Victory Congress" of January 1995, which called attention to the importance of ideology in the life of Kurds—and to the PKK in the progress of socialism across the globe.[6] In the two major documents that emerged from that congress, the "Brief History of the Kurdistan Workers Party (PKK)" and the "Party Program of the PKK," the organization portrays itself as the "vanguard of the global socialism movement, even though the Party hasn't yet come to power."[7] Perhaps to shore up its claim to the leadership of socialism internationally, the program states that the PKK from the very beginning tried to enlist support in other countries; that "a new phase of socialism" has begun; and that the PKK "is the embodiment of one of the most significant socialist movements during this new phase."[8] It is important to consider the timing of that statement—a decade after Mikhail Gorbachev initiated perestroika and glasnost and six years after the collapse of the Berlin Wall. What had the PKK to say about those events? It claimed that "Soviet socialism was a kind of deviation" and went so far as to call it "rough," "wild," and even "primitive." By contrast, "the PKK's approach to socialism is scientific and creative."[9]

The arrogance manifest in such declarations can be attributed directly to Öcalan's leadership style, which in its megalomania and iron-fisted grip on power borrows heavily from Stalin. Öcalan, simply put, created a personality cult with himself as its focal point, and has made his own name virtually synonymous with that of the organization he heads. He has always been identified as the sole author of any text of significant ideological impact (including all major documents of the Fifth Congress), the initiator of every political and military campaign, and the uncontested decision maker at the party's helm.[10] And yet Öcalan's personal background would seem to make him an unlikely leader of Kurdish workers, a fact that makes the PKK's purported nationalist aspirations all the more specious.

Öcalan was born in 1948 into a peasant family in the mostly Kurdish village of Omerli. Significantly, his mother was not Kurdish at all, but Turkoman, and it was she (described by Öcalan as an "independent, headstrong woman") who controlled the household and dominated his "helpless" Kurdish father. Equally notable is Öcalan's statement that his family "was poor and had lost its tribal traditions, but it continued with strong feudal values"[11]—rather a surprising admission from a self-declared socialist leader who claims to be fighting against the "colonial" oppression of Kurds. After studying at a vocational school in the provincial capital of Urfa, Öcalan moved on to Ankara University's School of Political Science in the early 1970s, a period during which Turkish universities were involved in revolutionary activism far more than education. Öcalan spent his time learning political organizing and Marxist doctrine, and he evidently learned well. As he later put it, "I dedicated myself completely to ideological work"—which included political violence, for which he was arrested and imprisoned for a few months in 1973.

The PKK itself was founded in 1978, and Öcalan's continuous control over it was only obtained by ruthlessly eliminating potential challengers to his absolute authority. Those who threatened his leadership or simply disagreed with him faced demotion, expulsion, or death. As he euphemistically described the fate of those unfortunates at his own trial, despite "comprehensive educational and organisational efforts against them, . . . the most deviated ones of them could only be neutralised by internal struggles."[12] According to Chris Kutschera, one of Europe's most active, sympathetic, and knowledgeable analysts of the PKK, "Five or six of [the PKK's] original central committee have been physically eliminated, three others committed suicide, [and] eight are still alive, acting semi-clandestinely. . . . Others have been driven underground."[13] Moreover, the purges continued for years. Kutschera goes on to quote Selahattin Çelik, the founder and first commander of the PKK's armed wing, the People's Liberation Army of Kurdistan (Artesa Rizgariya Gele Kurdistan/Kürdistan Halk Kurtuluş Ordusu— ARGK): "There were between 50 and 60 executions just after the 1986 Congress. In the end there was no more room to bury them!"[14] Among those "arrested" at that time was Duran Kalkan, who was later released and is now still a member of the PKK Presidential Council. Not surprisingly, perhaps, Kalkan is now rumored to have offered Ankara his surrender in exchange for amnesty.[15] Another reminder of the Stalinist purges of the 1930s is found in the career of Ali Omer Can, a Central Committee member who was arrested and tortured in the PKK's Beka'a jails in 1986 and then released and rehabilitated. After he again broke with the party and tried to establish a rival organization, the "PKK Refoundation," he was assassinated in November 1991.[16]

If Öcalan's leadership style was Stalin's, his strategy for conquest resembled Mao's. The PKK's first goal was to establish a credible military force within Turkey that would be sufficient to challenge the political power of the government. Once that was accomplished, the party would expand its control to Kurdish areas beyond Turkish borders. A unified, socialist Kurdistan could then serve as a base from which to promote socialism within the region and around the world.[17] In other words, the foundation of a Kurdish state was never an ultimate goal in itself, but rather a means to spread socialism.

Specious Nationalism

If a Kurdish state was at best only a secondary goal for the PKK, it is important to consider the nature of its purported nationalism. Upon closer examination, it becomes clear that the PKK's claim to be "the leading force in the liberation of Kurdistan" is sheer obfuscation. In reality, the organization is not representative of the Kurdish people, nor is it nationalist in any commonly understood sense.

From the PKK's beginnings, there have been several reasons to question its claim to be the legitimate representative of the Kurdish people. First, as noted above, ethnic Turks were a part of the party since its inception, and in the early years the PKK counted as many Turks as Kurds among its members. Second, the party's official history acknowledges that already by 1980 it had difficulty recruiting Kurds in Turkey, which suggests that many Kurds' interests—*as they perceived them*—did not coincide with the PKK's own. Third, Öcalan's own background makes him ill suited to be a standard-bearer of Kurdish interests. Not only was his mother of Turkoman origin, but his 1999 trial made clear that he never learned either of the two major Kurdish languages (Kurmandji and Zaza) and used Turkish in all communications with followers.

Surely the most damaging fact undermining the PKK's position as the representative of Kurdish interests is the party's adversarial and often hostile relationship with Kurds throughout the region. In its efforts to gain recruits and legitimize itself in the eyes of certain segments of the Kurdish population, particularly in Tunceli province, Öcalan's party has not only exploited but exacerbated historic regional divisions and clan rivalries. Kurds under PKK attack have then sought assistance from the Turkish government and joined in its successful counterinsurgency campaign. Partially as a result of this internecine conflict, more Kurdish civilians than Turks have died during the PKK's war against Ankara, which suggests that absolute power matters far more to Öcalan than do the aspirations and welfare of the people he claims to lead. His party has killed Kurds as reprisals for suspected collaboration with Ankara; it has killed Iraqi Kurds during hostilities with the two leading Kurdish groups there; and it has killed Kurds in Europe and Lebanon who disagreed with Öcalan or simply did not support him fervently enough.

Among other tactics, suicide bombings in Kurdish areas have figured prominently in the PKK's terror campaign and contributed to the group's reputation for indiscriminate violence. According to the Turkish government, quoting both internal PKK documents and statements by captured militants, the PKK decided at its Fifth Congress to engage in bombing, and reaffirmed the decision a year later.[18] By 1997 the group had formed "Suicide Guerrilla Teams" that relied on large numbers of potential volunteers. Perhaps not surprisingly, the "volunteers" came from the most vulnerable segments of society: the majority of the early bombings attributed to the PKK were carried out by young, impoverished, and poorly educated women.

The PKK's disregard for human life has also carried over into its collaborative arrangements with governments waging violent campaigns against their own Kurdish populations, most notably in Syria and Iraq, but also to a lesser extent in Iran. The incentive for such collusion is not immediately apparent. One PKK analysis of the general Kurdish situation acknowledges that large numbers of Kurds in Syria "play an active role" in the Kurdish struggle, and Öcalan himself admitted that during the late 1980s Syrian Kurds were an essential part of the PKK's recruitment base.[19] And yet Öcalan has not only refused to provide assistance to Kurds in Syria, he cooperated with the government in Damascus that brutally oppressed them. Similarly, for more than a decade he supported Saddam Hussein's offensives against Kurdish nationalists in northern Iraq (or "South Kurdistan," in PKK parlance). The PKK's machinations have left Kurds throughout the region, who were never united to begin with, more divided than ever.

The real motivation for PKK collaboration can be summed up as strategic necessity. The insurgents have almost always needed outside help and have been willing to accept it from any quarter. The official history of the PKK acknowledges that the group engaged in a "tactical retreat" into Syria in 1980, when Öcalan fled Turkey just ahead of a military coup that culminated in a violent crackdown on Marxists.[20] He and his followers were given relatively free rein in the Syrian-controlled Beka'a Valley in Lebanon, where they thrived. As recently as the early 1990s, the PKK took foreign journalists on Potemkin village tours of bases and training camps there. For Öcalan to have objected to his hosts' treatment of their own Kurdish population would have meant the loss of the PKK's center of operations, without which it

would have never been able to threaten extensive areas of southeastern
Turkey during the 1990s.

Öcalan's acceptance of safe haven from Syria marked only the
beginning of the PKK's heavy reliance upon support from governments
that, for reasons of their own, found common cause with it. The Persian
Gulf War created a power vacuum in northern Iraq, allowing the PKK
to expand its influence there in competition with the existing Kurdish
groups, principally the Patriotic Union of Kurdistan (PUK) and the
Kurdistan Democratic Party (KDP). Iran, because of its ambiguous
position vis-à-vis Kurdish separatism in Turkey and Iraq (but never at
home), likewise allowed the PKK to use Iranian territory to open new
fronts along Turkey's eastern frontier. With the collapse of the Soviet
Union, newly independent Armenia also provided enough help, or
tolerance, for the PKK to threaten northeastern Turkey. In addition to
these friendly outsiders, Greece supported, tolerated, and encouraged
the PKK for more than a decade, as the circumstances surrounding
Öcalan's arrest ultimately revealed.[21] It is noteworthy, however, that
although outside assistance greatly enhanced the PKK's effectiveness,
ultimately it was also a key factor in the party's rapid descent.

In light of the PKK's acceptance of foreign support and open
opposition to other Kurds, two questions suggest themselves: On what
basis can the PKK claim to be nationalist, and what advantage does it
gain from doing so? Despite ample evidence to the contrary, the PKK
has gone to some lengths to shore up its claim to represent Kurds—a
claim that has required no small amount of logical and linguistic
contortions. According to the Fifth Congress documents, the lineage of
the Kurds can be traced back to the ancient Medes, who as early as the
seventh century B.C. were engaged in a "long struggle which gave rise
to a national consciousness" and who "played a leading role in the
formation of our national values."[22] But the national consciousness
touted by the PKK is not any "bourgeois" consciousness of the Kurds
as an ethnically, culturally, or historically distinct group. Rather, the
PKK distinguishes "reactionary nationalism" from a "socialist national
consciousness" that takes into account "the fact of exploitation . . . a
class characteristic."[23] Presumably, then, a Turk of an "exploited" class
would be included within this "nation," whereas a Kurdish landowner
would not.

This patently Leninist definition of nationalism is incompatible with the usual understanding of the concept, but has nevertheless allowed the PKK to portray itself as a Kurdish nationalist organization since the class-based distinction seems largely lost on outsiders sympathetic to its calls for national self-determination. Thus, although not a single volume has been published in English on the PKK per se, the vast literature on the Kurds tends to assume, without further explanation, that the PKK is the legitimate representative of Kurdish interests. John Bulloch and Harvey Morris, for example, while aware of Öcalan's Stalinist beliefs, still described the PKK as "the latest in a long line of insurgent groups which has tried over the years to obtain basic human rights for the Kurds of Turkey."[24] Michael M. Gunter describes the PKK as "first a Kurdish nationalist movement."[25]

A European Life-Support System

Here the PKK's motivation to be called "nationalist" becomes clearer: the label has proved to be a highly successful part of its public-relations campaign and its principal means of gaining a degree of legitimacy around the world. Specifically, the survival of the PKK has depended not only on the cooperation of the various governments mentioned above, but also on the active support of some Westerners and the Kurdish diaspora in Western Europe. By virtue of its being considered a nationalist organization, the PKK seems to have inoculated itself against at least some of the damage that might be expected to result from reports of its murders, insurgent attacks, and collaboration with dictators. No such news, for example, dissuaded Danielle Mitterand, the radical widow of the former French president, from addressing Öcalan as "Dear President Öcalan" in a 1998 letter, which ended "[R]est assured, Abdullah, that I am committed to be beside you in the bid for peace. Sincerely yours, Danielle Mitterand."[26] As Öcalan's attempts to find political asylum in 1998 and early 1999 proved, he also enjoyed the support of leftist parties in Italy, France, and Greece. The most insidious, if not necessarily surprising, support came from Germany's and Italy's Marxist terrorists, who supported and occasionally even joined in PKK combat operations. At least two German women became PKK members. One was killed in combat, the other was captured in 1998.[27]

Nothing better demonstrates the PKK's public-relations capabilities than MED-TV, a satellite television channel that operated first under a British license from London and later from Brussels. Although it ostensibly existed to promote Kurdish culture, the channel was such a blatant propaganda outlet for the PKK (at a cost of some $200 million per year) that it was eventually expelled from Britain and later lost its operating license in Belgium as well.[28]

Its public-relations campaigns and prominent supporters gave the PKK a measure of legitimacy, but the party also needed something else: funding. It proved so adept at generating money that European assessments generally placed its annual income at between $200 and $500 million in the mid-1990s. Income came from two major sources in Europe. One was the sizable pool of West European Kurdish militants among the émigré population, especially in Germany. In 1997 Germany's Federal Ministry of the Interior estimated the number of PKK sympathizers in the country at 11,000, and claimed that the PKK possessed an ability to mobilize "tens of thousands" among the 500,000 resident Kurds.[29] The German government further stated that the PKK collected millions of marks at its annual fundraising events, including 20 million marks in 1996–97.[30]

The more important source of funds has been criminal activity, especially in Germany, Switzerland, France, Scandinavia, and the Benelux countries.[31] Operating among Europe's 800,000 Kurdish immigrants, the PKK has been involved in theft, extortion, arms smuggling, human smuggling, and heroin trafficking. Infamous for its violence, the PKK is widely known to rely on murder and beatings as enforcement measures. Apparently, its methods have had their desired effect. Some sources estimate the PKK's annual income from criminal activities at $86 million.[32] The PKK's bankrolls have likely suffered some setbacks due to the military decline of the PKK and factional disputes among the European front's leaders. One PKK representative, for example, disappeared with 2.5 million German marks in party funds and may have made them available to PKK dissidents.[33] Despite those losses, however, the magnitude of the PKK's income suggests that the group remains wealthy. It is also worth noting that in addition to providing considerable financial resources, the PKK's international criminal activities also attest to the organization's sophisticated logistical capabilities.

Foreign political support, well-padded bank accounts, and the backing of thousands of Kurds in Western Europe enabled the PKK to apply immense military and political pressure on Turkey throughout most of the 1990s. Ultimately, however, these same pillars of support pointed up the inherent weakness underlying the PKK's apparent strength. Émigrés and criminals underwrote the PKK, and prominent leftists legitimized it, but their backing never translated into the broad support of Kurds in Turkey, who were better apprised of the party's totalitarian nature.

This constellation of facts provided the kernel of the PKK's undoing, as became apparent in the late 1990s, when much of the external support started to unravel. Most prominently, Turkey's de facto alliance with Israel automatically raised the stakes for Syria's continuing support for the organization.[34] As a result, when in the summer of 1998 Ankara threatened military action because of Syrian aid to Öcalan, President Hafez al-Assad had to back down. In October of that year he expelled Öcalan and closed most PKK camps in Lebanon and Syria, including those along the Turkish border. Suddenly on the run, Öcalan had to find a new refuge farther away from his fighters (whom, one may add, he never personally joined in combat), first in Russia, then Italy and Greece. Pursued by the Turks and denied asylum in Western Europe, he accepted Greek offers to go to Nairobi, only to be captured there by Turkish commandos with Kenyan connivance and probably American and Israeli intelligence help. The Iraqi government is in no position to offer any significant assistance to the PKK, since it still does not control its own northern territories. Armenia, constrained by its vulnerability to Turkish reprisals, likewise cannot do much even if it were so inclined. Greece, apparently, was stung by the Kenya episode and U.S. criticism. It has made a concerted effort both to mute its traditional hostility toward Turkey and to limit aid to the PKK.

Ankara's Response

Deprived of external support and chronically short of it within Turkey, the PKK was left vulnerable to Ankara's crushing blows. As major insurgencies go, Turkey's campaign against the PKK is one of the few recent examples of clear victory by the state itself—only Peruvian president Alberto Fujimori's success against the Shining Path and the Tupac Amaru Revolutionary Movement was similarly decisive.[35] It took Ankara sixteen years and cost some 30,000 lives, but success ultimately resulted from a combination of military astuteness, political realism, and diplomacy.

For the first six years of PKK operations, Turkish forces failed to realize the magnitude of the PKK military threat and respond adequately. Among the most effective measures taken was the militarization of virtually the entire southeast. The army and militarized police seized de facto control of daily life and managed to ingratiate themselves with the population at least in part through initiatives such as education programs for girls. But the military also won support because a large portion of the Kurdish population found the protection of the Turkish government far more attractive than the terror of the PKK and its hostility to Kurds of rival clans or differing political views. The most dramatic result of the cooperation between government and people was the "village guards," which were local Kurdish self-defense forces specifically organized to counter PKK operations. At the height of their strength, the village guards numbered some 60,000 armed civilians.

Aside from the changed relationship between the Turkish government and the population, the military also took other tactical and strategic steps to harm the Kurdish rebels. Notable in this regard was the effective use of special forces to pressure PKK groups in their mountain strongholds. In addition, heavy use of air power, mostly helicopters, hindered PKK movements in border areas where limited natural cover left the insurgents vulnerable. The army also launched massive operations in northern Iraq—often in conjunction with local KDP elements—that succeeded in denying the PKK access to its rear bases there. Finally, improvements in intelligence led to the capture of at least three major PKK leaders abroad in 1998 and 1999, the most notable, of course, being Öcalan himself.

To be sure, the Turkish military also benefited from developments that lay at least partially beyond its control. Among the most important of these was the depopulation of the countryside and concentration of Kurdish civilians in defensible centers. This dramatic shift occurred for several reasons, including PKK atrocities against civilians (mostly Kurds from clans Öcalan could not control or intimidate), the government's own military operations (damage from air attacks, in particular, forced people to relocate), and the general poverty of the southeast, which the war exacerbated. Local residents fled many of the more isolated areas and migrated to Western Europe, other parts of Turkey, or regional centers such as Diyarbakir, Van, and Sirnak. In doing so, they deprived the PKK of the recruitment, logistical, and communications assistance on which it had depended. As Öcalan himself admitted, "The PKK has not succeeded to become a regular armed force," the implication being that the PKK's inability to attract willing recruits forced it to resort to violence and intimidation, which in turn led to indiscipline and indiscriminate attacks against civilians.[36]

Ankara also pursued other policies that greatly enhanced its position vis-à-vis Öcalan's rebels. As noted above, its increasingly assertive regional diplomacy, backed by credible threats of force, led Syria to expel Öcalan and close down PKK camps on its territory and in Lebanon. Domestically, Turkish leaders, from the late president Turgut Özal to the current prime minister, Bülent Ecevit, have gradually come to acknowledge the Kurdish issue as such and—without ever accepting any PKK connection to it—have made concessions on matters related to language and cultural grievances. In addition, the government has also initiated huge investments in the southeast, exemplified by the $32 billion Southeastern Anatolia Project, to improve the long-languishing region's economic prospects.[37] Indeed, between 1983 and 1992 the southeast received twice as much investment per capita as any other region in Turkey, with total spending during that time on the Southeastern Anatolia Project reaching $20 billion.[38]

Lastly, it should be noted that strong diplomatic support from the United States helped to convince a number of West European governments, particularly the Netherlands, Greece, and Italy (and to a lesser degree Russia and Armenia), to deny Öcalan political asylum. His failure to find refuge ultimately led him to Kenya and captivity.

The Prisoner Recants?

If the dramatic progress of the campaign against the PKK within Turkey exposed the weaknesses in its support there and the inadequacy of its outside assistance, then Öcalan's incarceration revealed the flaw in the party's Stalinist leadership structure. Once the supreme commander was arrested, rifts emerged throughout the entire organization that threatened its continued existence. Even more important than his imprisonment itself, however, was the effect on the PKK of Öcalan's apparent renunciation of his entire insurgent campaign.

Ever since his arrest in Nairobi in February 1999, Abdullah Öcalan has made repeated statements contradicting the ideological, military, and political positions he has advocated since the founding of the PKK. To begin with, in his wide-ranging final statement at his trial in June 1999, he acknowledged that Kurdish society in Turkey did not fit his long-standing analysis and strategy. Indeed, he admitted that the PKK "should have taken into account the development the country had undergone both when it was founded and in the 1990s." More astonishing still was his giving up pursuit of "a separate part of a state, something which . . . would have been very difficult to realize—and, if realized, could not be maintained and was not necessary either."[39] In one grand stroke Öcalan delegitimized all PKK positions on matters of ideology, strategy, and tactics. In other words, a socialist Kurdistan— for which the PKK had ostensibly fought for years—was, as Chris Kutschera phrased it, a "mad dream."[40] Not only did Öcalan ask the PKK to stop fighting and withdraw from Turkish territory, but in September 1999 he also ordered the symbolic surrender of a few units to Turkish authorities.

The obvious question is whether Öcalan's statements are representative of true changes of personal opinion or merely an expression of survival instincts, particularly given the prospect of capital punishment. His behavior at his trial hints at the latter, in light of his attempts to lay the responsibility for the PKK's record of violence at the feet of his field commanders by claiming that he was unable to "implement my own ideas and the official tactical line of the organization. . . . Individual or local initiatives were dominant." He even seemed to suggest that his followers' upbringing was at the root of their violence: "[I]t was hard to control the PKK . . . especially when one considers how the individuals [fighting in the PKK] had grown up."[41] He also claimed that he had never ordered or approved of suicide bombings—a dubious denial from the man who once said: "We shall come down to the cities. . . . No matter the price, it is not difficult to get on a bus, to get on an airplane. We have thousands of people who shall go with a bomb around them."[42]

It is probably impossible to determine the degree to which Öcalan's about-face was due to the threat to his own life, or to a realization that the insurgency was a lost cause, or to the collapse of vital Syrian support. What is clear, however, is that, in a manner befitting a Stalinist leader, he made these extraordinary changes without consulting anyone and simply expected the party to accept them. Amazingly enough, the PKK did largely follow Öcalan's lead. Nothing better symbolized the abandonment of the goal of a separate Kurdish state than the decision by the PKK's Presidential Council in February 2000 to drop the word "Kurdistan" from the name of both its dwindling armed wing, the ARGK, and the still-strong international political wing, the National Liberation Front of Kurdistan (Eniya Rizgariya Netewa Kurdistan—ERNK). Thus, the ARGK became the People's Legal Defense Force (HPG), and the ERNK became the Democratic People's Union.[43] The personality cult constructed around Öcalan that had for so long given the PKK its unity, coherence, and purpose ultimately allowed it to be undermined rapidly.

High-ranking Turkish military officials professed surprise at Öcalan's apparent change of heart.[44] In actuality, however, it matches rather closely the behavior of the Shining Path's founder and supreme leader, Abimael Guzmán, who renounced armed struggle after his own arrest. In both cases the result was similar: the party faithful, having lost their ideological anchor, became confused and descended into factionalism and intraparty violence. The Shining Path suffered defeat; the ultimate fate of the PKK is not yet known.

Many PKK hardliners found Öcalan's newly conciliatory stance intolerable. Subsequent to his orders issued from captivity, and particularly his lengthy concluding statement at trial, dissent within the ranks of the party appeared almost immediately from among Kurds in Europe as well as fighters in and around Turkey. An anonymous group that called itself the "PKK revolutionary line fighters" issued a starkly worded rejection of Öcalan's call for some PKK combatants to surrender to Turkish forces: "At this junction, we will either be simple executor of this plan, and therefore we would kill ourselves, or we will say 'No' with all our force against this liquidation plan."[45] Some of the most prominent PKK hardliners, including former Central Committee members and other leaders, accused Öcalan of no less than "treason." In proof of their opposition to his decisions since capture, they established the "Kurdish Initiative in Europe," which was intended as a possible alternative to the ERNK. They also threw their support to Hamili Yıldırım, a Central Committee member and field commander from Tunceli province who refused to obey Öcalan's call for a general retreat.[46] Yıldırım joined forces with Turkish Communist Party elements and continued fighting Turkish security forces.[47] Significantly, the dissident group chose January 12, 2000, for one such attack—the very date the Turkish government coalition was to decide whether to execute or give a reprieve to Abdullah Öcalan. In view of Turkish public sentiment in favor of execution, those attacks could be seen as nothing but an attempt to have Öcalan killed. However, Yıldırım's rebellion did not last. By May 2000 security forces had killed one of his fellow commanders and wounded Yildirim himself, whereupon he returned to the PKK fold and reintegrated his troops into the PKK's "Public Self-Defense Force," although they did not disarm. That outcome, in fact, demonstrates the disingenuous nature of Öcalan's current position: he has ostensibly renounced armed struggle, but continues to encourage "self-defense" and overlooks the PKK forces still active in northern Iraq.

For a group notoriously intolerant of internal dissent, it is not surprising that the PKK leadership has taken exceptional measures to ensure that its orders are followed. The party dispatched Presidential Council member Murat Karayılan to the Netherlands in 1999, ostensibly to seek political asylum, but in reality to enforce Öcalan's will among Kurds in Western Europe.[48] In early 2000 the PKK Presidential Council simply decided to abolish the Free Women's Movement of Kurdistan (Yekityia Azadiya Jinen Kurdistan—YAJK), which had long supplied the movement with suicide bombers and assassins, because of the YAJK's leaders' objections to Öcalan's "capitulationist" stance. Intimidation and credible threats of violence are also commonly used to enforce the party line. In 1998 Semdin Sakık, a Central Committee member and ARGK field commander, was expelled from the party and forced to flee to pro-Turkish areas in northern Iraq after facing death threats for disagreeing with Öcalan.[49] When it cannot silence dissidents, the PKK has also tried to discredit them. Sakık, for example, is now accused by the PKK of having sabotaged Öcalan's 1993 cease-fire declaration by attacking and killing some thirty unarmed Turkish recruits. This particular claim, however, is belied by the fact that he was reelected to the Central Committee in 1995—two years after his alleged transgression. In another case, Öcalan tried to destroy his estranged wife, Yesire Yıldırım, and her brother Hüseyin (who are not related to Hamili Yıldırım), both of whom had been expelled from the party in 1986, by accusing the pair of the 1986 assassination of Swedish prime minister Olof Palme—an unproven and probably unprovable charge. (Long-time suspect Christer Petterson confessed to this assassination in October 2001.)[50]

Yet for all its efforts, the PKK has still not entirely succeeded in silencing its disgruntled members. Some of the most telling statements have come from a co-founder of the ARGK, Selahattin Çelik, who was beaten up by PKK supporters in Cologne after criticizing Öcalan's behavior in captivity. In an interview given in Germany following that attack, he said,

> Most Kurds simply cannot understand this [Öcalan's statements since his capture]. And yet no one is allowed to raise their voice in opposition to this new line. While the PKK makes one concession after another to the Turkish state, they damn people who demand democracy in their own ranks and in Kurdish society.[51]

In a view paradoxically shared by Ankara, Çelik went on to state that the "Kurdish issue could increasingly become separated from the PKK . . . [and] contradictions could surface within the PKK, which would make internal clashes unavoidable."[52] In other words, the PKK could lose its relevance and descend into yet another round of purges.

What Future for the PKK?

Currently, however, as Öcalan faces the (admittedly unlikely) prospect of execution and his beleaguered party confronts political and military pressure on almost all fronts, the PKK leadership seems to understand that it cannot afford costly strife within its own ranks. In an August 2000 interview, Cemil Bayık, the only remaining PKK founder at large (now in Iran) and the most prominent member of the Presidential Council, announced a new strategy that emphasized "deepening party unity and national unity, adding new circles of friends to those that already exist, strengthening solidarity with the regional people, and securing internal peace among the Kurds."[53] It would appear, then, that the PKK may seek common ground with erstwhile rivals and dissidents. But his statement was by no means completely conciliatory. Bayık, Öcalan's closest collaborator, lashed out at rivals among Kurds in Iraq and had harsh criticism for those within and outside the party who sought to "tear us from our beloved President" and "liquidate the party and the revolution and sell out the people." He went on to declare that the conflict with Turkey was far from over and that the PKK was "carrying on a sacred war with the genuine lords of the manservants"—the "lords" being an apparent reference to Turkey, the "manservants" being collaborators.[54] As those strident words suggest, the "strategic" changes that ostensibly announced the end of the PKK's bid for a separate Kurdish state may have actually been a tactical ploy to buy time for the PKK to regroup. In fact, according to plausible estimates from Jalal Talabani, leader of the rival PUK in northern Iraq, the PKK now has approximately 7,000 fighters in Iraq and Iran, and is currently recruiting and rearming. He added, however, that the fighters' morale was low: "I think that if there is an amnesty . . . all of them will come back to Turkey."[55]

The PKK's tenacious survival despite its declining fortunes has, of course, not escaped the notice of the Turkish government. To its credit, Ankara does not trust Öcalan's peaceful intentions or those of his lieutenants still at large and, despite Öcalan's September 1999 announcement that the party laid down its weapons, has given the PKK no quarter. In fact, air attacks in 2000 on targets inside Iraq demonstrate the military's greater willingness to pursue the PKK wherever necessary in order to ensure its final destruction.[56] At the same time, however, Selahattin Çelik's prediction has come to pass, and the Turkish government has indeed separated the Kurdish issue from the PKK. The significant political and economic changes mentioned above—most initiated since Öcalan's capture—prove that the PKK has been not an advocate for Kurds, but rather the major obstacle to political and economic development in southeastern Turkey and to Kurdish interests in general. The critical question now is whether the PKK's sympathizers and supporters in Western Europe will make a similar distinction. For only when Öcalan and his followers are deprived of funds and legitimacy will their bloody campaign truly be "neutralized," and only then will peace and genuine reconciliation have a chance for success.

Is now on terrorist list ?

Militarily irrelevant as the PKK is at the end of 2001, it is still politically influential, or threatening enough—once again, outside Turkey and in Western Europe—to manage to stay out of the European Union's December 2001 list of terrorist organizations. For a group responsible for over 20,000 deaths, most of them civilian Kurds, that is a great propaganda victory indeed. That fact, if nothing else, suggests that Western democracies and Turkish/Kurdish terrorism have a relationship going further than justice, realism, or indeed common sense. It also demonstrates Öcalan's spectacular success in hitching his real goal—the establishment of a totalitarian state in southeastern Turkey, to be expanded to Iran, Iraq, and Syria later, to a misguided, emotional and irrational sympathy by Brussels for the loosely defined "Kurdish" cause.

Notes

[1] Franz Schurmann, "Kurdish Leader Is Key Player," *San Francisco Examiner*, Sept. 5, 1996, posted by Kurdistan Web Resources (http://www-personal.usyd.edu.au/~rdemirb1/PUBLIC/Leader.html). Except where otherwise noted, all web sites cited in this article were accessible as of October 2000.

[2] Ibid.

[3] Author's interviews in Şirnak and Van provinces, June 1999.

[4] "PKK Looks for Route Out of Turkey," *Turkish Daily News*, May 18, 2000, posted by the *Kurdistan Observer* (http://homepages.go.com/~heyvaheft1999). Many stories from the *Kurdistan Observer* (http://www.kurdistanobserver.com) are archived elsewhere. See especially (http://homepages.go.com/~heyvaheft1999/Archive-News.html) and (http://www.mnsi.net/~mergan95/).

[5] Most of the information here is taken from the PKK's own "Brief History of the Kurdistan Workers' Party (PKK)" (http://www.guerilla.hypermart.net/archives/pkkhist.htm). Site no longer accessible, but see note 7 below.

[6] See "PKK Fifth Victory Congress" (http://www.kurdstruggle.org/pkk/information/congress.html).

[7] "A Brief History of the Kurdistan Workers Party (PKK)" and "Party Program of the Kurdistan Workers Party," posted at a PKK web site earlier available through the BURN! Project from the University of California at San Diego (http://burn.ucsd.edu/). The BURN! Project's site, a major publicity outlet for violent Marxist groups around the world, was closed down in 2000 by the administration of UCSD, but was accessible in Oct. 2000. The "Party Program" is also posted by Kurdish Struggle (http://www.kurdstruggle.org).

[8] "Party Program."

[9] Ibid.

[10] Among other works, Öcalan is identified as the author of the PKK's manifesto, *The Road to the Kurdistan Revolution* (1982), *Problems of the Personality and Characteristics of the Fighter* (1982), 32 volumes of political reports (1981, 1990), *The People's War in Kurdistan* (1991), and *Selected Writings* (5 volumes, 1986–92). See "Biographical Notes on Abdullah Öcalan" (http://burn.ucsd.edu/~ats/APO/apo-bio.html) and "Abdullah Öcalan Biographical Notes" (http://www-personal.usyd.edu.au).

[11] Ibid.; see also Öcalan's own account of his life as given during his 1999 trial, "My Personal Status" (http://www.xs4all.nl/~kicadam/declaration/status.html).

[12] "The Final Statements of Defendant Abdullah Öcalan," June 17, 1999, posted by Kurdish Struggle (http://www.kurdstruggle.org/defence/final.html).

[13] Chris Kutschera, "Disarray inside the PKK," *Middle East*, May 2000 (http://www.africasia.com/me/may00/mebf0502.htm).

[14] Ibid.

[15] "Kurdistan: La situación del PKK," *Rebelión*, Aug. 5, 2000 (http://www.rebelion/internacional/Kurdistan_pkk020800.htm).

[16] Kutschera, "Disarray inside the PKK."

[17] "PKK Fifth Party Congress Resolution on the Function of Internationalism" (http://www.kurdstruggle.org/pkk/information/internationalism.html).

[18] Office of the Chief Public Prosecutor, State Security Court (DGM), *Indictment Regarding Accused Abdullah Öcalan* (Ankara: Republic of Turkey, Apr. 24, 1999), prep. #1997/514, principle #1999/98, indictment #1999/78, pp. 56Ü60.

[19] "Party Program of the PKK. Chapter One: The World Situation" (http://kurdstruggle.org/information/chap1.html). Öcalan neglected to mention, however, that many of those recruits were in fact infiltrators working for the Syrian government. See Michael M. Gunter, *The Kurds and the Future of Turkey* (New York: St. Martin's Press, 1997), pp. 26–27.

[20] "Brief History of the PKK."

[21] Ministry of Foreign Affairs, Republic of Turkey, *Greece and PKK Terrorism* (Washington, D.C.: Turkish Embassy, Feb. 1999) provides an admittedly biased but largely correct analysis of Greece's support for the PKK and other terrorist groups in Turkey.

[22] "Party Program of the PKK. Chapter Two: Kurdish Society" (http://kurdstruggle.org/information/chap2.html).

[23] "Nationalism and the Kurdish National Liberation Movement" (http://burn.ucsd.edu/~ats/PKK/nationalism.html).

[24] *No Friends But the Mountains: The Tragic History of the Kurds* (New York: Oxford University Press, 1992), p. 168.

[25] *The Kurdish Predicament in Iraq: A Political Analysis* (New York: St. Martin's Press, 1999), p. 32.

[26] Danielle Mitterand, "An open letter to President Öcalan," Sept. 1, 1998, posted by the American Kurdish Information Network (http://www. kurdistan.org).

[27] See "Juhnke to be Transferred to Amasya," *Kurdish Observer*, Dec. 28, 1999 (http://www.kurdishobserver.com/1999/12/28/hab06.html); and "ERNK Statement on the Death of Andrea Wolf," KURD-L archives, Nov. 29, 1998 (http://burn.ucsd.edu/archives/kurd-l/1998.11/msg00033.html). For more details on German anarchist and "anti-fascist" groups' ties with the PKK, see (German) Federal Ministry of the Interior, *Annual Report 1997* (http://www.bmi.bund.de). The latter web page is no longer accessible.

[28] MED-TV ceased operations in 1999, but its web site was still accessible as of October 2000 (http://www.med-tv.be/med/med-tv/medhome.htm).

[29] Federal Ministry of the Interior, *Annual Report 1997*.

[30] Ibid.

[31] Ministry of Foreign Affairs, *Drug Trafficking and Terrorist Organizations* (Ankara: Republic of Turkey, Aug. 1998).

[32] "Kurdistan Worker's Party (PKK)," International Policy Institute for Counter-Terrorism, Jan. 27, 2000 (http://www.ict.org.il/inter_ter/orgdet.cfm? orgid=20). This source quotes the British National Service of Criminal Intelligence to the effect that in 1993 the PKK obtained 2.6 million pounds sterling from extortion and 56 million German marks from drug smuggling.

[33] "Cracks Appear in the PKK," *Turkish Daily News*, Jan. 21, 2000; and Susanne Gusten, "Kurdish Rebel Leader Ocalan at the Mercy of the PKK," Agence France-Presse, Jan. 13, 2000, both posted by the *Kurdistan Observer* (http://homepages.go.com/~heyvaheft1999/21-1-00-TDN-pkk-cracks.html and /~heyvaheft1999/13-1-00-AFP-apo-mercy-pkk.html).

[34] See Raphael Israeli, "The Turkish-Israeli Odd Couple," *Orbis* vol. 45, no. 1, Winter 2001, pp. 65–79.

[35] The definitive analysis of the Shining Path is to be found in Coronel PNP Benedicto Jimenéz Bacca, *Inicio, Desarollo y Ocaso del Terrorismo en el Peru* (The beginning, development and decline of terrorism in Peru), restricted ed. (Lima: Servicios Graficos SANKI, 2000), vol. 2, pp. 759Ü65. See also Carlos Ivan Degregori, ed., *Las rondas campesinas y la derrota de Sendero Luminoso*

(Peasant self-defense goups and the defeat of the Shining Path) (Lima: IEP Ediciones, 1996). For a recent analysis in English, see Michael Radu, "The Perilous Appeasement of Guerrillas," *Orbis*, Summer 2000, pp. 363–82.

[36] "Final Statements of Defendant Abdullah Öcalan."

[37] Douglas Frantz, "As Price of Progress, Turkish Villages Are Flooded," *New York Times*, Aug. 21, 2000.

[38] Kemal Kirişçi and Gareth Winrow, *The Kurdish Question and Turkey: An Example of Trans-state Ethnic Conflict* (London: Frank Cass, 1997), p. 124. For details on the $20 billion project, see Bülent Topkaya, "Water Resources in the Middle East: Forthcoming Problems and Solutions for Sustainable Development of the Region" (http://www.geocities.com/RainForest/Jungle/1805/gap.html).

[39] "Final Statements of Defendant Abdullah Öcalan."

[40] Chris Kutschera, "Mad Dreams of Independence: The Kurds of Turkey and the PKK," *Middle East Report*, July–Aug. 1994, posted by the Kurdish Information Network (http://www.xs4all.nl/~tank/kurdish/htdocs/lib/dream.html).

[41] "Final Statements of Defendant Abdullah Öcalan."

[42] *Indictment Regarding Accused Abdullah Öcalan*, p. 58. The PKK occasionally mentioned having as many as 3,000 would-be suicide bombers.

[43] "PKK dropping the word 'Kurdistan' from the names of new wings," Associated Press, Feb. 9, 2000, posted by the *Kurdistan Observer* (http://homepages.go.com/~heyvaheft1999/10-2-00-AP-pkk-dropping-kurdistan .html).

[44] Author's interviews with army and *Jandarma* officials in Diyarbakır, Şırnak, Van, and Eruh, June 1999.

[45] "Statement from 'PKK revolutionary line fighters,'" KURD-L archives, Nov. 12, 1999 (http://burn.ucsd.edu/archives/kurd-l/1999.11/msg00000.html).

[46] Kutschera, "Disarray inside the PKK."

[47] "Cracks Appear in the PKK."

[48] Kutschera, "Disarray inside the PKK."

[49] In April 1998 Turkish special forces captured Şemdin Sakık in a KDP-controlled part of northern Iraq and brought him to Turkey, where he was tried and sentenced to death. He now, like his former leader, awaits a decision of the European Court of Justice regarding his fate.

[50] *Washington Post*, Oct. 28, 2001.

[51] Jorg Hilbert, "Interview with Selahattin Celik on the PKK," *Junge Welt*, Sept. 25, 1999, KURD-L archives, Oct. 11, 1999 (http://burn.ucsd.edu).

[52] Ibid.

[53] Cemal Uçar, "Cemil Bayık: We Will Be Victorious," *Özgür Politika*, Aug. 16, 2000, posted by the *Kurdistan Observer* (http://www.mnsi.net).

[54] Ibid.

[55] "Talabani: There Is No Assault against the PKK," *Özgür Politika*, Aug. 5, 2000, posted by the *Kurdistan Observer* (http://www.mnsi.net/~mergan95/7-8-00-OP-talabani-ankara-pkk.html).

[56] "Turkey Acknowledges Iraqi Air Raid, Probes Casualty Claims," Agence France-Presse, Aug. 18, 2000, posted by the *Kurdistan Observer* (http://www.mnsi.net/~mergan95).

7

Turkey's New Strategic Partner: Israel

by Efraim Inbar

Since Turkey upgraded its diplomatic relations with Israel to ambassadorial level at the end of 1991, the two states have exchanged many high-level state visits. Bilateral trade has grown significantly and the volume of civilian exchanges (tourist, academic, professional, sporting and cultural) has increased dramatically. Most indicative of the emergence of a special relationship is the signing of a series of military agreements between the two states, which led to close cooperation between the two defense establishments.

The present Turkish-Israeli entente constitutes a departure from the historic reluctance on the part of modern Turkey to be entangled in Middle Eastern affairs, given its aim to buttress its ties with the West and to strengthen its European identity. The Kemalist regime largely saw Islam and the Arab culture as a barrier to modernization. Moreover, the desire to avoid unnecessary conflict required minimizing interactions with the war-prone Middle East.[1] Therefore, Turkey preferred low-profile relations with Israel. Moreover, it did not want to burden itself with links to a regional pariah and thus, with the exception of a short period in the late 1950s, was unresponsive to Israeli overtures. In the 1970s, the dispute with Greece over Cyprus and the world energy crisis provided additional reasons for Turkey to court Arab and Islamic countries and to keep Israel at arm's length.

For its part, Jerusalem has always desired good relations with Ankara, a pro-Western regional power in its vicinity. Moreover, cordial relations with an important non-Arab Muslim country such as Turkey could have contributed to the diluting of the Islamic religious dimension in the Arab-Israeli conflict. As early as the late 1950s, Israel made serious efforts to develop good relations with countries such as Turkey, on the periphery of the Arab Middle East, in order to escape the immediate ring of Arab hostility around Israel.

Yet, only in the 1990s, Turkey changed its policy to Israel. The entente with Israel was part of a reorientation of Turkey's foreign policy following the demise of the Soviet Union. The new foreign policy was characterized by a high threat perception and by greater assertiveness than during the Cold War. It also meant a greater involvement with the Middle East. Relations with Israel were considered useful in facing Turkey's new security challenges, and the strategic glue between the two states is based on a similar outlook on regional and international affairs.

Turkey Returns to the Middle East

In contrast to most Western countries, Turkey emerged from the Cold War with a sense of high threat perception, which is more typical of countries of the Middle East than of Europe. It perceived itself to be encircled by many areas of instability and threatened by dangerous neighbors. Moreover, the internal threat to the integrity of the Turkish state as a result of the Kurdish insurgency, which was supported by Turkey's neighbors, was very vivid during the 1990s. These developments led to a widespread fear in Turkish political and military circles of being engulfed in international crises and military conflicts.[2] Moreover, after the elimination of the Soviet threat, Turkey's membership in NATO, the Western military alliance, seemed to be less relevant to its new security environment. Turkey gradually realized that NATO would not always provide effective responses to the security challenges emerging in Turkey's immediate neighborhood.

Parallel to the high threat perception and the perceived need to devise appropriate responses, Turkey started to consider itself an important actor in global politics, which was a departure from a more modest past self-perception. In the 1990s, Turkey aspired to become more active in the international arena as result of the changes in its geostrategic situation, a redefinition of Turkey's role in world politics, and the new opportunities for extending its influence in the former Soviet republics in Central Asia and the Caucasus.[3] Foreign Minister İsmail Cem and the Turkish foreign policy elite (bureaucrats and politicians) started articulating a vision of Turkey, as geographically situated at the center of Eurasia and exerting a transcontinental political influence.[4] The underlying implication of the geopolitical "Eurasia" concept was the centrality of Turkey in world politics. Turkey portrayed itself as a stabilizing force in its periphery and also regarded itself as the corridor for the passage of energy resources from the Caspian Basin and Central Asia to the Western world. The new activism and self-perception as an important actor in world politics was balanced, however, by the traditional caution, as well as by limited resources.

One aspect of the new Turkish assertiveness is its growing activism in the Middle East. In the past, Turkey preferred not to be entangled in Middle Eastern disputes, and its foreign policy to this region has largely been reactive and non-interventionist. The relations with its Middle Eastern neighbors have been tense, if not overtly hostile. Despite this reluctance to engage the Middle East, Turkey is linked to the Middle East by history, religion and geography. Islam still plays an important part in Turkey's culture and identity, while Turkey shares almost 60 percent of its total land borders with Middle Eastern countries: Iran, Iraq and Syria.

Thus, Turkey's detachment from Middle East international politics has never been total. During the energy crisis in the 1970s Ankara intensified its relations with Arab countries in order to secure oil on convenient financial terms, to attract petrodollars for investment, and to increase exports to oil producing countries. The 1979 Islamic revolution in Iran led to an increase in Turkish threat perception and the tensions between the two states increased. In the late 1980s, Turkey had to face a number of additional Middle Eastern challenges: the Kurdish problem and the water disputes with Iraq and Syria over the waters of the Euphrates and Tigris. The Kurdish problem has essentially been a Middle Eastern one, as the Kurds are spread beyond Turkey, primarily in Iran, Iraq and Syria.

International events in the aftermath of the August 1990 Iraqi invasion of Kuwait reinforced the perception among Turkish policy makers that their country cannot disengage itself from the Middle East, even should it wish to do so. Turkey paid a heavy economic price for the military campaign against Iraq and the subsequent sanctions regime. The creation of a Kurdish controlled safe haven in northern Iraq in March 1991, protected by the United States and its allies, complicated Turkey's Kurdish predicament. Above all, Ankara feared the disintegration of Iraq and the emergence of an independent Kurdish entity in Northern Iraq, adjacent to Turkey's southeastern border.[5] Moreover, since 1991, the disputes over water rights with Iraq and Syria intensified with the opening of the large Atatürk Dam. Baghdad and Damascus have seen this project as allowing Turkey to control the water flow to the downstream riparian countries.

Gradually, Turkey began to see itself as a Middle Eastern player. For example, a senior analyst argued, "Turkey is the strongest military and economic power in the Middle East."[6] Turkey also wanted to take a part in the Arab-Israeli peace process. It looked for a role in the multilateral talks begun after the October 1991 Madrid Peace Conference, sent observers to the international force to monitor the Hebron Agreement (January 1997) between Israel and the Palestinian Authority (PA), and offered its services to facilitate negotiations between Israel and the PA.

Moreover, Turkey displayed an unprecedented willingness to employ military force in Middle East scenarios. In 1990, Turkey concentrated troops along the Iraqi border parallel to the massive American deployment south of the Kuwait theatre. In the 1990s, Turkey invaded northern Iraq several times to fight the Kurdistan Workers' Party (*Partiya Karkeren Kurdistan*–PKK). In October 1998, it threatened Syria with a military confrontation and forced Damascus to oust the leader of the Kurdish insurgency, Abdullah Öcalan. Two months later, Ankara was also successful in coercing Cyprus not to deploy Russian-made S-300 surface-to-air missiles on the island. In October 2001, Turkey sent military personnel to Afghanistan to help the U.S.-led effort to fight the Taliban regime and Osama bin Laden's al-Qaeda organization after the latter's September 11 terrorist attacks on the United States.

The Rapprochement with Israel

One element in Turkey's foreign policy reorientation and its new approach to the Middle East has been better relations with Israel. A gradual reassessment process of Middle East policies began within the Turkish Ministry of Foreign Affairs as early as the late 1980s.[7] Then, Turkey's low-level relations with Israel and its consistent pro-Arab voting record at the UN were evaluated against an appraisal of the role of Israel in the region and the possible benefits to be accrued from becoming closer to Jerusalem. This led to a quiet upgrading of the level of the diplomatic personnel representing the two countries, which culminated in the decision to raise the relations to ambassadorial level at the end of 1991. A parallel reassessment of the policy towards Israel took place in the Turkish military, which led to a clear preference for closer ties with the Israeli defense establishment and its military industries.[8] Turkey discovered that its views of the emerging strategic environment overlapped in many ways with Israeli perceptions, an issue addressed in the next section.

Upgrading relations with Israel was also facilitated by the disappearance of several inhibiting factors. First, a change in the trends in the political economy of energy sources lessened the political leverage of the Arab bloc, and of the oil-producing states in particular. By the end of the 1980s, the substantial subsiding of fears of energy crises had diminished the weight of Arab objections to better relations with Israel.

Second, the Arab-Israeli peace process, reactivated by the Americans in the aftermath of the 1991 Gulf War, further marginalized the objections of Israel's regional enemies to third-party ties with Jerusalem. The October 1991 peace conference in Madrid, a formal gathering with Israel to which almost all Arab countries sent senior diplomatic delegations, served as a convenient pretext for formalizing the Turkish interest in a closer relationship with Israel.[9] This was true of other countries, too. For example, China and India, both major international players, also capitalized on the changes in the oil market and the better Middle Eastern atmosphere to establish full diplomatic relations with Israel. Similarly, Moscow renewed its diplomatic ties with Jerusalem in 1992, as well as countries previously in the Soviet orbit. The 1993 Oslo agreement between Israel and the Palestinians reinforced the trend to normalize relations with an increasingly important international actor, intended to tap Israel's advanced technologies and to profit from Jerusalem's good links in Washington.

During 1992–93, Israel was surprised at the Turkish desire to build a close relationship in the diplomatic and military spheres. Yet, Israeli diplomats immediately sensed the great opportunity and rose to the challenge by becoming a most willing and active partner.[10] From an Israeli perspective, the November 1993 visit of Foreign Minister

Hikmet Çetin, after several delays, was the diplomatic turning point. It was the first time a Turkish foreign minister had visited Israel. A stream of high-level Turkish dignitaries followed, including prime ministers, defense ministers, and foreign ministers, as well as the President Süleyman Demirel. The Israelis responded in kind. By the end of the 1990s, high-level visits by both sides became a routine affair.

Israel was generally pleased with the Turkish involvement in the peace process. Turkey also helped Israel in the diplomatic arena, particularly in Islamic forums. Moreover, Turkish official statements concerning Israeli policies (on the use of force, settlements, and Jerusalem) and its UN voting behavior were less critical during the 1990s than had previously been the case.

Political relations were complemented by the intensification of cultural ties. In the early 1990s, Israel's Ministry of Foreign Affairs actively encouraged and subsidized Israeli cultural and academic forays into Turkey. National museums exchanged exhibitions, and relations in the area of sports greatly improved. Generally, each country became more interested in learning about the other, which was reflected in a greater volume of media coverage, mostly positive.[11] The August 1999 earthquake in northwestern Turkey that claimed more than 17,000 lives consolidated ties between the two countries as Israel provided prompt and large-scale aid. The Israeli rescue team saved scores of lives after the quake, instilling in many Turks a belief that existed already in the political spheres—that a strong Israeli-Turkish alliance could benefit both countries.

The 1990s also witnessed a considerable increase in economic exchanges between Israel and Turkey, as the political restraints originating in Ankara were relaxed. While bilateral trade totaled $54 million in 1987, the figures rose to $100 million in 1991 and to $1.1 billion in 2000. Another facet of the economic relationship is Israeli tourism to Turkey, which has also increased enormously. Israeli entrepreneurs consider using Turkish partners to better penetrate Arab markets. In turn, Turkey has acquired better access to the American market, since Israeli firms process Turkish products and re-export them duty-free to the United States.

Turkey is also eager to export water to Israel, whose meager resources will increasingly be depleted by fast-growing demand. Water import has become an urgent issue in Israel by 2001, after several years of draught, and the Israeli government signed in April a ten-year agreement to purchase each year 50 million cubic meters of water (the final price has not been determined yet). Water import is viewed primarily as an interim solution before desalinization, the preferred option, is operational. Israel, like other Middle Eastern states, prefers not to be water-dependent on outsiders.

The economic aspect of the bilateral relationship is important, and the growing volume of bilateral trade has been matched by a relative decline in Turkey's trade with Iran and Arab countries. Yet, Turkey and Israel understand that their bilateral trade is only a small fraction of their total foreign trade (less than 2 percent), and that the well-being of both their economies is dependent primarily upon export growth to larger markets.

The Turkish military was a key actor in pushing its country closer to Israel. Both defense establishments feel that there are abundant areas of cooperation. In April 1992, the two defense ministries signed a document on principles for cooperation that was translated into a concrete protocol for cooperation in October 1994, designating specific areas of military co-operation.

As early as September 1995, the two air forces reached an agreement to allow training flights in each other's territory and to train together.[12] This exposed the two air forces to types of previously unknown terrain. In year 2000, the two air forces started training together, which enhanced the potential of operational co-operation.

During the February 1996 visit of the deputy of the Turkish Chief of Staff, Gen. Çevik Bir, a central figure in the Turkish-Israeli rapprochement, several additional military agreements were signed.[13] The first was in the area of intelligence, which formalized and expanded the previous ongoing cooperation. The two countries decided to act together in the area of electronic surveillance. The main target country was Syria, with Iran as the second priority. Turkey also receives information from Israel on Russian military systems used by its neighbors and receives access to information collected by the Israeli intelligence satellite Ofeq.

A naval agreement was also reached, permitting access by naval vessels to each other's harbors, and arranging joint exercises in the Mediterranean. The latter eventually took place off the Israeli coast in

January 1998, in the Reliant Mermaid naval search-and-rescue exercise, with U.S. ships also participating. Almost two years later, in December 1999, Israel, Turkey and the United States embarked again on joint naval maneuvers, this time off Turkey's Mediterranean coast. This exercise and the one conducted in January 2001 were presented again as search-and-rescue drills.

Since 1996, a formal common forum for exchange of strategic evaluations convenes biannually in alternate countries. Usually, the director-general of the Ministry of Defense leads the Israeli delegation to these talks, while the deputy chief of general staff heads the Turkish group. The chiefs of staff, their deputies and chiefs of services, as well as many in the senior echelons of the two armies often visit each other. The bilateral contacts generate greater familiarity with the *modus operandi* of the other military, an atmosphere of professional respect, as well as an ambience of social ease.

The co-operation extended also to the area of weapons sales and production. The main strategic rationale has been to lower dependency upon outside suppliers. For Turkey this is a new emphasis as it encountered difficulties in procuring weapons from its NATO allies (the United States and Germany), particularly because of the suppliers' sensitivities to Turkey's human rights record. Moreover, it developed aspirations to acquire advanced military technology that would be commensurate with its newly perceived international status. Oltan Sungurlu, Turkey's defense minister, outlined a new policy in 1996, which encouraged Turkey's leading companies to enter into the defense industry business in order to lessen Turkey's dependency on high-tech.[14] An important component of the multi-billion military modernization plans was technology transfer. The cumulative impact of the August 1999 earthquake, and then two serious economic crises, in November 2000 and February 2001, has forced the Turkish government to consider cuts in its budget, including military expenditures.

Israeli arms have been attractive because of their high quality and because Jerusalem allows the transfer of military technology to Turkish defense industries. According to Gen. (ret.) Sadi Ergüvenç, "Taking into consideration the shortcomings of the new European security architecture, Turkey figures a need to become more self-sufficient in meeting its own military requirements. This is perhaps the most rational explanation for Turkey's recent rapprochement with Israel."[15]

Moreover, Israel appeared to be a more reliable supplier than the United States and the Europeans, who tended to link arms sales to non-security issues, such as human rights.

The largest military deal involves the Israeli upgrading of Turkey's fleet of 54 Phantoms in a contract worth $630 million, finally approved by Ankara in December 1996. The first 26 jet fighters were to be upgraded at Israel Aircraft Industry (IAI) and the remaining 28 in Turkey. Part of the deal included the supply of 100 Popeye-1 standoff air-to-ground missiles. At the end of 1997, Turkey decided to increase the order to 200. Then the consortium between the IAI and the Singapore Aerospace Industries won a $75 million contract to modernize Turkey's 48 U.S.-made F-5A/B fighter aircraft.[16] Smaller deals were also secured, including the supply of airborne search-and-rescue systems, devices to detect plastic and conventional mines, tank shells, and the production rights for the Galil assault rifle. By early 1998, estimates of total Israeli arms sales to Turkey in recent years reached $1 billion.[17]

By May 2000, Turkey decided to put its new tank production program on hold due to its cost and to pursue instead the upgrading option. Israel has also been bidding for a deal, worth nearly $900 million, to upgrade 1000 U.S.–built M-60 tanks. In June 2000 Turkey decided to award the state-owned Israel Military Industries (IMI) the contract to upgrade a first batch of 170 M-60 tanks at a cost of $250 million. Despite the fact that the Americans have contested this deal, negotiations toward finalizing a contract with the IMI continued.

In addition, IAI (and the Russian Kamov helicopter manufacturer) competed for a coproduction contract worth nearly $4 billion for 145 attack-helicopters. The contract went to the American Bell Helicopter Textron, but, according to Turkey's prime minister Bülent Ecevit, if final negotiations over technology transfer with the company fail, or U.S. Congress denies an export license, his government would reopen talks with the Israeli-Russian team.[18] In June 2000, the IAI also lost to the competition for the supply of the Ofeq intelligence satellite to a French firm. Yet, Turkey canceled two large military contracts with France, including the satellite deal, after the French National Assembly passed legislation in January 2001 that labeled as genocide the killing of Armenians by the Ottoman Empire at the beginning of the century. This reopened the possibility for IAI to win the satellite bid, should the necessary budgets be available. IAI also lost the a multibillion dollar contract bid for an Airborne Early Warning system (in conjunction with Raytheon) to the American Boeing company at the end of 2000. A partnership between the Israeli firms IAI and Elbit is still competing for a $500 million unmanned aircraft vehicles (UAVs) contract.

In 1997, Turkey secured a preliminary agreement for the co-production of the advanced Popeye-2 (150 kilometers range).[19] According to Turkish defense experts, Israel's missiles and its advanced technology are of special interest to the Turkish defense establishment.[20] Indeed, Ankara expressed an interest in co-production of the Delilah (400 kilometers range) cruise missile, while the Phyton-4 air-to-air missile, and the Gil and NT-D anti-tank missiles are also on the Turkish acquisition list.

The most remarkable element of the security ties is the institutionalization of the strategic dialogue at the highest levels and the development of routine working relations between the two defense establishments at various levels. So far, both sides feel that the interactions are mutually extremely beneficial.

The changing circumstances with the end of the Cold War led to greater openness in Turkey to the idea of seeking significantly better relations with Israel. The peace process between Israel and its neighbors, reinvigorated after the 1991 Gulf War, made such an idea more palatable. Rapprochement with Israel was sought because of its divergence from the typical Middle Eastern actor. Turkey has been the more eager party in pursuing ties with Israel, perceiving in Israel an advanced modern state with a clear Western outlook and a close ally of the United States. In turn, the Israeli governments actively welcomed the rapprochement with such an important non-Arab Muslim state and a regional power. Within a few years, the degree of intimacy developed with Turkey ranked second only to the closeness of Israel-U.S. ties.

The Israeli-Turkish Strategic Partnership

The new close cooperation between Ankara and Jerusalem was driven primarily by national security concerns, which lent it a strategic quality. The entente between the two capitals is clearly not a military alliance in the traditional sense; the two states have not defined a *casus foederis*, the situation that would activate military action on behalf of the other. They both fear entrapment in crises of limited relevance to their own national security, and neither expects the other to participate actively in its wars. While expanding the scope of co-operation is possible, a formal defense pact is unlikely. Nevertheless, the current relationship between Turkey and Israel can be termed as a strategic partnership since it reflects a convergence of views on a wide range of global and regional issues, as elaborated below.

The two states publicize their high-level strategic dialogue and the current level of military cooperation has created an infrastructure for common military action in the future. Joint exercises, mutual visits, staff-to-staff coordination, and intelligence exchanges increase interoperability. Referring to the January 2001 naval exercise, Ephraim Sneh, the Israeli deputy defense minister said, "There is substance here. It would be naive to say it is just something technical."[21] This potential enhances deterrence, facilitates coercive diplomacy, and is the core for the entente's strategic implications.

The prevalent reading of international relations in the region also focuses on the military component in Israeli-Turkish ties. In both countries, as well as in the rest of the Middle East, military prowess is largely perceived as a crucial element of national power and the most important currency of regional influence.[22] In the Middle East, where the dominant prism for understanding international relations is power politics and informal alliances are at least as important as formal-explicit coalitions,[23] the interactions between Israel and Turkey, particularly the military dimension, are not perceived as innocent. An alternative paradigm for explaining regional dynamics, one stressing identity and culture, would still conclude that the Arabs will tend to see Turkish-Israeli closeness as some sort of alliance because of the nature of their past encounters with Turks and Israelis. Furthermore, the liberal vision of international politics, which regards the use of force as no longer relevant and suggests instead that economics become the dominant factor in international politics, was never accepted by other leaders in the region.[24] Therefore, the numerous Turkish and Israeli declarations that their alignment was not directed against any third party were usually not accepted at face value.

Moreover, Israeli and Turkish statements can be read as confirming an alliance politics behavior. Upon his return from Israel (November 1993), Foreign Minister Çetin announced that Turkey and Israel will co-operate "in restructuring the Middle East."[25] In August 1997, Prime Minister Mesut Yılmaz said that the Turkish-Israeli co-operation "is necessary to the balance of power" in the region.[26] Israeli prime minister Benjamin Netanyahu similarly concluded in 1998 that the two states were obliged to forge an "axis" in view of the volatile international security picture.[27] Israel's defense minister Yitzhak Mordechai said, "When we lock hands, we form a powerful fist . . . our relationship is a strategic one."[28]

So far, Turkey and Israel have reaped strategic dividends separately simply by being grouped together by other regional players and by rendering limited security services to each other. For example, the flights of Israeli aircraft in Turkey have a deterrent value versus Syria, Iraq and Iran, who view Israel's flights over Turkey as an extension of its strategic reach. During the Iraqi crisis of February 1998, the Turkish ambassador to the United States stated that Turkey would consider allowing Israel to use Turkish airspace for retaliation should Iraq launch missile attacks on Israel. According to Gen. Bir, the military agreement signed between Turkey and Israel paved the way for the resolution of the Turkish-Syrian crisis of autumn 1998.[29] Similarly, Turkey's threats to eliminate the Russian-made S-300 SAMs if deployed in Cyprus were credible, partly because of its Israeli connection.[30]

The strategic partnership between Turkey and Israel is not a classic balance of power act, as the two countries are militarily stronger than any combination of regional states. This partnership is characteristic of two satisfied (non-revisionist) powers cooperating primarily to preserve the regional status quo and to fend off common threats.[31] The common security prism on international relations in general, and on the Middle East, in particular, reinforces the balance of power perspective that brings Turkey and Israel together.

The Regional Prism

Both countries regard the Middle East as an unstable region, which generates considerable security risks. For example, Nüzhet Kandemir, former Turkish ambassador to the United States, described the Middle East as "long ravaged by terrorist and extremist tendencies."[32] According to Gen. Bir, Turkey's new self-perception as a Middle

Eastern "front country" facing new threats to its national security is the geostrategic context for understanding best the Ankara-Jerusalem relationship.[33] Indeed, a senior military official explained the rationale for the 1996 military accords: "we are surrounded on all sides by trouble. We are in the hot seat. It is critical for us to jump outside this circle of chaos and find friends in the region. Israel is the perfect choice."[34]

Israel continues to see the Middle East as a source of threat, too. While the evolving Arab-Israel peace process has reduced threat perception from its immediate neighbors, Israel fears threats from more distant countries.[35] Moreover, Israel's army continues to be regarded as the final guarantee for peaceful relations with its neighbors. Prime Minister Ehud Barak argued in August 1999 that "we live in a difficult region and environment, which resembles neither North America, nor Western Europe. In the Middle East there is no pity or esteem towards the weak: He who is unable to defend himself does not get a second chance."[36]

Turkey and Israel had unhappy encounters with Arabs, the dominant ethnic element in the core area of the Middle East. These have colored their perceptions of the region and could lead to similar, even if not fully coordinated, regional policies. For example, the two states would oppose any attempt coming from Cairo, Damascus or Baghdad to gain hegemony in the Arab arena and/or create an Arab united bloc. In the past, both states pursued policies intended to block pan-Arab impulses. As a result of a balance of power rationale, Israel and Turkey preferred a divided Arab world.

Adversarial Relations with Syria

One shared strategic concern revolves around Syria, the common neighbor and an adversary of both countries. Turkey and Israel have similar disputes with Syria. Turkey's defense minister Turhan Tayan, just back from a visit to Israel in May 1997, stated that the two governments share the same position against Syria due to its support for terrorism.[37] Despite repeated promises to stop aid to the Kurdish separatist activities, Syria hosted for years the PKK headquarters along with its leader Abdullah Öcalan (until October 1998), and allowed this organization to train in Lebanon—a Syrian protectorate. The Kurdish problem became more acute for Turkey, particularly after the establishment in 1991 of a no-fly zone in northern Iraq, free of Baghdad's intervention. This provided for greater autonomy for the Kurds, the dominant group in this region, as well as a freer hand for the PKK. In January 1996, Turkey's diplomatic note to Syria, which was leaked to the press, stated that unless Syria terminated aid to the PKK and extradited Öcalan, steps could be taken that might harm Syria's interests.[38] In April 1996, Prime Minister Yılmaz warned Syria of the possibility of punitive measures.[39] The greater Turkish assertiveness coincided with the rapprochement with Israel.

Similarly, Damascus has hosted the headquarters of the Hamas, the Islamic Jihad, and leftist Palestinian rejectionist groups, which shared the commitment to destroy Israel and the peace process. Moreover, Syria controls the flow of military equipment from Iran to Hizbullah in Lebanon and to a great extent has calibrated the operations against Israeli targets. One manifestation of the Israeli-Turkish strategic cooperation became known in June 2000. Iran complained that Turkey demanded to be informed about the cargo of Iranian aircraft transiting Turkish airspace en route to Syria, insisting on its right to force down Iranian planes suspected of carrying unmanifested cargo to Turkey.[40]

An additional common dispute is over territory; the Syrians claim the Turkish Hatay province Iskenderun (formerly known as Alexandretta), which was handed over to Turkey in 1939 by France, the mandatory power at that time in Syria. From Israel, Syria claims the Golan Heights, which it lost in the Six-Day War in 1967.

Finally, both Israel and Turkey quarrel with Syria over water—a scarce resource for Syria and Israel. Syria has complained that upstream Turkey denies it valuable amounts of water. Syrian territorial demands from Israel include control of two of the Jordan's tributaries, and access to the Lake of Galilee—Israel's main water reservoir.

The parallel disputes with Syria are an incentive for the two countries to coordinate their foreign policies in containing revisionist Syria, while Israeli attempts to reach a peace treaty with Syria evoked concern in Turkey. During the negotiations held by the Rabin government (1992–95), Ankara was unhappy with the suggested "carrots" to Syria: its removal from the American blacklist of states supporting terror and drug-trafficking, and an increase in its share of water from Turkey. The Turkish concern peaked during the 1995–96 winter, when the Shimon

Peres-led government attempted to induce Syria's president Hafez al-Assad to close a deal by offering him massive American financial support and by greatly elevating his regional status.[41]

Indeed, the apprehensions concerning the negotiations with Syria led the Turkish Foreign Ministry undersecretary Onur Öymen, during his visit in Israel (January 1996), to demand of Israel greater sensitivity to Turkish interests in the dialogue with Syria. He even described the Israeli policy towards Syria as "appeasement." When Prime Minister Barak revived the Israeli-Syrian talks in the fall of 1999, Turkey clarified its opposition to American military aid to Syria, in the framework of an Israeli-Syrian agreement, before relations between Ankara and Damascus improve considerably. A successful conclusion of the Israeli-Syrian negotiations would have enhanced President Assad's status in the eyes of the Americans, and would have lowered his fears of Israeli-Turkish cooperation against him, both developments inimical to Turkish interests.

President Assad's position in his dealings with Israel guaranteed that Syria remained an issue of accord rather than discord between Turkey and Israel. Yet should Israel and Syria sign a peace treaty, we cannot expect more than a "cold peace" at best, between the two states, parallel to the Egyptian-Israeli relations, which amounts to an armed peace. Such a state of affairs will continue to be conducive to an Israeli-Turkish entente. Similarly, the Turkish attempts to improve relations with Syria, after the expulsion of Öcalan and the Adana Protocol signed in October 1998, were only partially successful due to the Syrian refusal to give up its claim to Iskenderun and to its demands for more of the Euphrates' waters. Ankara presumably would welcome the emergence of a moderate pro-Western Syria. Yet, it would need a lot of proof and the passage of many years to convince skeptic Turkey on the issue of Syrian moderation.[42]

Fear of Islamic Extremism

Both countries share the need to curb the influence of radical Islam in the region. Turkey has always seen itself as a secular model for development. The competing Islamic religious model offered by Iran undermines the basis of the Turkish contemporary political system and the legitimacy of its secular leadership. The Turkish secular leadership has feared the activities of Iran or even Saudi Arabia within Turkey, which strengthen the domestic Islamic groups.

While Iran's Islamic fervor and its support for terrorism elevated her position on Turkey's list of opponents, Ankara usually behaved with caution. The relations with the Islamic Republic were strained and were punctuated by mutual accusations. In the late 1990s, Turks wondered whether Iran replaced Syria as its chief enemy. In February 1997, Gen. Bir described Iran as a terrorist state trying to export its anti-secular ideology to Turkey and Central Asian countries.[43] Turkey also accused Iran of supporting the Kurdish separatists.

Turkey also faces a serious domestic problem, as militant Islamic organizations have been active and segments of its society identify with the Islamist platform of the Welfare (or Prosperity) Party (Refah Partisi–RP), its predecessors and its offshoots. The RP is largely perceived by Turkey's political, military and intellectual elites as intent on undermining the secular-democratic order of modern Turkey. As such, it is a serious domestic challenge, which became particularly potent in the 1990s when the RP and its successor, the Virtue Party (Fazilet Partisi–FP), scored surprisingly well in several electoral contests. The constitutional steps taken against the Islamists have not removed their political appeal. There was also concern that radical Islamic organizations active in the Turkish diaspora were channeling financial support for Islamic causes in Turkey.[44]

Israel, too, has an interest in curbing the influence of radical Islam in the region because Muslim extremists oppose the very existence of the Jewish state, and they act violently against Israeli targets. In the 1990s, Islamic extremism became a major perceived threat for Israel. For Rabin, Iran became Israel's archenemy as it represented a particularly dangerous fusion of fanatic Islamic hostility to Israel with an active program to develop weapons of mass destruction. Moreover, the Islamic-inspired terrorism of the Palestinian Hamas and Islamic Jihad, once just a military nuisance, became in Israeli eyes a strategic threat. Rabin warned that Iran-backed Islamic fundamentalism could spill beyond the Arab world, especially to countries with Muslim communities.[45] These perceptions were shared by all of Rabin's successors, although suggestions for a more nuanced policy towards Iran were occasionally raised within the defense community.

At the end of the 1990s, Israel also developed domestic fears about the appeal of Islamic extremism among Israeli Arabs. The Islamic movement in Israel was infiltrated by Hamas elements and even participated in isolated terrorist acts during 1999–2001. Moreover, since August 2000, the security services investigate links to Osama bin Laden and the al-Qaeda in Afghanistan. Such fears were amplified after the September 11 terrorist attacks on the United States and the ensuing support for bin Laden among Israeli Arabs and the Palestinians.

Indeed, both states supported wholeheartedly the American campaign against the Taliban regime in Afghanistan and the attempt to destroy bin Laden's organization. The Turkish and Israeli leadership are also afraid of the growth of radical influence in pro-Western countries, such as Jordan or Egypt, which might destabilize these regimes. Generally, the two states would like the Turkish model towards modernization and democratization to gain the upper hand among the Muslims in the Middle East and in Central Asia.

The Threat of Weapons of Mass Destruction and Long-range Missiles

Another issue on the common strategic agenda is the spread of weapons of mass destruction (WMD) and their means of delivery, primarily long-range surface-to-surface missiles (SSMs). The 1991 Iraqi missile attacks on Israel developed a greater awareness than previously of a threat to its population centers. Israel was further sensitized to nuclear proliferation in the area in the 1990s, as the magnitude of the Iraqi nuclear program was disclosed, and as Iran intensified its interest in missile and nuclear technology. Israel has regarded the proliferation of missiles capable of reaching its territory and the WMD technology as an existential threat. Israel became painfully aware that it was increasingly difficult to deal with the new situation unilaterally and turned to look for allies for assistance.

For Turkey this is a relatively new concern. In the early 1990s, Turkish officials still displayed a surprisingly nonchalant attitude on this issue. When asked about the ramifications of a nuclear-armed Iraq or Iran, they typically claimed to be NATO members and beneficiaries of an American umbrella.[46] This attitude has since been replaced by a higher threat perception concerning a WMD attack by Iran or Iraq.[47] In

May 1997, Defense Minister Tayan noted that the WMD programs of its Middle Eastern neighbors (Iran, Syria and Iraq) "threaten regional peace."[48]

The higher threat perception was complemented by a more sober evaluation of the problematic NATO and/or American extended deterrence. Turkey also lacked an SSM capability, hampering its deterrence. In the late 1990s, Turkey felt inadequately equipped versus the growing missile capabilities of its neighbors, particularly in light of its claim to be a regional power.

The Turkish and Israeli concerns grew significantly after the Iranian tests of the Shihab-3 long-range SSM (1,300 kilometers) in August 1998 and July 2000. Since the August 1998 collapse of the UN-imposed arms control inspections in Iraq, this country has rebuilt its capability to manufacture chemical and biological weapons. The missile tests conducted in July 2000 indicated a reactivation of the capacity to produce long-range SSMs. Syria purchased from North Korea a Scud-D long-range SSM (700 kilometers), tested in September 2000. These developments reinforced the Turkish interest in cooperation with Israel.[49]

The Turks believed that Israel could help them build a long-range missile capability and showed an interest in acquiring active defense capabilities against theatre missiles, particularly the American-Israeli Arrow anti-ballistic missile. This missile is appealing to Turkey because it is the only operational system available (since year 2000). Yet, Washington, which has control over the export of the Arrow technology (as stipulated by its agreement to fund most of its development costs), objected to the sale of the missile to Ankara. Israel and Turkey still hope to convince the United States to allow the deployment of an American-produced Arrow in Turkey.

The Newly Independent Republics

The collapse of the Soviet order in Central Asia and the Caucasus allowed for the renewal of their political and cultural links with the Middle East. Indeed, they are considered by Israel and Turkey to be part of their more immediate region. Other Middle Eastern states such as Iran and Saudi Arabia similarly see this area as an extension of the Middle East and therefore a natural arena for their presence. While the expectations for the creation of a Turkish zone of influence in this region failed to materialize, Israelis preferred a greater Turkish presence in Central Asia and the Caucasus rather than that of Iran or Russia.

This is why Israel favored the linking of the energy resources from the newly independent states (the Caspian Basin) to Turkey, from Baku in Azerbaijan to the Turkish port Ceyhan in the Mediterranean, rather than to Russia or Iran. This energy project was seen as strengthening Turkey, politically and economically; preventing Russia from reasserting its hegemony in the Caspian Basin; blocking Iranian influence and detracting from the Gulf's importance as an energy outlet.

Israel also sought to forge good ties with newly independent states that had Muslim populations and secular nationalist governments. The new states see relations with Israel as unaffected by the Arab-Israeli conflict, while easing their access to technology and to the West, Washington in particular.[50] If they happened to border its foe—Iran— there was an even greater interest. For example, Israeli friendship for Azerbaijan (allied with Turkey) dovetails with Israel's deepening relationship with Turkey.

The Global Prism

Israel and Turkey share foremost a strong American orientation in their foreign policy. Moreover, there are similarities in their approach to Europe and they remain suspicious of Russian intentions in their immediate region.

The American Orientation

For the two countries, the United States remains the most important bilateral partner and the cornerstone of their foreign policy. Basically, they want the United States to be actively engaged in world affairs, with a clear strategic vision of the identity of its friends in a still turbulent world. Both regard themselves among America's best friends, having a long record of support for U.S. policies. While both welcomed the American victory in the Cold War, which brought about improvements in their strategic environment, they share the evaluation that in the new era their role as American allies in the region has been affected negatively. With the Soviet threat not longer palpable in the West, they are less needed for the protection of Western interests.

Currently, Turkey and Israel have apprehensions (of uneven intensity) of a reduced U.S. presence in the East Mediterranean, as the Americans focus primarily on the Persian Gulf, because of its oil. Moreover, both are afraid that the United States might adopt policies in their region that counter their vital interests. Much distrust existed in Ankara, particularly towards the Clinton administration's policy on Iraq, fearing its disintegration and the establishment of a Kurdish state in the north, as result of American pressure. Israel questions the effectiveness of the American counter-proliferation efforts in the Middle East-an issue of paramount importance to Jerusalem. It also resents the American attempts to control its arms sales abroad. Israel and Turkey also see the United States as the only country able to influence Russia, China and North Korea to slow the export of sensitive technologies to Middle Eastern states in the area of missile development and nuclear weaponry. Thus Turkey and Israel, are interested in solidifying the American commitment to their security needs (as they define them) and in upgrading their relations with the United States.

Turkey realized that Israel was better positioned in Washington, and hoped that Israel's influence and particularly its lobby could be harnessed to further Turkish interests, such as arms transfers. In 1996, Turkish ambassador to the United States Şükrü Elekdağ lauded the Jewish lobby and stated that "Whenever this lobby has worked for us, Turkey's interests have been perfectly protected against the fools in the U.S."[51] In the 1990s, Turkey's presidents and foreign ministers added the major American Jewish organizations to the agenda of meetings they conduct in the United States.

In the late 1990s, Israel conducted a concerted effort to instruct American Jewry on the strategic significance of Turkey. For example, American-Jewish organizations were induced to add Turkey to the itinerary of many high-level missions regularly sent to Israel. These organizations initiated regular interactions with the Turkish authorities and with the Turkish Jewish community. In July 1999, an American Jewish Committee official noted that the Jewish-American community has decided over the last two to three years that the relationship between Israel and Turkey, and Turkey's importance on a host of other issues, requires that it become an active friend of Turkey in the United States, particularly in Congress.[52]

The Israeli lobby helped Turkey in Congress with the campaign against the stationing of Russian-made S-300 SAMs in Cyprus, toning down the criticism of Turkey in Congress over human rights issues, and removing sanctions against Azerbaijan. Jewish organizations also engaged in explaining in the United States the importance of the Baku-Ceyhan oil pipeline. They also demanded U.S. support for Turkey during its period of economic duress.

The aid lent in Congress created high expectations in Turkey, which Israel and the American-Jewish organizations have tried to lower, while encouraging at the same time Turkey's diplomats to become more effective in their relations with Congress and the public at large. From an Israeli perspective, its efforts on behalf of Turkey on the Capitol Hill also had a negative side, since the better chances for American arms transfers limited the Turkish incentive to buy from Israel.

Ambivalent Attitudes towards Europe

Both countries complain about West European behavior towards them. Turkey suffered from arms embargoes imposed by European states that have shown sympathy to the Kurdish cause. Turkey has been excluded from the European Security and Defense Identity (ESDI). The EU accepted Turkey's candidacy for membership only in December 1999, but negotiations for membership in the EU would take years. Israel also experienced European arms embargoes until as recent as 1994, when the UK removed its twelve-year restrictions on arms deals with Israel. Moreover, Israel feels that the Europeans tilt politically towards Arab positions, particularly on the Palestinian issue, and are not sensitive enough to Israel's security concerns.

The European concepts of behavior during conflict and particularly the attitude towards the use of force are different from those of Turkey and Israel. In the relaxed atmosphere of the post–Cold War era, Europeans tend to believe that most military threats have been eliminated. Therefore, the discrepancy between the traditional notions of national security, still prevalent in Turkey and in Israel, and the contrasting developing concepts of national security in Western Europe, reinforce the gulf in perspectives on international relations in general, and specifically on Middle Eastern developments. European criticism of Turkish and Israeli military actions is often viewed at home as unfair and based on a misunderstanding of regional realities.

Moreover, Turkey and Israel view Europe's reservations towards them as partly culturally rooted and linked to religious differences. In European history and consciousness, Jews and Turks (both non-Christian) have evoked negative reactions, although in different ways; Jews have been for centuries the scapegoat of European society, while European folklore is abundant with fears of Turkish aggression. Both sides have noted this cultural parallel.

According to one Israeli approach, Israel benefits from the gulf between Europe and Turkey. The tensions with Europe push Ankara further into the Middle East and reinforce the search for regional allies. The dominant approach argues, however, that long-term Israeli interests are better served by anchoring Turkey in Europe. Negative European attitudes towards Turkey could weaken those elements bound by the Kemalist modernist pro-Western outlook, strengthening the Pan-Turkic and Islamist sectors of Turkish society that are less keen on preserving Turkey's pro-Western orientation. Israel has a vital interest in preventing Turkey from becoming embroiled in attempts to have its regime changed by Islamic revolutionaries, as had happened in Iran. Indeed, Israel has favored Turkey's bid to enter the EU. In 1995, it extended diplomatic assistance to Turkey with the long-awaited Custom Union agreement with the EU. Moreover, Turkey's entrance into the EU extends Europe eastward and brings it closer to Israel.

Persistent Suspicions of Russia

Ankara and Jerusalem retain serious concerns about residual risks from Russian conduct in their neighborhood, despite the improvement in relations with Moscow in the 1990s. Old suspicions and rivalries over the Caucasus and Central Asia still affect Russian-Turkish relations, as well as conflicts over planned energy routes and Russian arms transfers to Cyprus and Iran.[53] Similarly, Israeli-Russian differences are considerable. Israel's current main concerns evolve primarily around the Russian transfer of sensitive technologies for the development of missiles and WMD to Iran and Iraq. Turkey is not at ease with the expanded Russian-Iranian strategic cooperation.

Generally, Turkey and Israel fear a more assertive Russia in the Middle East and the East Mediterranean. So far, Moscow's Middle East policy seems to cultivate relations with Syria, Iran and Iraq, which are seen as potential allies in curbing American influence in the region. It is no coincidence that both Israel and Turkey see these countries in a similar light.

Conclusion

The many similarities in the strategic outlook of Israel and Turkey in the post-Cold War regional environment strengthen the bilateral relations. They share similar regional concerns regarding Syria, the proliferation of weapons of mass destruction, the challenge of Islamic radicalism, and the geopolitical destiny of Central Asia. These mutual concerns intensified in the 1990s as result of the end of the Cold War, which allowed for greater freedom of action of the revisionist states in the region, while Turkey adopted a more assertive foreign policy. At the global level, the two states display a strong pro-American orientation in their foreign policy, have a problematic relationship with Europe and are suspicious of Russian aspirations. The parallels outlined here are clear also to the other players in the region who generally see the entente in strategic terms.

Notes

This article largely draws from Prof. Inbar's *The Turkish-Israeli Entente* (London: King's College Mediterranean Studies, 2001).

[1] Kemal Karpat, *Turkey's Foreign Policy in Transition* (Leiden: E.J. Brill, 1975), pp. 108–11; Soli Özel, "Of Not Being a Lone Wolf: Geography, Domestic Plays, and Turkish Foreign Policy in the Middle East," in Geoffrey Kemp and Janice G. Stein, eds., *Powder Keg in the Middle East* (Lanham: Rowman and Littlefield, 1995), pp. 161–94.

[2] See inter alia Şükrü Elekdağ, "2 ½ War Strategy," *Perceptions*, March–May 1996; Şadi Ergüvenç, "Turkey's Security Perceptions," *Perceptions,* June–August 1998; Malik Mufti, "Daring and Caution in Turkish Foreign Policy," *Middle East Journal,* Winter 1998, pp. 33–41.

[3] Mufti, "Daring and Caution in Turkish Foreign Policy," pp. 32–50; Alan Makovsky, "The New Activism in Turkish Foreign Policy," *SAIS Review*, Winter–Spring 1999, pp. 92–113.

[4] *Turkish Probe*, May 10, 1998, p. 15.

[5] Ali L. Karaosmanoğlu, "Turkey: Between the Middle East and Western Europe," in Kemal H. Karpat, ed., *Turkish Foreign Policy* (Madison: University of Wisconsin Press, 1996), p. 14.

[6] Seyfi Taşhan, "A Review of Turkish Foreign Policy in the Beginning of 1998," *Diş Politika,* vol. 22, nos. 1–3 (1998), p. 22.

[7] Interview with Barlas Özener, Ambassador of Turkey to Israel (1995–99), Aug. 24, 1998.

[8] Interviews with Turkish senior officers.

[9] Interview with Özener.

[10] Interview with Uri Gordon, Israel's chargé d'affaires (1990–92) and ambassador to Ankara (1992–94), May 6, 1998; interview with Eytan Bentsur, director-general of Ministry of Foreign Affairs, Feb. 13, 2000.

[11] Anat Lewin, "Turkey and Israel: Reciprocal and Mutual Imagery in the Media, 1994–1999," *Journal of International Affairs*, Fall 2000, pp. 239–51.

[12] Interview with Maj. Gen. (ret.) David Ivry, National Security Advisor, Nov. 30, 1999.

[13] *Ha'aretz*, April 1996.

[14] *Jane's Defense Weekly*, July 3, 1996, p. 40.

[15] Ergüvenç, "Turkey's Security Perceptions," p. 41.

[16] *Defense News*, Jan. 5–11, 1998, p. 2.

[17] "Turkey, Israel, tanks and spies," *Foreign Report*, Feb. 10, 1998.

[18] *Defense News*, Aug. 21, 2000, p. 18.

[19] *Turkish Daily News*, Dec. 4, 1997.

[20] *Defense News*, Oct. 20–26, 1997, p. 14.

[21] *Jerusalem Post*, Jan. 18, 2001, p. 2.

[22] Efraim Inbar, "Contours of Israel's New Strategic Thinking," *Political Science Quarterly*, Spring 1996, pp. 42–45; Ahmed Hashim, "The State, Society and the Evolution of Warfare in the Middle East: The Rise of Strategic Deterrence?" *Washington Quarterly*, Autumn 1995, pp. 54–55; Ali L. Karaosmanoğlu, "The Evolution of the National Security Culture in Turkey,"

Journal of International Affairs, Fall 2000, pp. 199–201.

[23] Yair Evron, "Gulf Crisis and War: Regional Rules of the Game and Policy and Theoretical Implications," *Security Studies*, Autumn 1994, p. 125.

[24] Michael N. Barnett, *Dialogues in Arab Politics: Negotiations in Regional Order* (New York: Columbia University Press, 1998), pp. 229–31.

[25] *Newspot*, Nov. 18, 1993.

[26] *Newsweek*, Aug. 11, 1997.

[27] *Turkish Daily News*, Sept. 3, 1998.

[28] *Near East Report*, Jan. 26, 1998, p. 6.

[29] Çevik Bir, "Reflections on Turkish-Israeli Relations and Turkish Security," *Policywatch*, no. 422, Nov. 5, 1999, p. 1.

[30] Interview with Cypriot officials. Turkish planes that trained in Israel were suspected of exercises that simulated attacking SAM sites. In November 1998, two Israeli Mossad agents were caught with surveillance equipment in Cyprus, fuelling rumors about Israeli assistance to Turkey.

[31] For such a rationale in creating alliances, see Randall L. Schweller, "Bandwagoning for Profit: Bringing the Revisionist State Back In," *International Security,* Summer 1994, p. 79; balancing threats as the main reason for alliance formation was suggested by Stephen M. Walt, *The Origins of Alliances* (Ithaca: Cornell University Press, 1987).

[32] www.turkey.org/speeches/atlanta.htm, Nov. 18, 1996.

[33] Bir, "Reflections on Turkish-Israeli Relations," p. 1.

[34] *Turkish Daily News*, June 5, 1996, p. A4.

[35] Inbar, "Contours of Israel's New Strategic Thinking," p. 47.

[36] *Yediot Aharonot*, Aug. 13, 1999, p. 3.

[37] *Turkish Daily News*, May 4, 1997, p. 2.

[38] *Milliyet*, Feb. 18, 1996.

[39] *Milliyet*, Sept. 23, 1996.

[40] *Ha'aretz*, June 13, 2000, p. A3.

[41] For this chapter in Israeli-Syrian relations, see Itamar Rabinovitch, *The Brink of Peace: Israeli-Syrian Negotiations* (Princeton: Princeton University Press, 1998).

[42] Kemal Kirişci, "Turkey and the Muslim Middle East," in Alan Makovsky and Sabri Sayari, eds., *Turkey's New World: Changing Dynamics in Turkish*

Foreign Policy (Washington, D.C.: Washington Institute for Near East Policy, 2000), p. 47.

[43] *Turkish Daily News*, Feb. 21, 1997, p. 1.

[44] Metin Heper and Aylin Güney, "The Military and the Consolidation of Democracy: The Recent Turkish Experience," *Armed Forces and Society*, Summer 2000, p. 640.

[45] Efraim Inbar, *Rabin and Israel's National Security* (Baltimore: Johns Hopkins University Press, 1999), pp. 138–39.

[46] Interviews with senior officials.

[47] Duygu Bazoğlu Sezer, "Turkey's New Security Environment, Nuclear Weapons and Proliferation," *Comparative Strategy*, Apr.–June 1995, pp. 149–72.

[48] *Turkish Daily News*, May 4, 1997, p. 2.

[49] Ian O. Lesser, *NATO Looks South: New Challenges and New Strategies in the Mediterranean* (Santa Monica: RAND, 2000), p. 31.

[50] Bülent Aras, "Post–Cold War Realities: Israel's Strategy in Azerbaijan and Central Asia," *Middle East Policy,* vol. 5, no. 4, p. 69.

[51] Elekdağ, "2-½ War Strategy."

[52] *Turkish Daily News*, July 29, 1999.

[53] Duygu Bazoğlu Sezer, "Turkish-Russian Relations a Decade Later: From Adversity to Managed Competition," *Perceptions*, March-May 2001, pp. 79–98.

8

Turkish-U.S. Relations

by Birol A. Yeşilada

Since the end of the Cold War, Turkey's geopolitical importance to U.S. interests has grown steadily. As Alan Makovsky and Sabri Sayarı explain, Turkey's position in American foreign policy soared as efforts to curtail Saddam Hussein became a key U.S. policy objective.[1] Other post–Cold War developments in the Balkans, the Caucasus, and the eastern Mediterranean region combined with the Iraq problem to make relations with Turkey crucial to achieving U.S. strategic goals. More recently, the events of September 11, 2001, and the subsequent international war on terrorism further demonstrated Turkey's pivotal role in U.S. policy. Yet Turkey's growing importance to U.S. strategic and political interests does not mean that the relationship between the two allies is free of potential problems. Among many issues, the following issues in Turkey are critical areas of concern: (1) domestic political and economic reforms as they affect the degree of support the United States can offer; (2) its European Union (EU) candidacy; (3) the Cyprus problem and other conflicts with Greece; (4) Turkey's objections to the European Defense and Security Identity/Initiative (ESDI); (5) its energy needs; (6) its transregional interests; and (7) ethnic pressure groups and their effect on U.S. policy toward Turkey. This paper provides an overview of developing U.S.-Turkish relations with a special emphasis on how the post–September 11 war on terrorism is likely to affect relations between the two countries. Before this assessment, however, it is important to examine Turkey's critical role in the war against terrorism and the consequences of the war in Afghanistan.

Turkey's Decision to Support the War Against
Terrorism in Afghanistan

During the last decade, Turkey's geopolitical environment changed dramatically. No longer trapped in Cold War politics, Turkey found itself in an environment of fluid developments stretching from the Balkans to the Caucasus and from the Black Sea to the Middle East. In this new environment, Turkish officials and private businessmen engaged in a series of complex international relationships that resulted in major economic and political initiatives. On the economic front, Turkey initiated a regional economic cooperation agreement with its neighbors to the north (the Black Sea Economic Cooperation Zone–BSEC), signed a Customs Union (CU) agreement with the EU, provided economic assistance to the Turkic states in Central Asia and the Caucasus, and integrated its economy with global capitalism. On the political front, Turkish leaders supported the United States in the 1991 Gulf War, provided access to Incirlik Airbase for the American and British airplanes that observe the no-fly-zone established after that war in northern Iraq, signed a defense cooperation agreement with Israel, defeated the terrorist Kurdistan Workers Party (Partiya Karkeren Kurdistan—PKK), and sent troops to take part in NATO peacekeeping operations in Somalia and the Balkans. In short, Turkey has emerged in a mere ten years as a regional power center.[2] These developments have brought Turkey both benefits and risks. While Turkey's international and regional influence grew, a similar success did not materialize in its domestic scene. Successive coalition governments failed to carry out domestic economic and political reforms. The financial crisis that hit Turkey in February 2001 further added to uncertainties about Ankara's ability to stabilize the economy and pave the way for stable economic growth. As Turks struggled with these problems, the events of September 11, 2001, brought new challenges to the Turkish government. As a NATO member, Turkey agreed to support the United States in the war against terrorism. Yet the uncertainty over this obligation's impact on Turkish economic recovery makes Ankara nervous.

Turkey's decision to open its air bases and airspace to U.S. forces and to send an elite, 90-men special anti-guerrilla mountain warfare unit to Afghanistan drew mixed reaction from Turkish citizens, as well as from the media and politicians. Turkish troops were to train opposition Northern Alliance fighters[3] and provide support for humanitarian aid operations, but in a statement made shortly after September 11, the Turkish General Staff and the government left the door open for possible combat operations that could involve additional special Turkish forces.[4] The "Bordeaux berets," as these special forces are called in Turkey, are experienced in guerrilla warfare, having fought the terrorists of the PKK for more than 15 years in the mountains of southeastern Turkey and northern Iraq. They were involved in the abduction of key PKK leaders including Abdullah Öcalan as he left the Greek ambassador's residence in Kenya. Nonetheless, opinion surveys showed that Turks were apprehensive about their country's involvement in this new war and opposed sending their soldiers to fight in Afghanistan by a margin of 8 to 2.[5] While few respondents felt uncomfortable with fighting another Muslim country, most worried about the war spreading to other regions, notably northern Iraq, and eventually to Turkey.   Nonetheless, in light of Turkey's economic difficulties, the decision by the pro-Western government was a bold one and it could very well pay off in badly needed financial assistance from the United States and other Western countries.

Turkish prime minister Bülent Ecevit justified his government's decision by noting that having fought terrorism for so long, Turkey would have denied itself if it chose to opt out of this war. Furthermore, Turkey clarified that it will take part in NATO's collective decision under Article 5 of the Atlantic Charter. He stated that "It is [Turkey's] natural duty to participate in the front lines along with our friend and ally, the United States."[6] Foreign Minister İsmail Cem repeatedly emphasized this position in interviews with Turkish and international media, emphasizing that terrorism had no geography, religion, or nationality and required international collaboration to fight. The commander of the Turkish Armed Forces, General Hüseyin Kıvrıkoğlu, also indicated that the United States was the only of Turkey's NATO partners that consistently supported its war against the PKK.

To obtain additional support for its position, the Ecevit government obtained a majority decision from the National Assembly authorizing the sending of Turkish troops to foreign territories.[7] It is worth noting that most of the politicians who opposed sending troops to Afghanistan were members of Turkey's two new Islamist parties, the Happiness (or Felicity) Party (Saadet Partisi—SP) and the Justice and Development *Party* (Adalet ve Kalkınma Partisi—AKP); both established in summer 2001 by members of the Virtue Party (Fazilet Partisi—FP), which was banned in June 2001. At the time of writing (November 2001), the Islamist parties were planning to file an appeal with the Constitutional Court to reverse the Grand National Assembly's decision to support the government's sending of troops to Afghanistan. With this commitment, Turkey can expect a degree of support from the United States in policy issues that are vital to its economic, political, and strategic national interests. Yet, it would be naive to assume that the United States would simply back Turkey with a carte blanche on all the issues Turkish officials would like to advance in their favor (e.g., the Turkish option to resolve the Cyprus problem). It is crucially important that policy makers and academics understand the potential consequences of the events of fall 2001 on these issues in Turkish-U.S. relations.

Key Issues in Turkish-U.S. Relations

If there has been any constant in U.S.-Turkish relations that has survived the end of the Cold War, it is the general belief in U.S. policy circles that the U.S. does not want to see an inward-looking Turkey governed by paranoid and xenophobic elected officials who do not trust their citizens. American policy makers would prefer to see Turkey be integrated with the West (preferably as a member of the European Union), maintain a strong and secular political system, achieve a stable and growing market economy, and be an important player in global markets. Recent public statements by officials following Turkey's decision to stand by the United States after the events of September 11, 2001, further underline this observation. Policy makers in Ankara and Washington point to Turkey's crucial position as a role model to countries of Central Asia and the Middle East as a secular republic with a predominantly Muslim population. Yet, Turkish-U.S. relations face many challenges that cannot be underestimated.

Bilateral Issues with Multilateral Implications:
Domestic Reforms in Turkey

Turkey's political and economic development is crucial to U.S. interests and presents an important component of EU-Turkey relations. As such, the two relationships are interrelated. The reforms are part of the EU's membership requirements (the "Copenhagen criteria"), which require commitment to the EU's *acquis communautaire,* i.e., the adoption of all of the legislation and provisions of the EU Treaties by the time of accession.[8] Required political reforms include the presence of a democratic political system characterized by free and fair elections, the rule of law, respect of human rights, and protection of minorities. Over the years, the United States and the EU have criticized Turkey for falling short of these goals. The required economic reforms include the presence of a strong market economy measured on the relative strength of a functioning market economy and the capacity to withstand competitive pressure and market forces within the EU. Furthermore, free movement of goods, capital, services, and people must be in place for accession. For Turkey, economic development is intimately related to the structural adjustment program signed with the International Monetary Fund to overcome problems created by the financial crisis of February 2001.

Democratization

Washington consistently points to Turkey as the only Muslim country that has a secular democratic political system. But Turkey's experiment with democracy has been shaky. Since the beginning of its multiparty democracy in 1950, Turkey has experienced three coup d'états and one indirect intervention in politics. Moreover, its most recent constitution was written under the military government of General Kenan Evren in 1982 and included numerous restrictions on individual civil and political rights.[9] Since transition to civilian rule in 1983, there has been a gradual return to pluralist democracy in Turkey, but the process has been slow and difficult. U.S. administrations have encouraged Turkish officials to push ahead with these reforms, but Ankara found a less-than-sympathetic audience in the U.S. Congress. Congressmen with close ties to the American-Greek and American-

Armenian lobbies have repeatedly criticized Turkey for its democratic shortcomings and blocked or delayed sales of military hardware to the country.[10]

Turkey's transition to a full liberal representative democracy with extensive individual and human rights is in the interests of the United States for the reasons stated above. From a U.S. perspective, Turkey's membership in the EU is central to the future stability of transatlantic relations as the EU and NATO attempt to find new arrangements for the Union's defense policy. In interviews last year, U.S. officials pointed out that if Turkey carries out democratic and economic reforms that satisfy the Copenhagen criteria—which, along with EU Commission reports, give it a roadmap for the democratic targets it must satisfy[11]—it would be next to impossible for the EU to reject its accession to membership.[12] Therefore, the United States is likely to continue supporting the Turkish government's reform efforts.

During 2000 and 2001, the Ecevit government made significant improvements in Turkey's democratization. Turkey presented a National Program to the EU in March 2001 and outlined its plan for economic and political reforms.[13] At that time, the proposed economic reforms dominated the report, and the vagueness of the political reforms drew criticism from the EU. However, progress in democratization accelerated, and on October 3, 2001, the Grand National Assembly approved thirty-four of the Ecevit government's thirty-seven proposed constitutional amendments. This is not the first time that Turkey undertook significant constitutional reforms. In 1995, after signing the CU agreement with the EU and in order to secure its ratification by the EU Council, there was a limited constitutional amendment. The most recent reforms are far more comprehensive and include Articles 13 and 14, dealing with the basic human rights, and Article 38, dealing with the death penalty. Amendments include improvements in freedom of thought and expression, freedom of association and the press, civil rights, individual liberties, and gender equality. They also restrict the imposition of the death penalty to cases of treason and terrorism.[14] The amendments also lifted the ban on the use of languages other than Turkish in broadcasting, thus making it possible for the Kurdish population in southeastern Turkey to use their mother tongue in radio and television broadcasts. These reforms drew praise from Washington as well as from EU member states' capitals.

However, the amendments still fall short of meeting the requirements of the Copenhagen criteria—e.g., they do not entirely eliminate the death penalty—and so require more work. Nevertheless, they represent a remarkable achievement in that the Turkish government accomplished these reforms in just one month. Furthermore, the reforms weaken the ability of ethnic lobbies in Washington to portray Turkey as a terrible state that violates its citizens' human rights.

Economic Development

Economic development is another important issue in Turkish-U.S. relations. Turkey needs U.S. support in securing fresh loans to carry out its economic reforms, while the United States needs for Turkey to succeed in its economic development so that it can showcase the country as a model for other states in Central Asia and the Middle East. In this regard, Turkey's move away from import substitution growth to an open market economy has a mixed record of success. On the one hand, Turkey has the sixteenth largest economy in the world, with a dynamic private sector. The Turkish economy also successfully integrated with the world financial markets, and the Istanbul Stock Exchange (ISE) became a star among emerging stock markets. On the other hand, successive Turkish governments, including that of Turgut Özal, failed to complete the necessary economic reforms required for a stable market economy. They prevented transparency of the economic system, postponed difficult reforms, continued with expansionary monetary policies and, when problems mounted, blamed individuals who were simply doing what they were told to (since the Central Bank was not an independent institution), and took part in corruption on a massive scale. In short, Turkey is far from meeting the Euro criteria (the earlier Economic and Monetary Union requirements) of the Copenhagen criteria for economic integration with the EU. Following the financial crisis of February 2001, Turkey's report card has become even worse.

The February 2001 financial crisis followed a textbook sequence of events previously observed in other emerging market countries: Mexico in 1994, Thailand, Indonesia and South Korea in 1997, Russia and Brazil in 1998, and Argentina in 2000. The cost of the crisis to the Turkish banking sector was $20 billion (for state-owned banks), with the total exposure for commercial banks totalling some $43.9 billion.[15] At the same time, $7.5 billion fled Turkey's portfolio market during the first 48 hours of the crisis.[16] In addition, the government's decision to switch the monetary policy to the free-float system resulted in a 48-percent devaluation of the Turkish lira against the U.S. dollar. The expected cost of the crisis and economic restructuring for the Turkish economy is for GNP to fall by 7.5 percent in 2001 and to enter positive figures in 1002 and 2003 (estimated at 5 percent and 6 percent, respectively); for inflation to rise to 75 percent in 2001 and fall to 20 percent in 2002; and for the public sector borrowing requirement to increase to 17 percent of GDP in 2001. The consolidated net public debt is expected to increase to 79 percent of GNP, from 58 percent in 2000, due to the foreign exchange crisis and banking restructuring that required new borrowing from the IMF and the World Bank.[17]

Turkey responded to this crisis by inviting former World Bank vice president Kemal Derviş to lead the economic recovery as a cabinet minister and by seeking financial assistance from the IMF and the United States. The United States immediately supported Turkey's economic reform package, encouraged the IMF to extend fresh loans to Turkey, and assisted in forming an international consortium of creditors to extend additional credit. The U.S. action was key, since at the time no private international financial institution was willing to extend new credits to Turkey.

Many Turks saw Washington's response as a sign of good relations between the two countries. It reinforced in their minds the importance of Turkey to Western interests. Yet their own response to the crisis at home is far more important to the market's confidence than what others say or do. This is because Turkey's monetary credibility has suffered as a result of the failed crawling peg fixed exchange rate (FX) system. Basically, the Turkish officials tried to use this FX regime as a disinflationary policy but failed to anticipate its complications or to know when to bail out. Under the crawling peg FX system, profits can be made by borrowing in foreign currency to buy domestic assets that have higher interest rates. Many Turkish banks followed this and relied on the government's announced rates for the future. They all lost when the peg failed. Businesses that invested based on announced policies and foreign exchange rates also faced large losses. Another serious problem was that the government created a shadow treasury in the form of two state banks (Ziraat and Halk). For far too long, Turkish governments pushed these banks to meet government obligations such as guaranteed floor price payments to farmers and credits to small businessmen (*esnaf*). In the past, when these banks failed to meet their obligations, like paying their loans to other private banks, the Central Bank intervened as the lender of last resort. Yet, when this problem arose in October and December 2000, the Central Bank could not intervene due to an austerity package signed earlier with the IMF. The combined obligations of Ziraat Bank and Halkbank stood at $20 billion. Add to this the increases recently seen in global interest rates on emerging market debt and the government's balance of payments receives a tremendous shock.

The structural reforms that Derviş outlined seem to be the only hope for recovery at this time, and they have the complete support of the Bush administration, as indicated by President Bush and the U.S. ambassador to Turkey. These reforms focus on reorganization of the banking sector, increased financial transparency to eliminate the government's historical practice of extra-budget accounts, privatisation (more serious than the previous attempts under earlier governments), fighting against corruption, and structural adjustments in economic sectors to attract direct foreign investment.[18]

Completion of these reforms is crucial for two reasons according to the U.S. perspective. First, success will make Turkey a role model for other Turkic states of the former Soviet Union as well as for countries of the Balkans and the Middle East. Second, reform is necessary for Turkey's quest for membership in the EU. Thus, the United States firmly supports the reform policies of the Ecevit government and favors rapid implementation of Kemal Derviş's economic reform package and the other political reforms the government has identified in its National Program given to the EU.

Multilateral Issues in Turkish-U.S. Relations

Several important U.S. foreign policy interests overlap with those of Turkey's. They are:

- The Cyprus-Greece-EU triangle and U.S. interests;
- The ESDI-NATO relations;

- Turkey's transregional interests and energy security; and
- The war in Afghanistan.

The Cyprus-Greece-EU Triangle and Turkey-U.S. Relations

The Cyprus problem has been a sore point in Greek-Turkish-U.S. relations for over four decades. Since the Republic of Cyprus became a candidate for EU membership in 1998 (it is likely to join the Union in 2002), the situation has worsened. The Turkish government stated in November 2001 that if Cyprus were admitted into the EU, then it would consider annexing northern Cyprus (Turkish Republic of Northern Cyprus) notwithstanding the cost to it.[19] This announcement drew immediate criticism from Greece, the Greek government of Cyprus, and the EU. The implications of such an action for Turkish-EU and Turkish-Greek relations are immense. First, it will most likely end Turkey's hopes for membership in the EU. Second, relations between Greece and Turkey will deteriorate and result in additional confrontation in the Aegean. Third, Cyprus will become permanently divided. And fourth, the Greek and Armenian lobbies in the United States would pressure Congress to punish Turkey and probably succeed in their efforts. This will be a great blow to Washington's efforts to promote better relations between Greece and Turkey, find a solution to the Cyprus problem, and assist Turkey's entry into the EU.

It is ironic that, once again, an EU action will necessitate U.S. intervention to minimize damage to relations between the transatlantic allies. At the December 1998 Luxembourg summit, the EU excluded Turkey from the list of candidates for membership but included Cyprus when Greece threatened to block the enlargement process if it did not. The EU had already taken Greece's side in the 1996 Greek-Turkish disagreement over the islet of Imia (or Kardak) in the Aegean, and Ankara viewed this as another victory for Greece. Furthermore, Greece had succeeded in getting the EU's backing on the Cyprus problem despite U.S. pressure. During this time, the Clinton administration was planning to launch a major diplomatic initiative led by Special Presidential Envoy Richard Holbrooke to resolve the Cyprus problem. The Luxembourg decision was an enormous setback for this.

Turkey's reaction to these developments was harsh. Ankara announced that it would match the EU step for step and would integrate northern

Cyprus with Turkey if the EU launched accession talks with the Republic of Cyprus.[20] Turkey also informed the EU that it no longer welcomed the EU in the mediation efforts in Cyprus.

Not surprisingly, these developments caused serious concern in Washington. The EU resolved the problem when it invited Turkey to become a candidate for membership at the December 1999 Helsinki summit. During the year between Luxembourg and Helsinki, several developments had helped improve relations between all concerned. First, the United States had brought had brought its pressure to bear on all parties. Second, the Greek government was in an embarrassing position following the Turkish special forces' capture of PKK leader Abdullah Öcalan in February 1999 as he was leaving the residence of the Greek ambassador in Kenya. And third, Greek and Turkish citizens had rushed to each other's assistance following the devastating earthquake in Turkey in August and the minor earthquake in Greece shortly thereafter.[21]

The ESDI-NATO Dilemma

Another problem affecting Turkish-U.S. relations is the EU's ESDI. At the heart of the problem is the EU's plan to establish a 60,000-men strong rapid deployment force as part of its integrated defense structure. The EU recommendation, supported by the United States, called for NATO to provide equipment and intelligence for the European-only missions as long as the former did not undermine the Atlantic Alliance by creating its own bureaucracy and independent capabilities. In getting access to NATO equipment and facilities, the EU would consult with NATO's non-EU members but would not include these countries in the decision-making mechanism unless the Alliance was taking an active part in the military deployment. NATO's EU and EU-candidate members accepted this plan. The rationale behind their decision was twofold. First, if NATO were to reject the proposal, the EU would be forced to spend capital and energy to duplicate what is already present in Europe. Secondly, this duplication would most likely result in weakening NATO's role in the European theater.

Such arguments failed to convince either the Turkish government or the Turkish General Staff (TGS) to accept the EU proposal. And since NATO decisions required unanimity, Turkish dissent translated to a veto of the ESDI-NATO agreement. Why did the Turks reject the proposed agreement and risk alienating the Europeans? Turkey feared that exclusion from the ESDI decision-making mechanism, even when NATO troops were not involved, would further distance it from Europe. It insisted that the terms offered to it were not consistent with the arrangement it had had with the former Western European Union (WEU), since the new arrangement would keep it out of the decision making structure and give it only a consultatative status in operations that did not call on NATO's assistance on the field.[22] At the root of this crisis, however, is Ankara's suspicion of a Greek plot to expand Greek-Turkish problems into EU-Turkish problems. Ankara argues that unless it has a say in how these forces would be deployed, resources could be used against Turkey's interests, possibly in disputes with Greece over the Aegean or Cyprus.[23] Ankara assumes that its position on the ESDI–that Europe cannot exclude or ignore Turkey's pivotal position in security and defense matters—has gained additional credibility with the war against terrorism and the war in Afghanistan.

Transregional Power of Turkey

The United States favors closer relations between Israel and Turkey with regard to security policy in the greater eastern Mediterranean region. This relationship serves more than one purpose. First, it strengthens ties between the only two democracies in the region. Second, it gives Turkey another channel of access to sophisticated defense technologies that the U.S. Congress frequently denies or delays due to domestic political pressures from American lobbies. Finally, it creates a stronger pro-U.S. military cooperation among the region's powers. In addition to the priority of security relations, Turkish-Israeli cooperation is also apparent in other areas. The two countries signed a free trade agreement in March 1996 that began on May 1, 1997.[24] An agreement to prevent double taxation followed in May 1998 and led to a third agreement, on mutual encouragement and protection of investments. Since then, economic relations between Israel and Turkey have grown steadily and spilled over into the higher education sector with the signing of mutual cooperation agreements between Israeli and Turkish universities.

Improved relations with Israel naturally translate into wary relations with the Arab countries in the Middle East, which in turn affect Turkish-U.S. relations in the Middle East. Until the Persian Gulf War in 1991, Turkey chose to distance itself from U.S. strategic interests in the Arab world. It had stayed out of the 1980-88 Iran-Iraq war. In fact, the Özal government chose a combined policy of commercial and Islamic cultural interests to increase Turkey's ties to the Arab world.[25] This policy began to change as Iraq took a threatening posture toward Turkey after the Iran-Iraq war, and with its 1990 invasion of Kuwait and Syria's support for the PKK. By supporting the U.S.-led war against Iraq and lending assistance for Operation Northern Watch (as Operation Provide Comfort was renamed in 1996), Turkey quickly became a key player in most U.S. regional policy goals. However, there are areas of disagreement between the two allies. Turkey would like to see the sanctions against Iraq and Iran eased. It is also wary of some U.S. policy makers' support for an independent Kurdish state in northern Iraq.

A November 5, 2001, article by William Safire in the *New York Times*, "The Turkey Card," suggesting that the United States should encourage Turkey to invade northern Iraq, drew considerable attention from Turkish policy makers and media. This is a sensitive issue among the Turks because many fear that the war in Afghanistan will spread to Iraq and engulf Turkey. While most Turkish leaders do not trust Saddam Hussein, they favor the current political arrangement in Iraq— a unitary state. If for whatever reason the Kurds were going to be outside of the control of Iraq's central government, Turkey would prefer that the two main Kurdish political parties in Iraq, Massoud Barzani's Kurdistan Democratic Party (KDP) and Jalal Talabani's Patriotic Union of Kurdistan (PUK), not be united. The Turks fear that an independent Kurdish state in northern Iraq could make future territorial demands from Turkey. For this reason, Turkey is more likely to invade and occupy northern Iraq than accept the establishment of a Kurdish state to its southeast.

As for Iran, Turkey, like the United States, is very concerned about the threat of fundamentalist Islam originating from this country. For Turkey, Iran is the antithesis of Atatürk's secular republic. The secular Turkish elites are therefore extremely suspicious of Iran's political and economic policies. During the past two decades, Turkish officials accused Iran of supporting Islamic extremists and PKK terrorists in Turkey and training these groups' members in Iranian camps. Some of these individuals are currently serving time in Turkish prisons for killing writers, academics, and journalists in Turkey. Furthermore, Turkey and Iran are engaged in a power struggle in the Caspian region. In July 2001, when the Iranian navy threatened an Azeri oil vessel conducting research in the Caspian Sea and the Iranian air force invaded Azerbaijan's airspace, Turkey responded with a sharp note to Iran. It also sent its F-16 fighter jets to Baku when Turkish Armed Forces (TSK) chief of general staff Hüseyin Kıvrıkoğlu visited Azerbaijan the next month.[26]

However, unlike the United States, Turkey favors good economic relations with Iran and opposes American efforts to isolate this country. It is well aware of the economic costs it had to bear as a result of the U.S. sanctions against Iraq and the Iran-Libya Sanctions Act (ILSA) passed by the U.S. Congress in 1996. Turkey's estimated losses from the first totaled more than $40 billion, while the ILSA has cost it billions of dollars in lost opportunities in the energy sector. Despite U.S. disapproval, Turkish governments have been pursuing potential joint ventures with Iranian companies to diversify Turkey's energy imports.

In the Balkans, the post-earthquake Greek-Turkish rapprochement could potentially be a key stabilizing factor for the region, and the United States views collaboration between these two countries in Balkan peacekeeping operations as an important component of American security policy. During the 1992-95 war in Bosnia and the 1999 war in Kosovo, U.S. officials justified American intervention in the Balkans in terms of preventing the escalation of hostilities that would engulf Greece and Turkey in a greater regional war.[27] There were valid reasons behind these concerns as Greece and Turkey displayed support to the Serbs and Bosnians respectively during the crises. Greece accused Turkey of wanting to reclaim the former Ottoman influence and hegemony in the Balkans, while Turkey accused Greece of supporting Serbian genocide against the Muslim Bosnians. Therefore, when the Greek and Turkish governments started to talk to each other about the crisis in Macedonia following their rapprochement, President Clinton's administration welcomed this development. The participation of Turkish troops in NATO peacekeeping operations in the Balkans further underlines the multilateral nature of Turkey's Balkan policy. Turkey supports Bulgaria and Romania's entry into NATO and endorses the free trade goals of the BSEC zone for the entire region.

Turkey's interests in the Caucasus and Central Asia are more complex and should be considered in the context of a new Great Game characterized by competition for influence in the greater Caspian area between Turkey, Iran, and Russia. This competition is further complicated by the intervention of outside players such as the United States, Saudi Arabia, and Western oil companies. In this environment, there is a large degree of overlap between American and Turkish interests. First, both countries want to prevent the reentry of Russia into the region and its attempts to influence the energy policies (particularly with respect to oil and natural gas exports) of the former Soviet states. The desire of these states to maintain their distance from Russia also supports the American and Turkish positions. In this regard, among the Transcaucasian states, only Armenia maintains close ties with Russia. The reasons for this can be found in the war between Armenia and Azerbaijan and the Armenian claim of a security threat from Turkey. Georgia and Azerbaijan feel threatened by Russia and seek security guarantees from Turkey. Both countries have signed defense cooperation agreements with Turkey. Turkish officers provide education and training for the Azeri military students, Azerbaijan being the Turkic cousin with which Turkey's relations are strongest. Second, the United States supports the Baku-Ceyhan oil pipeline, which suits Turkish interests. And third, both Turkey and the United States would like to prevent the spread of Iranian and Saudi-based fundamentalist Islam in these countries.

Following the fall of the Soviet Union, many Turkish government officials and their nationalist counterparts in the Turkic states dreamed of forming some form of a Turkish unity among theses countries. This did not materialize for several reasons. Rivalries among the leaders of the Turkic states prevented genuine cooperation among these countries. Second, Turkey's "big brother" approach to the Central Asian republics did not sit well with peoples who had just rid themselves of another big brother. Third, while Turkey provided a significant amount of economic and educational assistance to the Turkic states, there were numerous cases of Turkish business corruption in these countries.

Perhaps the worst consequence of these developments was that the Turkic states did not rush to adopt the "Turkish model" for economic and political development. However, the war in Afghanistan and the United States' emphasis on the dangers of radical fundamentalist Islam could enable the Turkish model of economic and political models to advance.

Achieving a delicate balance in all of the above areas is extremely important to Turkey's ability to meet its energy needs in the future. As an energy importer, Turkey needs to diversify its sources of imported natural gas and oil. Several projects that occupy Ankara's agenda include the Baku-Ceyhan oil pipeline, a natural gas pipeline from Turkmenistan to Turkey via Iran, the Blue Stream natural gas pipeline from Russia to Turkey under the Black Sea, the reopening of the Turkish-Iraqi pipeline, and expanded cooperation with Iraq to develop additional energy options and direct imports from the Gulf States and Libya.

The Iraqi option includes the Turkish Petroleum Company (Türk Petrolleri Anonim Ortaklığı—TPAO) and private Turkish companies Tekfen and Botas' partnering with Western companies to develop five non-associated gas fields in northeastern Iraq (Anfal, Chemchemal, Jeria Pika, Khashim al-Ahmar, and Mansuriya) with proven reserves of 9.5 trillion cubic feet (270 billion cubic meters) for the supply of 10 bcm a year of exports to Turkey.[28] Companies would also build a pipeline to Turkey at an estimated total cost of $2.7 billion. However, U.S. sanctions on Iraq and the threat of the war on terrorism spilling over into this country threatens all of these agreements.

Many questions surround the plan for the Baku-Ceyhan pipeline. The United States has been promoting the pipeline as a pivotal contribution by the United States to Turkey's future. To Turkish officials, this project now represents a promise the United States must keep. There is a general feeling in Ankara that construction of the pipeline should begin regardless of the uncertainties surrounding its economic viability. Can Turkey meet its own financial obligation to the pipeline given the state of economic crisis the country faces? After all, Turkey is obliged to pay for any cost overruns on the pipeline on its territory. The ability to meet this "cost overrun guarantee" will be important for financiers when they assess the project's economics and risks. Any overruns will drive up the cost of the project's financing, given Turkey's current economic situation. Turkey must also operate the pipeline at a low fixed cost. It would not be surprising if Turkey seeks to extract guarantees from the United States in return for its support for the U.S.-led war on terrorism. No matter the project's outcome, it is clear that it will result in a serious conflict of interest between the United States, Russia, and Iran. Moscow does not want to see the pipeline completed, preferring the Russian option of exporting Caspian oil from Russian oil terminals on the Black Sea. Iran, on the other hand, opposes growing cooperation between Azerbaijan and Turkey and the building of an alternative pipeline from Baku to existing Iranian pipelines to the Gulf, as has been proposed. Ironically, the Iran Libya Sanctions Act (ILSA) eliminates the third option altogether for Western oil companies, despite the fact that it is the most logical and cost efficient alternative.

The Armenian Issue

Turkey's relations with its eastern neighbors cannot be complete without addressing the Armenia problem. Turkey's relations with Armenia have direct implications for U.S.-Turkish relations. The Armenian lobby in Washington encourages the passage of the "Armenian resolution" acknowledging the actions of the Ottoman Empire against the Armenians in World War I as genocide. Intervention from President Clinton and others resulted in the resolution's being pulled in fall 2000, but it continues to be probably the single most dangerous issue that could threaten U.S.-Turkish relations in years to come.

When Armenian-Americans realized that they had little chance of winning their war against Turkey in the Congress, they embarked on a grassroots political campaign aimed at state legislators and public opinion. One by one, state legislatures are passing resolutions supporting the Armenian position. Turkish-American efforts to stop this campaign have been ineffective in the face of the sheer organizational and monetary superiority of the Armenian-Americans, who have bloc-voting powers in many states and include very rich constituents. In contrast, Turkish-Americans are thinly spread out across the United States and their relations are often marked by discord. The Assembly of Turkish American Associations has been attempting a good counterargument but lacks the Armenian-Americans' clout with state legislators. It is probable that once 35-40 state legislatures pass the Armenian Resolution, the U.S. Congress will be forced to consider this matter and most likely pass a similar resolution. Perhaps it is time for Ankara to rethink its Armenia strategy and send the whole matter to an international board of inquiry that could open all parties' archives. The United States would most certainly support this. So far, Ankara's traditional strategy of threats of economic and political sanctions (e.g., France after President Chirac signed a similar bill in 2001) only served to reinforce the American public's anti-Turkish sentiments, especially given the Armenians' effective media campaign. Even many of the pro-Turkish politicians in Congress privately admit that this resolution will likely clear the U.S. Congress eventually. It is therefore high time for the Turkish government to undertake an international campaign, not designed by itself but by a powerful public relations firm in the West, to tell the Turkish human rights story of 1908–1923 and simultaneously take the matter to an international board of inquiry recognized by the UN Human Rights Commission. Reactionary policies by Ankara would only hurt its relations with Washington in years to come. The U.S. could also help to defuse future problems by undertaking concrete steps that should include: (1) providing constructive information to the senators and congressmen about Turkey's pivotal role in U.S. security interests, (2) assisting and advertising the current efforts of the joint Armenian-Turkish committee in promoting better relations between Armenia and Turkey, (3) discouraging the nationalist Armenian government from its international anti-Turkish campaign, and (4) providing economic assistance for joint Armenian Turkish business ventures. The U.S. could also point out that objective investigation of historical facts needs to include opening of the archives of all parties relevant to the question at hand (e.g., Armenia, Britain, Russia, Turkey, and the United States) and to permit the investigation of all acts of atrocities, from the Balkans to the Caucasus.

Political Islam

Islam has been one of the most delicate issues in Turkish-U.S. relations for several reasons. The staunchly secular Turkish political elite and military believe that the Islamists' participation in politics is aimed at weakening the secular state and replacing it with a theocratic

Islamic republic. This view has been articulated in numerous statements and publications by the secularists and the military. [29] From the American perspective, the United States has treated Turkey's repeated dissolution of the Islamist political parties with some degree of uneasiness because of its implications for the consolidation of democracy in Turkey. Also, the United States views restrictions on Islam as interference in religious freedoms. Until recently, Turkey felt that the Americans failed to understand the inherent dangers that political Islam presents to Turkey. Their fears were not unfounded. For example, President Clinton raised the United States' uneasiness over Turkey's secularist-Islamist tensions when he addressed the Turkish Parliament in November 1999. As Alan Makovsky noted:

> Without referring specifically to secular-Islamist disputes, Clinton appeared to urge the Turkish parliament to support greater freedom of religious expression in speaking of his hope for 'a future in which people are free to pursue their beliefs and proclaim their heritage.' He philosophized, 'when people can celebrate their culture and faith in ways that do not infringe upon the rights of others, moderates do not become extremists, and extremists do not become misguided heroes.'

Yet, the history of an Islamist-secular divide in Turkish politics has repeatedly demonstrated the inability of either camp to compromise. The Turkish secular elite has historically felt that the United States failed to see the hidden aspiration of the Turkish Islamists to undermine the secular Turkish republic and to turn it into an effectively Islamic state. It is unlikely that the Turkish secular establishment will change its views on this subject in the future. At present, the state prosecutor is looking into the activities of the two new Islamist political parties, Saadet and AKP, that were formed after the June 2001 dissolution of Fazilet. The war in Afghanistan has also caused a rift between the Islamists and the mainstream political parties in Turkey, with the former criticizing the United States and its allies and accusing the Ecevit government of being a puppet of Washington. For its part, the Islamist media, with the exception of the Fethullah group's *Zaman* newspaper, runs daily accounts of U.S. "atrocities" in Afghanistan and publishes editorials glorifying Islam and the Islamist fighters.

The most tragic aspect of the Turkish experiment with democracy may be that while political parties are essential for democratic development and pluralist participation is necessary for the consolidation of democracy, Islamist political parties' track record demonstrates a darker strategy aimed at undermining the basic foundations of the secular Turkish republic. During the last four decades, Islamist political parties from the National Order Party (Milli Nizam Partisi—MNP) to the Virtue Party attempted to use democratic politics to end democracy in Turkey. While scholars and other Turkey observers may disagree on this issue, the decisions of Turkey's Constitutional Court closing these parties supports the observation. Moreover, the Virtue Party's appeal to the European Human Rights Court to nullify the closure of its predecessor Welfare Party was rejected on similar ground.[30] Given the complex nature of the secular-Islamist divide in Turkey, the United States should refrain from making any statement that could be perceived as pro-Islamist in Turkey until is it absolutely clear that Islamist parties are truly committed to the democratic state. Otherwise, this is one issue in Turkish-U.S. relations that could cause serious damage to bilateral relations between the two allies.

Conclusions and Prospects

Turkish-U.S. relations have survived the end of the Cold War and become more complex. From the U.S. perspective, Turkey is a pivotal country for American interests in the region. The war in Afghanistan has clarified this. In turn, U.S. support is crucial for Turkey's efforts at democratic and economic reforms and its bid for EU membership. However, serious threats to this relationship exist in the form of anti-Turkish lobbies in the United States, anti-American forces in Turkey, and the aspirations of Turkey's enemies in the region. Successful relations in the future depend on Washington and Ankara's ability to use proactive policies in meeting these challenges. Future Turkish-U.S. relations will turn on the outcome of the war in Afghanistan, whether or not the United States spreads the campaign to countries near Turkey's borders, the Turkish reaction to this should it happen, the future of oil and gas politics in the region, the outcome of the Cyprus problem and relations with Greece, ESDI-NATO relations, the Armenian issue, and

Turkey's domestic reform. In this regard, we can imagine the convergence of three vectors of developments (measures as low/bad to high/good) that capture these issues: the EU membership process, relations with neighbors, and domestic reforms.

From the U.S. perspective, the best scenario is one where Turkey makes good progress all around, achieving a democratic political system with extensive individual civil and political rights, a dynamic market economy, stable and good relations with neighboring countries, and EU membership. Achieving these objectives requires substantial help from the United States, particularly with regard to resolving the Cyprus problem and preventing the EU from engaging in any behavior that would distance Turkey from the West. The worst scenario is a Turkey that has failed miserably on the domestic reform fronts, economically bankrupt, saber rattling at Greece and Armenia, distanced from becoming a member of the EU, and suspicious of U.S. intentions in the region. The prospects of achieving good outcomes on the three avenues of development depends on how much the United States is willing to play the role of stabilizer in EU-Turkey and Turkey-Greece relations. The United States needs to champion secular Turkey's image in the region and provide much needed economic assistance to Turkey.

Notes

[1] Alan Makovsky and Sabri Sayarı, "Introduction," in *Turkey's New World: Changing Dynamics in Turkish Foreign Policy,* Alan Makovsky and Sabri Sayarı, eds. (Washington, D.C.: The Washington Institute for Near East Policy, 2000), p. 3.

[2] For a detailed assessment of this period see Makovsky and Sayarı, *Turkey's New World,* and Morton Abramowitz, ed., *Turkey's Transformation and American Policy* (New York: The Century Foundation Press, 2000).

[3] Turkey has long had contacts with Afghan opposition groups, especially the forces of General Rashid Dostum, one of the Northern Alliance's Uzbek leaders. Dostum's fighters are largely Uzbeks, a group that has close ethnic links with Turks.

[4] In point of fact Turkey made it clear on September 15, 2001 that it would not object to any U.S. request for support from NATO. See *Sabah* (Turkish Daily) Sept. 15, 2001.

[5] ANAR survey of monthly public opinion, October 2001 (Ankara: ANAR).

[6] *Hürriyet* (Istanbul), Nov. 1 and 3, 2001.

[7] For official documents see Belgenet.com (http://www.belgenet.com /teror/t_011101.html). Grand National Assembly Decision No. 722, Oct. 10, 2001, published in the *Official Gazette,* Oct. 12, 2001 (10/10/2001-24551).

[8] For a detailed discussion of the Copenhagen criteria, see David Wood and Birol Yeşilada, *The Emerging European Union,* 2nd ed. (New York: Longman, 2002), Ch. 10.

[9] Birol A. Yeşilada, "Problems of Political Development in the Third Turkish Republic," *Polity,* Winter 1998, pp. 345–72.

[10] Alan Makovsky, "U.S. Policy Toward Turkey," in Abramowitz, ed., *Turkey's Transformation,* pp. 249–51.

[11] European Commission, *Progress Report on Accession: Turkey 1999 and 2000* (Brussels: European Commission official publications, Nov. 1999 and Nov. 2000).

[12] Interviews of U.S. State Department officials by the author in August 2001 and officials of the U.S. embassy in Ankara in April 2001.

[13] *Ulusal Program* (The National Program), (Ankara: Başbakanlık, 2001).

[14] For a complete listing of the amendments see Belgenet Arsiv [Archives] (http://www.belgenet.com/2001/anayasa37_03.html).

[15] *Financial Times,* Feb. 23, 2001.

[16] Associated Press, "Chronology and key events leading to Turkish Currency Float," Feb. 22, 2001.

[17] Birol Yeşilada, "Turkey's EU Candidacy," *Middle East Journal,* vol. 56, no. 1 (2002).

[18] For a detailed list of the reforms and their justification, see *The New Economic Program* (http://www.belgenet.com/eko/yeniprogram_2001.html). For the letter of intent and the subsequent additions to this letter by the Turkish government (in June and July 2001), see Letter of Intent (http://www.belgenet.com/eko/mektup_030501.html), Additional Letter of Intent of June 2001 (http://www.belgenet.com/eko/mektup_260601.html), and Additional Letter of Intent of July 2001 (http://www.belgenet.com/ eko/mektup_310701.html).

[19] *Hürriyet*, Nov. 6, 2001.

[20] *Milliyet*, Dec. 14, 1998. It is important to note that the threat to integrate the TRNC with Turkey was made in 1998 and that it is repeated again in response to yet another EU position on Cyprus's accession to membership.

[21] Yeşilada, "Turkey's EU Candidacy."

[22] Ibid.

[23] Interviews with members of the Turkish General Staff, *Milliyet* (Turkish Daily), June 12, 2001.

[24] Meliha Benli Altunışık, "Turkish Policy toward Israel," in Makovsky and Sayarı, eds., *Turkey's New World*, p. 67.

[25] Birol Yeşilada, "Turkey's Foreign Policy Toward the Middle East," in Atila Eralp, Muharrem Tunay, and Birol Yeşilada, eds., *The Political and Socioeconomic Transformation of Turkey* (Westport, Conn.: Praeger, 1993), pp. 169-192.

[26] *Sabah* (Turkish Daily) "F-16 Huzursuzluğu" (The F-16 Uneasiness), Aug. 20, 2001.

[27] Morton Abramowitz, "The Complexities of American Policymaking on Turkey," in *Turkey's Transformation*, p. 158.

[28] TPAO, *Türkiye'nin Doğal Gaz İhtiyaçları ve Proje Çalışmaları* (Turkey's Natural Gas Needs and Project Studies) (Ankara: TPAO, 2001).

[29] Political Islam in Turkey is a very complex topic and it is beyond the scope of this paper to provide justice to this subject. For further analysis of this topic see Howard Reed, "Islam and Education in Turkey: Their Roles in National Development," *Turkish Studies Association Bulletin*, March 1988, pp. 3–4; Uriel Heyd, "Revival of Islam in Modern Turkey," *Universities Field Staff Report* (March 1968), pp. 1–27; Mustafa Haki Okutucu, *İstikamet Şeriat: Refah Partisi* (Direction Sheria: The Refah Party) (Istanbul: Yeryüzü Yayınları, 1996); Sayarı Sabri, "Turkey's Islamic Challenge," *Middle East Quarterly*, Sept. 1996, pp. 35–43; Mehmet Ali Soydan, *Dünden Bugüne Türkiye'nin Refah Gerçeği* (From Yesterday to Present: The Welfare Reality of Turkey) (Erzurum: Birey Yayın, 1994); Birol A. Yeşilada, "The Refah Party Phenomenon in Turkey," in Birol A. Yeşilada, ed., *Comparative Political Parties and Party Elites: Essays in Honor of Samuel J. Eldersveld* (Ann Arbor:

University of Michigan Press, 1999), pp. 123–50; and Yeşilada, "The Virtue Party," *Turkish Studies*, vol. 3, no. 1 (2002).

30 Associated Press, July 31, 2001.

Index

Contributors

Michael Radu is a Senior Fellow with the Foreign Policy Research Institute, Director of its Center for the Study of Terrorism and Political Violence, and contributing editor of its journal, *Orbis*. He received his Ph.D. from Columbia University and is the editor or main author of many volumes on terrorism and political violence and has also written a number of articles on Turkish terrorism and politics.

Hüseyin Bağcı is a professor in international relations at Middle East Technical University in Ankara. He received his Ph.D. from Bonn University and is a professional member of the Foreign Policy Institute Ankara, the Deutsche Atlantische Gesellschaft, and the IISS of London. He has written numerous articles in Turkish, German, and English, as well as several books on Turkish foreign policy and Turkey's relevance to the region.

Svante E. Cornell is a lecturer and researcher at the departments of East European Studies and Peace and Conflict Research in Uppsala University, Sweden. He has made numerous appearances on Swedish television and radio, commenting on events and developments in Turkey, the Caucasus, Central Asia, and the wider Middle East. Cornell has also published numerous articles and several books on the subjects of the Caucasus region and Turkey in international relations.

Aslan Gündüz received his LL.B from Istanbul University Faculty of Law (1976), his Ph.D. in International Law from Istanbul University (1983), and his M.Phil. in Human Rights and Security from University of Essex (1993). His publications include five books and more than thirty articles (both in English and Turkish) on various aspects of international law including human rights, European Union law, law of the sea, and Greek-Turkish relations. He is currently a professor of international law at Istanbul Kultur University.

Paul Henze is a retired U.S. diplomat and consultant in the Washington office of RAND. He headed the National Security Council's Nationality Working Group from 1977-80. He spent thirty years in U.S. government and government-related positions, including at Radio Free Europe and American embassies in Turkey and Ethiopia. Henze specializes in Caucasian history and politics. His history of modern Turkey, *Ataturk's Legacy* (1998), has a published translation in Turkish.

Efraim Inbar is a Professor in Political Studies at Bar-Ilan University. He received his M.A. and Ph.D. from the University of Chicago and has been appointed a Manfred Warner NATO Fellow. He has served in the Israel Defense Force as a paratrooper and is currently posted (in reserve) at the IDF College of Staff and Command. His area of specialization is Middle Eastern Strategic issues and Israeli national security. He has edited several collections of articles and authored a number of books, including *Outcast Countries in the World Community* (1985), *Labor Party Positions on National Security* (1991), and *Rabin and Israel's National Security* (1999).

Ali Murat Köknar received his B.Proc. and MBA degrees from the University of Witwatersrand in Johannesburg and has worked in commercial aviation in Turkey. After spending five years in South Africa, where he worked in international business and law enforcement, he moved to the United States in 1994. In Washington, Koknar works as an independent writer and consultant on counterterrorism, low-intensity conflict, missile defense and nuclear proliferation issues. His research focus remains on the Caucasus, the Balkans, and subsaharan Africa.

Birol A. Yeşilada is a professor of political science at Portland State University. He received his Ph.D. from the University of Michigan and is currently an endowed chair of its Contemporary Turkish Studies. He is a policy consultant to the U.S. State and Defense Departments, as well as to private sector companies doing business in Cyprus and Turkey. He has written several articles and books, most recently *The Political and Socioeconomic Transformation of Turkey* (1993).